Revenue Statistics in Asian and Pacific Economies 2020

1990-2018

This work is published under the responsibility of the Secretary-General of the OECD. The opinions expressed and arguments employed herein do not necessarily reflect the official views of the member countries of the OECD or its Development Centre.

This document, as well as any data and map included herein, are without prejudice to the status of or sovereignty over any territory, to the delimitation of international frontiers and boundaries and to the name of any territory, city or area.

Please cite this publication as:
OECD (2020), *Revenue Statistics in Asian and Pacific Economies 2020*, OECD Publishing, Paris, *https://doi.org/10.1787/d47d0ae3-en*.

ISBN 978-92-64-89727-4 (print)
ISBN 978-92-64-18269-1 (pdf)

Revenue Statistics in Asian and Pacific Economies
ISSN 2617-9172 (print)
ISSN 2617-9180 (online)

Foreword

Revenue Statistics in Asian and Pacific Economies is a joint publication by the OECD Centre for Tax Policy and Administration, the OECD Development Centre with the co-operation of the Asian Development Bank (ADB), the Pacific Island Tax Administrators Association (PITAA), and the Pacific Community (SPC) and the financial support from the governments of Ireland, Japan, Luxembourg, Norway, Sweden and the United Kingdom. It presents detailed, internationally comparable data on tax revenues for 21 Asian and Pacific economies: Australia, Bhutan, People's Republic of China, the Cook Islands, Fiji, Indonesia, Japan, Kazakhstan, Korea, Malaysia, Mongolia, Nauru, New Zealand, Papua New Guinea, the Philippines, Samoa, Singapore, the Solomon Islands, Thailand, Tokelau and Vanuatu. It also provides information on non-tax revenues for Bhutan, the Cook Islands, Fiji, Kazakhstan, Mongolia, Nauru, Papua New Guinea, the Philippines, Samoa, Thailand, Tokelau and Vanuatu. Four of these economies are OECD members (Australia, Korea, Japan and New Zealand). The approach used in Revenue Statistics in Asian and Pacific Economies is based on the well-established methodology of the OECD Revenue Statistics (OECD, 2020), which has become an essential reference source for OECD member countries. Comparisons are also made with the averages for OECD economies, Latin American and Caribbean (LAC) countries and 26 African countries.

In this publication, the term "taxes" is confined to compulsory, unrequited payments to general government. As outlined in the Interpretative Guide to the Revenue Statistics, taxes are "unrequited" in the sense that benefits provided by government to taxpayers are not normally in proportion to their payments. The OECD methodology classifies a tax according to its base: income, profits and capital gains (classified under heading 1000), payroll (heading 3000), property (heading 4000), goods and services (heading 5000) and other taxes (heading 6000). Compulsory social security contributions paid to general government are treated as taxes, and are classified under heading 2000. Greater detail on the tax concept, the classification of taxes and the accrual basis of reporting is set out in the Interpretative Guide in Annex A.

Information is also presented on non-tax revenues in twelve economies. The term "non-tax revenue" includes all general government revenue that does not meet the OECD definition of tax revenues. Non-tax revenues include grants (e.g. foreign aid), returns on government market investments, rents on the extraction of resources from public lands, sales of government-produced goods and services, and the collection of fines and forfeits. More details on the definition of these revenues are available in Annex B.

Chapter 1 of this report provides an overview of the main tax revenue trends in the 21 economies and non-tax revenue trends in the 12 relevant economies from 2007 to 2018. A special feature on tax policy and administration responses to COVID-19 in the region is found in Chapter 2, while Chapter 3 contains comparative tables on the level and structure of taxation in the 21 economies since 1990. Chapter 4 contains detailed information on tax revenues on a country-by-country basis. Chapter 5 includes information on the level and structure of non-tax revenues in selected economies.

Acknowledgements

Revenue Statistics in Asian and Pacific Economies is jointly produced by the Organisation for Economic Co-operation and Development (OECD)'s Centre for Tax Policy and Administration (CTP) and the OECD Development Centre (DEV) with the co-operation of the Asian Development Bank (ADB), the Pacific Island Tax Administrators Association (PITAA), and the Pacific Community (SPC) and financial support from the governments of Ireland, Japan, Luxembourg, Norway, Sweden and the United Kingdom. The authors like to thank the ADB for co-organising with the OECD and the Study Group on Asian Tax Administration and Research a technical workshop on *Revenue Statistics* in Manila, Philippines, on 13 September 2019. PITAA and SPC have also provided invaluable support and advice.

The staff with responsibility for producing the publication were: Michelle Harding, Head, Tax Data and Statistical Analysis, Emmanuelle Modica, Statistician/Analyst, Leonie Cedano, Statistician, Talita Yamashiro Fordelone, Advisor and Koji Ono, Senior Advisor, Global Relations of the OECD Centre for Tax Policy and Administration under the supervision of the Director Pascal Saint-Amans, Deputy Director Grace Perez-Navarro and the Head of the Tax Policy and Tax Statistics Division David Bradbury; Jingjing Xia of the OECD Development Centre under the supervision of the Director and Special Advisor to the OECD Secretary-General on Development, Mario Pezzini, Deputy Director Federico Bonaglia, Kensuke Tanaka, Head of the Asia Unit, and Alexander Pick, Coordinator of *Revenue Statistics* for the Development Centre. The special feature was written by Donghyun Park, Principal Economist, Yasushi Suzuki, Public Management Specialist, and Go Nagata, Public Management Specialist at the ADB, and by Leonie Cedano, Michelle Harding, Emmanuelle Modica, Alexander Pick, Jingjing Xia and Talita Yamashiro Fordelone (OECD), drawing on the presentations and research of speakers at an ADB-CATA-OECD-PITAA-SGATAR virtual meeting that was held on 14 May 2020, including Peter Green and David Bradbury (OECD), Dr Sabin Samitah (Malaysia), Dr Lamy Mong (Cambodia), Iain Steel (ODI), and David Phillips (IFS). Elizabeth Nash and Delphine Grandrieux at DEV and Marie-Aurélie Elkurd, Karena Garnier and Natalie Lagorce at CTP assisted with the production and publication of this report.

The authors would like to thank other officials for their invaluable help in completing this publication. Support was also provided by Piera Tortora, Economist/Policy Analyst at the OECD Development Co-operation Directorate; Heike Buss, Tax Advisor, Ben Dickinson, Head of the Global Relations and Development Division, Varsha Singh, Deputy Head of Division of the Global Relations and Development Division of the OECD Centre for Tax Policy and Administration; Policy Officer Vincent Bigot, Head of Domestic Revenue Mobilisation Sector Stefan Agne, Head of Sector for Domestic Revenue Mobilisation Benedikt Madl, Head of Budget Support, Public Finance Management, Domestic Revenue Mobilisation Unit Erica Gerretsen, at the European Commission; Team leader Economic Cooperation and Agriculture Section Emmanuelle Guiheneuf, Programme Manager Budget Support Marga Peeters, and Programme Manager Economic Cooperation and Agriculture Section Shaleshni Prasad at the Delegation of the European Union for the Pacific; Nilima Lal, Economic Statistics Advisor at the SPC; Koni Ravono, Head of Secretariat, and Petero Maivucevuce, Training Coordinator at PITAA. The authors would like to thank their colleagues working in national administrations with whom they have consulted regularly. These institutions include finance ministries, national tax agencies and national statistical institutes of the participating countries. The authors are also very grateful to all participants at the technical workshop in Manila,

Philippines in September 2019 and at the ADB-CATA-OECD-PITAA-SGATAR virtual meeting that was held on 14 May 2020.

This document was produced with financial support from the governments of Ireland, Japan, Luxembourg, Norway, Sweden and the United Kingdom. The views expressed herein can in no way be taken to reflect the official opinion or policies of the governments of Ireland, Japan, Luxembourg, Norway, Sweden and the United Kingdom.

Table of contents

Foreword   3

Acknowledgements   4

Executive summary   9

1 Tax revenue trends in Asian and Pacific economies   11

2 Tax policy and administration responses to COVID-19   39

3 Tax levels and tax structure, 1990-2018   52

4 Country tables, tax revenues, 1997-2018   73

5 Comparative and country tables, non-tax revenues, 2007-2018   115

Annex A. The OECD Classification of Taxes and Interpretative Guide   132

Annex B. Interpretative Guide to non-tax revenue in Revenue Statistics in Asian and
      Pacific Economies   160

Tables

Table 1.1. Attribution of tax revenues to sub-sectors of general government   31
Table 1.2. Non-tax revenue of main headings as a percentage of GDP in selected Pacific economies (2007-
18)   33
Table 3.1. Total tax revenue as percentage of GDP, 1990-2018   53
Table 3.2. Total tax revenue (excluding social security contributions) as percentage of GDP, 1990-2018   54
Table 3.3. Tax revenue of main headings as percentage of GDP, 2018   55
Table 3.4. Tax revenue of main headings as percentage of total taxation, 2018   56
Table 3.5. Taxes on income and profits (1000) as percentage of GDP   57
Table 3.6. Taxes on income and profits (1000) as percentage of total taxation   58
Table 3.7. Social security contributions (2000) as percentage of GDP   59
Table 3.8. Social security contributions (2000) as percentage of total taxation   60
Table 3.9. Taxes on property (4000) as percentage of GDP   61
Table 3.10. Taxes on property (4000) as percentage of total taxation   62
Table 3.11. Taxes on goods and services (5000) as percentage of GDP   63
Table 3.12. Taxes on goods and services (5000) as percentage of total taxation   64
Table 3.13. Taxes on general consumption (5110) as percentage of GDP   65
Table 3.14. Taxes on general consumption (5110) as percentage of total taxation   66
Table 3.15. Taxes on specific goods and services (5120) as percentage of GDP   67

Table 3.16. Taxes on specific goods and services (5120) as percentage of total taxation 68
Table 3.17. Gross domestic product for tax reporting years at market prices, in national currency 69
Table 3.18. Gross domestic product for tax reporting years at market prices, in millions of US dollars at market exchange rates 70
Table 3.19. Total tax revenue in millions of US dollars at market exchange rates 71
Table 3.20. Exchange rates used, national currency per US dollar 72
Table 4.1. Australia 74
Table 4.2. Bhutan 76
Table 4.3. China 78
Table 4.4. Cook Islands 80
Table 4.5. Fiji 82
Table 4.6. Indonesia 84
Table 4.7. Japan 86
Table 4.8. Kazakhstan 88
Table 4.9. Korea 90
Table 4.10. Malaysia 93
Table 4.11. Mongolia 95
Table 4.12. Nauru 97
Table 4.13. New Zealand 99
Table 4.14. Papua New Guinea 101
Table 4.15. Philippines 103
Table 4.16. Samoa 105
Table 4.17. Singapore 107
Table 4.18. Solomon Islands 109
Table 4.19. Thailand 111
Table 4.20. Tokelau 112
Table 4.21. Vanuatu 114
Table 5.1. Total non-tax revenue as percentage of GDP in selected economies, 2008-18 116
Table 5.2. Non-tax revenue of main headings as percentage of GDP in selected economies, 2018 117
Table 5.3. Non-tax revenue of main headings as percentage of total non-tax revenues in selected economies, 2018 118
Table 5.4. Total non-tax revenue in selected economies in millions of US dollars at market exchange rates 119
Table 5.5. Bhutan 120
Table 5.6. Cook Islands 121
Table 5.7. Fiji 122
Table 5.8. Kazakhstan 123
Table 5.9. Mongolia 124
Table 5.10. Nauru 125
Table 5.11. Papua New Guinea 126
Table 5.12. Philippines 127
Table 5.13. Samoa 128
Table 5.14. Thailand 129
Table 5.15. Tokelau 130
Table 5.16. Vanuatu 131

Figures

Figure 1.1. Tax-to-GDP ratios in Asian and Pacific economies, including and excluding social security contributions (2018) 13
Figure 1.2. Tax-to-GDP ratios and GDP per capita (in PPP) in Asian and Pacific economies, Latin America and the Caribbean, OECD and African countries (2018) 16
Figure 1.3. Annual changes in tax-to-GDP ratios (2017-18) 17
Figure 1.4. Net changes in tax-to-GDP ratios between 2017 and 2018 by main type of tax 18
Figure 1.5. Changes in tax-to-GDP ratios (2007-18 and 2007-12) 19
Figure 1.6. Net changes in tax-to-GDP ratios between 2007 and 2018 21
Figure 1.7. Tax structures as a percentage of GDP (2018) 22
Figure 1.8. Tax structures as a percentage of total taxation (2018) 24
Figure 1.9. Revenue from value added tax and other taxes on goods and services as a percentage of total tax revenue (2018) 25

Figure 1.10. Revenue from corporate income tax and personal income tax (2018)   27
Figure 1.11. VAT revenue ratios (VRRs) in Asian countries (2018)   28
Figure 1.12. Environmentally related tax revenue in Asian and Pacific economies, by main tax base (2018)   29
Figure 1.13. Structure of non-tax revenue (2018)   33
Figure 2.1. Changes of tax-to-GDP ratios in Asian and Pacific economies during the global financial crisis (2007 and 2009)   42

Boxes

Box 1.1. Enhancing domestic resource mobilisation in Small Island Developing States through revenue statistics   14
Box 1.2. VAT revenue ratios in Asian countries   27
Box 2.1. Tax policy and administrative responses to COVID-19 in Malaysia   45
Box 2.2. Tax policy and tax administration responses to the COVID-19 crisis in Cambodia   47

Follow OECD Publications on:

http://twitter.com/OECD_Pubs

http://www.facebook.com/OECDPublications

http://www.linkedin.com/groups/OECD-Publications-4645871

http://www.youtube.com/oecdilibrary

http://www.oecd.org/oecddirect/

This book has...

StatLinks
A service that delivers Excel® files from the printed page!

Look for the StatLinks at the bottom of the tables or graphs in this book. To download the matching Excel® spreadsheet, just type the link into your Internet browser, starting with the *https://doi.org* prefix, or click on the link from the e-book edition.

Executive summary

In light of the United Nations' 2030 Agenda for Sustainable Development, awareness of the need to mobilise government revenue in developing countries to fund public goods and services is increasing. *Revenue Statistics in Asian and Pacific Economies* presents key indicators to track progress on domestic resource mobilisation and to inform tax policy and reform.

Revenue Statistics in Asian and Pacific Economies 2020 is published at a time when the world confronts an unprecedented crisis due to the COVID-19 pandemic, which has posed severe challenges to health systems and economies across the Asia and Pacific region, as well as to citizens themselves. A special feature in this report examines the ways in which tax revenues across the region will be affected by the pandemic, as well as the central role that tax policy and administration play in supporting households and individuals during the crisis, and stimulating economic and fiscal recovery once it has passed.

Revenue Statistics in Asian and Pacific Economies presents detailed, internationally comparable data on tax revenues for 21 Asian and Pacific economies: Australia, Bhutan, People's Republic of China, the Cook Islands, Fiji, Indonesia, Japan, Kazakhstan, Korea, Malaysia, Mongolia, Nauru, New Zealand, Papua New Guinea, the Philippines, Samoa, Singapore, the Solomon Islands, Thailand, Tokelau and Vanuatu. It also provides information on non-tax revenues for Bhutan, the Cook Islands, Fiji, Kazakhstan, Mongolia, Nauru, Papua New Guinea, the Philippines, Samoa, Thailand, Tokelau and Vanuatu. The data on fiscal revenues demonstrate the strength of the region's tax systems going into the crisis and are a valuable tool to understand how the crisis might affect different countries, and also to support countries to build more resilient fiscal systems in its aftermath.

Tax-to-GDP ratios in Asian and Pacific economies

In 2018, tax-to-GDP ratios in the Asia and Pacific region ranged from 11.9% in Indonesia to 35.4% in Nauru. The tax-to-GDP ratio refers to total tax revenue, including social security contributions, as a percentage of gross domestic product (GDP). All economies in this publication had lower ratios in 2018 than the OECD average of 34.3%, with the exception of Nauru, whereas ten of the economies included in this publication had tax-to-GDP ratios above the Latin American and the Caribbean (LAC) average of 23.1%. There is also a difference in tax-to-GDP ratios across the regions: eight of the eleven Asian countries covered in this publication had a tax-to-GDP ratio below 20.0% (the exceptions being Japan, Korea and Mongolia) whereas seven of the ten Pacific economies had a tax-to-GDP ratio above 23.0% (the exceptions being Papua New Guinea, Tokelau and Vanuatu).

Since 2017, nearly two-thirds of the economies included in this publication experienced increases in their tax-to-GDP ratios. The largest increases were seen in Nauru, Tokelau and Mongolia (6.4 percentage points (p.p.), 3.8 p.p. and 2.5 p.p., respectively), largely due to increases in tax rates. In Mongolia, increases in personal income tax rates and in the excise rates on tobacco and alcohol drove higher revenues. Higher tobacco duties also contributed to the increase in Tokelau; and higher employment tax rates for non-residents, service tax rates and various business tax rates drove the increase in Nauru. Four other economies (Solomon Islands, Korea, the Cook Islands and Samoa) had increases greater than 1 percentage point. By contrast, most of the decreases were less than one percentage point: only Bhutan experienced a larger decrease of 1.4 p.p., mainly due to the removal of the excise duty on fuel imports.

Over a longer timeframe, eleven economies included in the publication have increased their tax-to-GDP ratios over the last decade. The highest increases between 2007 and 2018 were observed in the Solomon Islands, Samoa and the Cook Islands (10.6 p.p., 7.0 p.p. and 4.9 p.p., respectively). Across the same period, Mongolia, Papua New Guinea and Kazakhstan experienced the largest decreases in their tax-to-GDP ratios (4.3 p.p., 8.6 p.p. and 9.3 p.p., respectively), driven in all three cases by decreases in corporate income tax (CIT) revenues due to lower resource prices.

Tax structures in Asian and Pacific economies

Economies in Asia and the Pacific rely on goods and services taxes and on income taxes. In ten economies in this publication (the Cook Islands, Fiji, Kazakhstan, Mongolia, the Philippines, Samoa, the Solomon Islands, Thailand, Tokelau and Vanuatu), taxes on goods and services accounted for the largest share of tax revenues in 2018. In most of these economies, VAT is less significant than other taxes on goods and services, such as excises and import duties, with seven economies recording higher revenues from other taxes on goods and services (ranging from 31.1% of total tax revenues in Kazakhstan to 73.2% in the Solomon Islands), and three economies receiving a larger share of revenue from VAT (Mongolia (28.2%), Samoa (40.1%) and the Cook Islands (44.6%)).

Income taxes provided the main share of tax revenues in the remaining economies, except in Japan. Among these economies, the share of income tax revenues varied from 34.1% in Korea to 70.2% in Nauru. Corporate income tax revenues were higher than personal income tax revenues in four Asian countries (Bhutan, Indonesia, Malaysia and Singapore), while all Pacific economies in this group (Australia, New Zealand, Papua New Guinea and Tokelau) and Korea raised higher shares of personal income taxes.

As discussed earlier, social security contributions played a small role in revenues for most Asian and Pacific economies, with a few exceptions. Japan derived the largest share of total tax revenues from social security contributions, at 39.9% in 2017. Social security contributions also played a significant role in revenues in Mongolia (20.1%) and Korea (25.4%) in 2018, similar to the OECD average (26.0% in 2017).

Non-tax revenues in selected economies

This publication includes data on non-tax revenues for twelve economies (Bhutan, the Cook Islands, Fiji, Kazakhstan, Mongolia, Nauru, Papua New Guinea, the Philippines, Samoa, Thailand, Tokelau and Vanuatu). In 2018, non-tax revenues as a percentage of GDP were significant for Bhutan, the Cook Islands, Nauru, Tokelau and Vanuatu but lower than 6.5% of GDP in the remaining economies.

Grants were an important source of revenue in 2018 for six economies for which non-tax revenues are presented (Papua New Guinea, the Cook Islands, Bhutan, Tokelau, Samoa and Vanuatu). In each of these economies they exceeded 30% of total non-tax revenues and they were the main source of non-tax revenues for Papua New Guinea (62.6%), the Cook Islands (46.7%) and Samoa (33.8%). Property-related income was the main source of non-tax revenues for Kazakhstan (81.5%) and Tokelau (60.0%), but also contributed more than 36% of total non-tax revenues in eight other economies (Papua New Guinea, the Cook Islands, the Philippines, Fiji, Mongolia, Bhutan, Nauru and Thailand).

1 Tax revenue trends in Asian and Pacific economies

Chapter 1 provides information on trends in tax and non-tax revenues in 21 Asian and Pacific economies, including changes in tax-to-GDP ratios, tax structures, taxes by level of government and non-tax revenue structures.

Achieving the Sustainable Development Goals in the 2030 Agenda for Sustainable Development requires mobilising additional resources – in particular government revenues – to fund public goods and services in developing countries. Taxation provides the largest share of government revenues in almost all countries and is relatively predictable and sustainable, in contrast with non-tax revenue sources such as official development assistance and royalties.

Revenue Statistics in Asian and Pacific Economies 2020 is published at a time when the world confronts an unprecedented crisis as a result of the coronavirus (COVID-19) pandemic, which has posed severe challenges to health systems and economies across the Asia and Pacific region, as well as to citizens themselves. Chapter 2 of this report examines the ways in which tax revenues across the region will be affected by the pandemic, as well as the central role that tax policy and administration play in supporting households and individuals during the crisis, and stimulating economic and fiscal recovery once it has passed. Data on fiscal revenues discussed in Chapter 1 demonstrate the strength of the region's tax systems going into the crisis and are thus a valuable tool not only for understanding how the crisis might affect different countries, but also for supporting countries to build more resilient fiscal systems in its aftermath.

This report presents detailed and internationally comparable data on tax revenues in 21 Asian and Pacific economies: Australia, Bhutan, People's Republic of China (hereafter "China"), the Cook Islands, Fiji, Indonesia, Japan, Kazakhstan, Korea, Malaysia, Mongolia, Nauru, New Zealand, Papua New Guinea, the Philippines, Samoa, Singapore, the Solomon Islands, Thailand, Tokelau and Vanuatu. It also provides information on non-tax revenues for Bhutan, the Cook Islands, Fiji, Kazakhstan, Mongolia, Nauru, Papua New Guinea, the Philippines, Samoa, Thailand, Tokelau and Vanuatu. This chapter discusses key tax indicators for these 21 economies: the tax-to-GDP ratio; the tax structure and the share of tax revenue by level of government; and non-tax revenue for selected economies. The discussion is supplemented by detailed information for each economy in Chapters 4 and 5.

Tax ratios

Tax-to-GDP ratios in 2018

In 2018, tax-to-GDP ratios in the Asia and Pacific region ranged from 11.9% in Indonesia to 35.4% in Nauru (Figure 1.1). Ten of the 21 economies had tax-to-GDP ratios above the Latin American and the Caribbean (LAC) average of 23.1% in 2018, and all economies in the publication had lower ratios than the OECD average of 34.3%, with the exception of Nauru. Most of the Asian countries covered in this report had a tax-to-GDP ratio below 20%, with the exceptions of Japan (31.4%, 2017 figure), Korea (28.4%) and Mongolia (24.0%). Among the Pacific economies, seven of the ten included in this publication had a tax-to-GDP ratio above 23%, with the exception of Papua New Guinea (12.1%), Vanuatu (18.0%) and Tokelau (18.1%).

The tax-to-GDP ratio measures tax revenues as a proportion of gross domestic product (GDP). Taxes are defined as compulsory, unrequited payments to general government. In the OECD classification, taxes are classified by the base of the tax and include taxes on incomes and profits, compulsory social security contributions (SSCs) paid to the general government, taxes on payroll and workforce, taxes on property, taxes on goods and services and other taxes.

Tax-to-GDP ratios in Asian and Pacific economies, exclusive of SSCs, are shown in Figure 1.1. In countries that levy social security contributions, the tax-to-GDP ratios exclusive of SSCs range from 11.5% of GDP in Indonesia to 21.2% of GDP in Korea in 2018. Six countries in Asia had tax-to-GDP ratios exclusive of SSCs between 15% and 20% of GDP (the Philippines (15.7%), Kazakhstan (16.4%), Thailand (16.5%), China (17.0%), Japan (18.8%) and Mongolia (19.2%)], while four countries had tax-to-GDP ratios exclusive of SSCs below 15% (Indonesia (11.5%), Malaysia (12.2%), Bhutan (12.3%) and Singapore (13.2%)). While excluding revenues from social security contributions does not impact the tax-to-GDP ratios in Pacific economies, where SSCs are rarely used, it plays a more significant role in the ratios of all Asian economies except Bhutan.

Figure 1.1. Tax-to-GDP ratios in Asian and Pacific economies, including and excluding social security contributions (2018)

Percentage of GDP

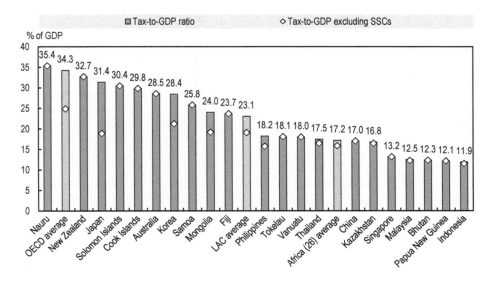

Notes: The figures do not include sub-national tax revenue for the Cook Islands, Fiji, Malaysia, Papua New Guinea, Samoa and the Solomon Islands.
The averages for Africa (26 countries), for LAC (25 Latin American and Caribbean countries) and the OECD (36 countries) are unweighted.
Australia, Japan, Korea and New Zealand are part of the OECD (36) group. Data for Australia, Japan, Korea, New Zealand and the OECD average are taken from *Revenue Statistics 2019* (OECD, 2019[1]).
2017 data are used for the Africa (26) average, Australia and Japan, as 2018 data are not available.
The tax-to-GDP ratio for China does not include revenue from social security contributions (SSCs) as detailed data were not available. The OECD Secretariat estimates SSCs to be approximately 4.0% of GDP in 2018 based on publicly available data from China's Ministry of Human Resources and Social Security (MOHRSS, 2015[2]; MOHRSS, 2016[3]; MOHRSS, 2017[4]; MOHRSS, 2020[5]).
Source: Authors' calculations based on Table 3.1 in Chapter 3.

StatLink https://stat.link/vruexd

Structural economic factors are a key determinant of tax-to-GDP ratios across economies. These include the importance of agriculture in the economy, openness to trade and the size of the informal economy. Agriculture, for example, is a challenging sector to tax: most people in the agriculture sector in developing economies are on low incomes and many are not registered for tax purposes (PEAKS, 2013[6]). In addition, agriculture benefits from numerous tax exemptions. For example, Malaysia allows an agriculture allowance to be deducted from profits of eligible businesses (Inland Revenue Board of Malaysia, 2016[7]), and goods and services related to the agriculture sector are exempt from import duty and excise duty (Ministry of International Trade and Industry of Malaysia, 2016[8]).

In addition to structural economic factors, tax policy and tax administration settings also strongly influence the level of tax revenues. These include the power of tax administrations, the levels of corruption within these administrations and tax morale (i.e. willingness of people to pay taxes) (OECD, 2014[9]). For example, Aizenman (2015[10]) found that in Asia, government effectiveness and institution quality are positively correlated with the level of tax-to-GDP ratio. Finally, in general, GDP per capita is also related to tax-to-GDP ratios. Tax-to-GDP ratios tend to be higher in high-income economies, although the relationship is not direct and is less pronounced at lower levels of income due to the influence of other factors. It is in particular less pronounced in Asian and Pacific economies (Figure 1.2).

The proportion of agriculture in an economy also influences its tax-to-GDP ratio. For example, a relatively high share of agriculture in Indonesia's economy (above 10% of GDP) compared to the other Asian countries in this publication, as well as a low openness to trade, contribute to its low tax-to-GDP ratio, together with high levels of informality (estimated to amount to around 57.6% of employment), tax evasion and narrow tax bases (OECD, 2019[11]). Indonesia has undertaken reforms to strengthen tax administration, increase tax revenues and reduce its dependence on oil revenues. It has set a goal of increasing its tax-to-GDP ratio to 17% of GDP by 2019 (OECD, 2018[12]). These reforms have focused on modernising processes and systems, building human capacity and enhancing the tax administration's integrity (OECD, 2018[12]). Since 2014, Indonesia has also reformed its social insurance system. It has created or restructured several social security programmes, including work accident insurance and pensions for formal and non-formal workers. A new health insurance programme for all Indonesians covered 78% of the population in 2018 (OECD, 2019[11]). More details are provided further in the chapter.

The relationship between GDP per capita and tax levels across the Asian and Pacific economies in this publication is less direct than that observed across LAC or OECD countries. Six Asian and Pacific economies (China, Fiji, Kazakhstan, Mongolia, Samoa and Thailand) have broadly similar GDP per capita and tax-to-GDP ratios as the majority of LAC countries. Papua New Guinea, Vanuatu and the Solomon Islands have similar per capita levels of income but their tax-to-GDP ratios differ markedly. In contrast, Australia, Japan, Korea and New Zealand have higher per capita income and tax-to-GDP ratios. Finally, Singapore has the highest GDP per capita of the 21 economies considered here and one of the lowest tax-to-GDP ratios. The high GDP per capita in Singapore results from significant inward flows of foreign direct investment (FDI) due to its attractive business climate and stable political environment (UNCTAD, 2012[13]), whereas the tax-to-GDP ratio is explained by lower income tax rates (particularly on corporate income) and value added tax (VAT) rates compared to other Asian and Pacific economies (UNESCAP, 2014[14]).

Box 1.1. Enhancing domestic resource mobilisation in Small Island Developing States through revenue statistics

Small Island Developing States (SIDS) comprise a diverse group of the smallest and most remote economies in the world. They are located across the African, Asian, Latin American and the Caribbean, and Pacific regions. They share a common and unique set of development challenges owing to their small populations and landmasses, spatial dispersion and remoteness from major markets, and exposure to severe climate-related events and natural disasters. With small and undiversified economies, SIDS are highly vulnerable to external shocks, as they rely strongly on the global economy for financial services, tourism, remittances and concessional finance.

One common challenge faced by SIDS is the achievement of adequate domestic resource mobilisation and debt sustainability. Domestic revenues are often erratic due to narrow economic productive bases, often concentrated in sectors that are exposed to external fluctuations, such as natural resources or tourism. At the same time, SIDS typically have large current expenditures, as the high unit costs of providing services to small and scattered populations increase public sector expenditures above the average levels of other developing countries [31.7% of GDP in SIDS, compared to 21.3% in other developing countries (World Bank, 2020[18])]. Severe climate events and natural disasters also tend to have heavy fiscal and economic impacts. These factors lead to high levels of public debt for many SIDS [59.5% of GDP, compared to 44.6% for other developing countries (World Bank, 2020[19])] and reduce the fiscal space to invest in development.

Taxes are an important and relatively more stable source of revenues in many SIDS, although economies' ability to raise domestic revenues varies significantly. The *Global Revenue Statistics* publications and database (OECD, 2020[20]) show that among the Pacific SIDS, tax-to-GDP ratios ranged from 12.1% in Papua New Guinea to 35.4% in Nauru in 2018. Among African SIDS, Cabo Verde had a tax-to-GDP ratio of 20.1%, Mauritius of 19.8% and Seychelles of 31.5% in 2017 (OECD/ATAF/AUC, 2019[21]). Finally, SIDS in Latin America and the Caribbean had the biggest variation, from Dominican Republic's tax-to-GDP ratio of 13.2% to Cuba's ratio of 42.3% in 2018 (OECD et al., 2020[22]).

SIDS' ability to mobilise and improve the stability of domestic revenues may be hampered in future years due to the impact of the COVID-19 pandemic. Public revenues in SIDS may be affected by the crisis via a variety of channels, most notably the sharp decline in global and domestic trade (as many SIDS have a high share of revenues coming from taxes on goods and services), declines in commodity and natural resource prices, and the fall of tourism activity. To recover from the COVID-19 crisis, enhanced management of key sectors, including fisheries, tourism and natural resource extraction, may provide opportunities to enhance domestic revenue mobilisation in SIDS. Policies to reduce "leakages" from these sectors – especially tourism – and to support backward and forward linkages with other domestic sectors (e.g. food and agriculture, consumer goods and construction) could expand the taxable production base.

Improving the efficiency of revenue collection, enlarging the tax base and employing efficient tax policies are also essential to increase the resources required to sustain development. The *Global Revenue Statistics* project supports 20 SIDS in these efforts by providing accurate, comparable and detailed data on their tax revenues. This information is essential for tax policymaking and administrative reforms, and forms a common evidence base for mutual learning across SIDS on how to scale up domestic resource mobilisation. The OECD is deepening analysis on the role of domestic revenue mobilisation in financing sustainable development in SIDS.

Source: Piera Tortora and Talita Yamashiro Fordelone, based on OECD (2018[23]), (World Bank, 2020[19]), (World Bank, 2020[18]) and on the *Global Revenue Statistics* database (OECD, 2020[20]).

Figure 1.2. Tax-to-GDP ratios and GDP per capita (in PPP) in Asian and Pacific economies, Latin America and the Caribbean, OECD and African countries (2018)

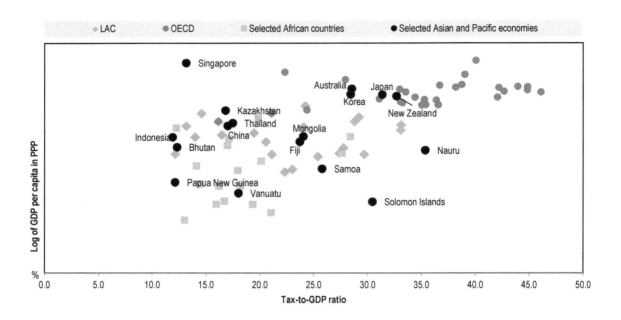

Notes: The y-axis is on a logarithmic scale.

Source: The tax-to-GDP ratio for China does not include revenue from social security contributions (SSCs) as detailed data were not available. The OECD Secretariat estimates SSCs to be approximately 4.0% of GDP in 2018 based on publicly available data from China's Ministry of Human Resources and Social Security.

The Cook Islands and Tokelau are excluded as GDP per capita data was unavailable for these countries.

The purchasing power parity (PPP) between two countries is the rate at which the currency of one country needs to be converted into that of a second country to ensure that a given amount of the first country's currency will purchase the same volume of goods and services in the second country as it does in the first. The implied PPP conversion rate is expressed as national currency per current international dollar. An international dollar has the same purchasing power as the US dollar has in the United States. An international dollar is a hypothetical currency that is used as a means of translating and comparing costs from one country to the other using a common reference point, the US dollar (definitions derived from (IMF, 2019[15]) and (WHO, 2015[16])).

Source: GDP per capita from World Economic Outlook, April 2020 (IMF, 2020[17])

StatLink 🔗 https://stat.link/q6hv5y

Changes in tax-to-GDP ratios in 2018

Since 2017, more than two-thirds of the economies in this publication for which 2018 data are available have experienced increases in their tax-to-GDP ratios (Figure 1.3). Fourteen economies had higher tax-to-GDP ratios in 2018 relative to 2017, whereas five had lower ratios than in 2017. The largest increases were seen in Nauru, Tokelau and Mongolia, at 6.4 percentage points (p.p.), 3.8 p.p. and 2.5 p.p., respectively. Four other economies had increases greater than 1 p.p. (the Solomon Islands, 1.8 p.p.; Korea and the Cook Islands, both at 1.5 p.p.; and Samoa, 1.2 p.p.). Most of the decreases between 2017 and 2018 were less than 1 p.p.: Fiji decreased by 0.5 p.p., Malaysia and Singapore both by 0.9 p.p., with only Bhutan experiencing a larger decrease of 1.4 p.p.

Figure 1.3. Annual changes in tax-to-GDP ratios (2017-18)

Percentage point (p.p.) change

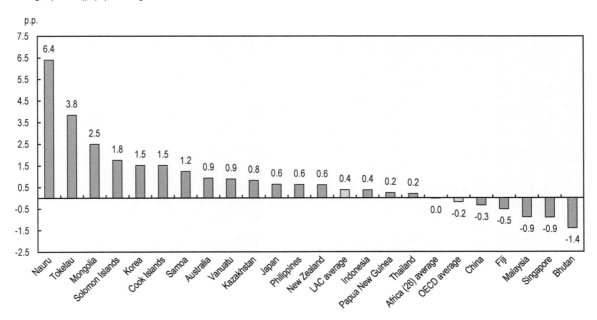

Notes: The figures do not include sub-national tax revenue for the Cook Islands, Fiji, Malaysia, Papua New Guinea, Samoa and the Solomon Islands.

The averages for Africa (26 countries), for LAC (25 Latin American and Caribbean countries) and the OECD (36 countries) are unweighted.

Australia, Japan, Korea and New Zealand are part of the OECD (36) group. Data for Australia, Japan, Korea, New Zealand and the OECD average are taken from *Revenue Statistics 2019* (OECD, 2019[24]).

Data for the change between 2016 and 2017 are used for the Africa (26) average, Australia and Japan.

The tax-to-GDP ratio for China does not include revenue from social security contributions as detailed data were not available.

Source: Authors' calculations based on Table 3.1 in Chapter 3.

StatLink ⬛️ https://stat.link/6g910r

Different factors accounted for the large increases in tax-to-GDP ratios of Nauru, Tokelau and Mongolia between 2017 and 2018 (Figure 1.4). In Mongolia, increases of personal income tax (PIT) rates, as well as several increases in the rates on tobacco and alcohol, contributed to the increase of 2.5 p.p. in the tax-to-GDP ratio between 2017 and 2018 (news.mn, 2018[25]). Value added taxes (VAT) contributed the most due to a 23% decrease in VAT refunds in 2018. This decrease was due to a timing issue with a large VAT reimbursement, requested in December 2018 and processed in 2019,[1] so consequently not included in the 2018 data. The second largest increase was seen in Tokelau, where, to reach the policy goal of being tobacco free in 2020 (Tokelau, 2017[26]), Tokelau increased tobacco duties,[2] leading to a rise in tax-to-GDP ratios of 3.8 p.p. in 2018. The largest increase occurred in Nauru, mostly due to higher revenue from income taxes, which increased by 6.0 p.p. in 2018. These increases were due to higher employment tax rates for non-residents, service tax rates and various business tax rates (Nauru, 2019[27]). Due to the government's commitment to a positive fiscal budget and expected decreases in revenues from the Regional Processing Centre (RPC) and from phosphate mining, the government has been seeking to increase tax revenues to offset possible future declines in public revenues, including by increasing various tax rates (IMF, 2020[28]). The remaining increases of 0.4 p.p. in other taxes on goods and services were the result of higher revenue from the passenger levy, departure tax and the telecom tax.

Figure 1.4. Net changes in tax-to-GDP ratios between 2017 and 2018 by main type of tax

Percentage point (p.p.) change

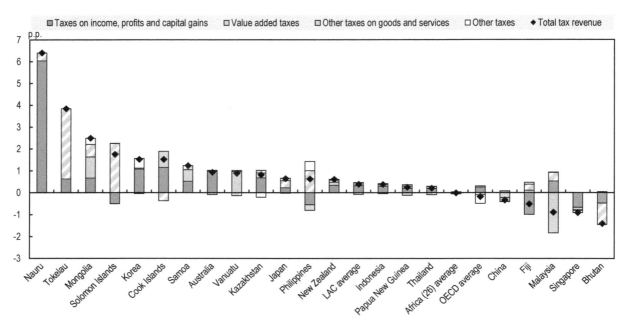

Notes: The averages for Africa (26 countries), for LAC (25 Latin American and Caribbean countries) and the OECD (36 countries) are unweighted.

Australia, Japan, Korea and New Zealand are part of the OECD (36) group. Data for Australia, Japan, Korea, New Zealand and the OECD average are taken from *Revenue Statistics 2019* (OECD, 2019[1]).

2017 data are used for the Africa (26) average, Australia and Japan.

The tax-to-GDP ratio for China does not include revenue from social security contributions as detailed data were not available.

Source: Authors' calculations based on (OECD, 2020[29]), "Revenue Statistics - Asian and Pacific Economies: Comparative tables", *OECD Tax Statistics* (database).

StatLink https://stat.link/olzput

A variety of factors drove the decreases in tax-to-GDP ratios in Malaysia, Singapore and Bhutan between 2017 and 2018. Malaysia changed the standard rate of the goods and services tax (GST) – introduced in 2015 – from 6% to 0%, resulting in a large decrease from revenues on goods and services, and reintroduced the sales tax and service tax (ASEAN, 2018[30]). Revenues from VAT thus decreased by 1.8 p.p. in 2018 and were offset only partially by increases in revenue from income taxes (0.5 p.p.) and other taxes of goods and services (0.4 p.p.). The second largest decrease in tax-to-GDP ratios occurred in Singapore: revenues from income taxes decreased by 0.7 p.p. because of lower revenue from statutory board contributions, which had been exceptionally high in 2017 due to a surplus generated by the Monetary Authority of Singapore, and have since returned to previous levels (Business Times, 2018[31]). The largest decrease in tax-to-GDP ratios occurred in Bhutan, where revenues from income taxes decreased by 0.5 p.p. and revenues from other taxes on goods and services fell by 1.0 p.p. in 2018. This was due to the removal of the excise duty on fuel imports from India (Bhutanese, 2017[32]), decreasing revenue from other taxes on goods and services.

Evolution of tax-to-GDP ratios since 2007

Across a longer time horizon, 11 economies in the publication have increased their tax-to-GDP ratios since 2007 (OECD, 2019[24]),[3] whereas 9 have not (Figure 1.5).

Figure 1.5. Changes in tax-to-GDP ratios (2007-18 and 2007-12)

Percentage point (p.p.) change

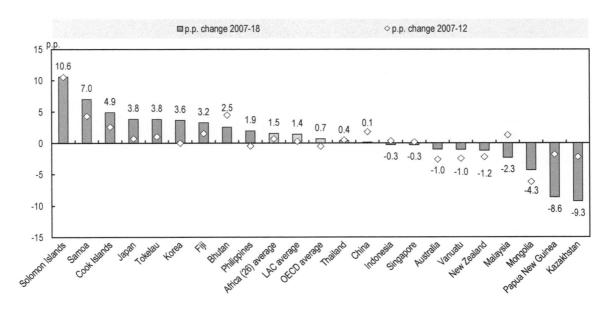

Notes: The figures do not include sub-national tax revenue for the Cook Islands, Fiji, Malaysia, Papua New Guinea, Samoa and the Solomon Islands.

The averages for Africa (26 countries), for LAC (25 Latin American and Caribbean countries) and the OECD (36 countries) are unweighted.

Australia, Japan, Korea and New Zealand are part of the OECD (36) group. Data for Australia, Japan, Korea, New Zealand and the OECD average are taken from Revenue Statistics 2019 (OECD, 2019[1]).

2017 data are used for the Africa (26) average, Australia, Japan and the OECD average.

Data for the Africa (26) average, Bhutan and Fiji start in 2008.

The tax-to-GDP ratio for China does not include revenue from social security contributions as detailed data were not available.

Data for Nauru are only available from 2014 onwards and therefore excluded from this graph.

Source: Authors' calculations based on Table 3.1 in Chapter 3.

StatLink ⌗⌗ﬦ https://stat.link/hkcmq0

Across the period, the largest decreases in tax-to-GDP ratios were observed in Mongolia, Papua New Guinea and Kazakhstan (by 4.3 p.p., 8.6 p.p. and 9.3 p.p., respectively), which were affected by the fall in mineral resource prices between 2007 and 2018. By contrast, the tax-to-GDP ratios of the Solomon Islands, Samoa and the Cook Islands grew by over 4.5 p.p. during the same period. The change in the tax-to-GDP ratios for the remaining economies ranged from a decrease of 2.3 p.p. in Malaysia to an increase of 3.8 p.p. in Japan and Tokelau.

Across the Asian countries included in the publication, the change in tax-to-GDP ratios ranged from -9.3 p.p. in Kazakhstan to 3.8 p.p. in Japan, with ratios increasing in 6 of the 11 Asian economies considered here and decreasing in 5. Across the Pacific economies in this publication for which data were available between 2007 and 2018, tax-to-GDP ratio changes ranged from -8.6 p.p. in Papua New Guinea to 10.6 p.p. in the Solomon Islands. The distribution of changes across the period was similar to those of the Asian economies: ratios decreased in 4 Pacific Island economies and increased in 5.

Changes in tax-to-GDP ratios between 2007 and 2018, by tax category

Between 2007 and 2018, corporate income tax (CIT) revenues were the driver of the major decreases observed in tax-to-GDP ratios in many economies, whereas other taxes on goods and services contributed to several of the increases, although to a lesser extent (Figure 1.6). These changes reflect a diverse range of policy measures and economic developments in Asian and Pacific economies over this period.

Of the nine economies where tax-to-GDP ratios declined between 2007 and 2018, lower CIT revenues contributed in six. The declines in the tax-to-GDP ratios in Mongolia (4.3 p.p.), Papua New Guinea (8.6 p.p.) and Kazakhstan (9.3 p.p.) resulted from lower CIT revenues, which decreased by 7.6 p.p., 7.9 p.p. and 7.2 p.p., respectively. As noted, the three economies were strongly affected by declines in natural resource prices. Kazakhstan also reduced its corporate tax rate from 30% in 2008 to 20% in 2009. An additional factor contributing to the decrease in revenues from CIT in Mongolia was the abolishment of the windfall tax on profits in 2011, which accounted on average for around 20% of total tax revenue in previous years (World Bank, 2011[33]).

Eleven economies recorded increases in their tax-to-GDP ratios between 2007 and 2018. The highest increases were seen in Samoa and the Solomon Islands. In Samoa, the increase in the tax-to-GDP ratio of 7.0 p.p. was due to VAT increasing by 3.2 p.p., other taxes on goods and services by 2.4 p.p. and income taxes by 1.5 p.p. Samoa has implemented a variety of reforms to broaden the tax base and remove exemptions, improve tax administration efficiency and tax compliance (IMF, 2018[34]; Cullen, 2017[35]). All these measures contributed to the increase in tax revenue over the years. The increase by 10.6 p.p. of the tax-to-GDP ratio for the Solomon Islands was mainly driven by increases in other taxes on goods and services (7.2 p.p.) and taxes on income (1.7 p.p. from both corporates and individuals). The growth in revenues from taxes on income can be explained by favourable conditions in the Solomon Islands' economy. The consistently strong performance of the logging sector, which accounts for over 50% of the country's GDP (IMF, 2018[36]) and over 70% of total exports (IMF, 2020[37]) contributed to large increases in revenue from export duties.

Levels of revenues from tax categories in 2018 (as a percentage of GDP)

Australia, New Zealand and Tokelau had the highest levels of personal income tax (PIT) revenues as a percentage of GDP in 2018 (Figure 1.7). Revenue from PIT equated to 12.1% of GDP in New Zealand and 11.5% of GDP in Australia (2017 figure). Tokelau, with a ratio of 8.6% of GDP, had a similar level of PIT revenue to the OECD average in 2017 (8.3%). In the other Pacific economies covered in this publication, revenue from PIT was above 3.0% of GDP except in Fiji (1.9%) and Vanuatu (which does not have a PIT). For Nauru, it is not possible to distinguish between revenues from PIT and CIT. However, Nauru has the highest level of revenue from income taxes of all economies included in the publication, at 24.8% of GDP. In the Asian countries included in this publication, with the exceptions of Japan and Korea, revenue from PIT in 2018 ranged from 0.9% of GDP in Bhutan to 2.5% of GDP in Mongolia.

Figure 1.6. Net changes in tax-to-GDP ratios between 2007 and 2018

Percentage point (p.p.) change, by main type of taxes

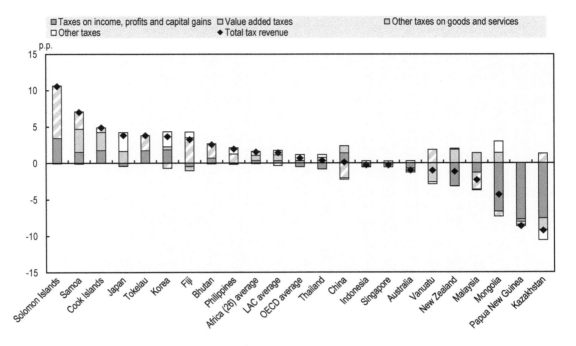

Notes: The figures do not include sub-national tax revenue for the Cook Islands, Fiji, Malaysia, Papua New Guinea, Samoa and the Solomon Islands.

The averages for Africa (26 countries), for LAC (25 Latin American and Caribbean countries) and the OECD (36 countries) are unweighted.

Australia, Japan, Korea and New Zealand are part of the OECD (36) group. Data for Australia, Japan, Korea, New Zealand and the OECD average are taken from *Revenue Statistics 2019* (OECD, 2019[1]).

2017 data are used for the Africa (26) average, Australia, Japan and the OECD average.

Data for the Africa (26) average, Bhutan and Fiji start in 2008.

Nauru is excluded from this analysis as data are only available from 2014 onwards.

The tax-to-GDP ratio for China does not include revenue from social security contributions as detailed data were not available.

Source: Authors' calculations based on (OECD, 2020[29]), "Revenue Statistics - Asian and Pacific Economies: Comparative tables", *OECD Tax Statistics* (database).

StatLink ᏗᎶᏍᏉ https://stat.link/cz6vy5

Figure 1.7. Tax structures as a percentage of GDP (2018)

Percentage of GDP

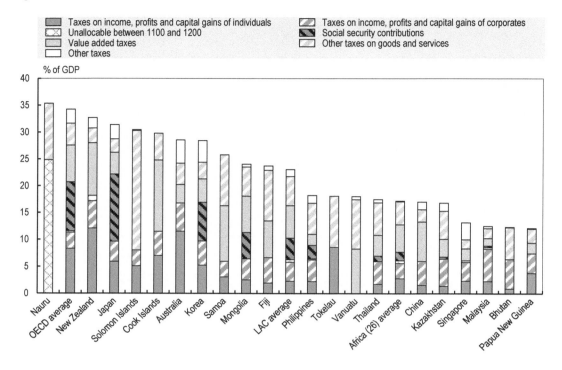

Notes: The figures do not include sub-national tax revenue for the Cook Islands, Fiji, Malaysia, Papua New Guinea, Samoa and the Solomon Islands.

The averages for Africa (26 countries), for LAC (25 Latin American and Caribbean countries) and the OECD (36 countries) are unweighted.

Australia, Japan, Korea and New Zealand are part of the OECD (36) group. Data for Australia, Japan, Korea, New Zealand and the OECD average are taken from *Revenue Statistics 2019* (OECD, 2019[24]).

2017 data are used for the Africa (26) average, Australia, Japan and the OECD average.

The tax-to-GDP ratio for China does not include revenue from social security contributions (SSCs) as detailed data were not available. The OECD Secretariat estimates SSCs to be approximately 4.0% of GDP in 2018 based on publicly available data from China's Ministry of Human Resources and Social Security.

Source: (OECD, 2020[38]), "Revenue Statistics - Asian and Pacific Economies: Comparative tables", *OECD Tax Statistics* (database).

StatLink ᫿ https://stat.link/drc5l0

Revenues from corporate income tax (CIT) were higher than revenues from PIT in 10 of the 18 economies considered here (excluding Tokelau and Vanuatu, which do not have a corporate tax, and Nauru, for which a distinction between PIT and CIT revenues is not possible). Revenues from CIT ranged from 2.9% of GDP in the Solomon Islands and Samoa, to 6.0% in Malaysia. CIT revenue exceeded 5% of GDP in five countries: Kazakhstan and New Zealand (both at 5.1% of GDP), Australia (5.3% of GDP), Bhutan (5.5% of GDP) and Malaysia (6.0% of GDP).

Social security contributions (SSCs) play a small role in the tax revenues of Asian and Pacific economies. Eleven of the economies in this publication, including all Pacific economies, do not levy SSCs. In most of the remaining economies, revenues from SSCs were relatively low in 2018, including in Malaysia (0.3% of GDP), Indonesia and Kazakhstan (0.4% of GDP), Thailand (1.0% of GDP) and the Philippines (2.5% of GDP). These levels are significantly below the LAC average (4.0% of GDP) and the OECD average (9.1% of GDP in 2017). Three Asian countries reported higher shares of SSCs. Mongolia recorded a share of SSCs at 4.8% of GDP, and Korea and Japan also have high shares of revenue from SSCs, at 7.2% and 12.5% of GDP (2017 figure), respectively.[4]

Although the level of SSCs remains relatively low in Indonesia (0.4% of GDP), the government has recently undertaken intensive reforms to increase it:

- A new pension system (*Jaminan Pensiun* (JP)) was introduced in 2014 and is a compulsory insurance for formal workers in the private sector (OECD, 2019[11]).
- New institutions responsible for health and employment-related social security were created to replace the previous ones. The *Badan Penyelenggara Jaminan Sosial* (BPJS) is responsible for policy development, implementation of social security schemes, and monitoring of social security funds. The BPJS has two independent management bodies: *BPJS Kesehatan* (Health); and *BPJS Ketenagakerjaan* (Labour). They began operations in January 2014 and July 2015, respectively (OECD, 2019[11]).
- The coverage and contribution rates for these programmes (both for employees and employers) have increased, which has led to higher social security contributions (The United States Social Security Administration, 2018[39]).

In most of the Asian economies in this publication, revenues from taxes on goods and services as a percentage of GDP are below 10.0%, with the exception of Mongolia, which raised an equivalent of 12.2% of GDP in 2018. In contrast, the majority of the Pacific economies in this publication raised levels of revenues from taxes on goods and services above 10.0% of GDP, ranging from 10.5% of GDP in Nauru to 22.3% in the Solomon Islands in 2018. The exceptions are Papua New Guinea (4.6% of GDP), Australia (7.4% of GDP, 2017 figure) and Tokelau (9.5% of GDP).

Tax structures

The tax structure, measured as the composition of tax revenues of different types, is the second key indicator in *Revenue Statistics*. Different taxes have different economic and social effects. Across the 21 economies in this publication, the composition of taxes varies widely, reflecting economies' different policy choices, economic structures and conditions, tax administration capabilities and historical factors.

Tax structures in 2018 and evolution since 2007

The tax structure of the economies covered in this publication varied greatly in 2018. In ten economies, the main source of tax revenue was taxes on goods and services, while nine economies obtained the primary share of tax revenues from income taxes (Figure 1.8). Japan is the only country in which the greatest share of revenues was derived from social security contributions.

In 2018, income taxes were the largest source of revenue for Australia (2017 figure), Bhutan, Indonesia, Korea, Malaysia, Nauru, New Zealand, Papua New Guinea and Singapore. Among these economies, the share of income tax revenues varied from 34.1% in Korea to 70.2% in Nauru. CIT revenues were higher than PIT revenues in four Asian countries (Bhutan, Indonesia, Malaysia and Singapore), while all Pacific economies in this group (Australia, New Zealand, Papua New Guinea and Tokelau), as well as Korea, raised higher shares of revenue from PIT.

Taxes on goods and services were the main source of tax revenue in the Cook Islands, Fiji, Kazakhstan, Mongolia, the Philippines, Samoa, the Solomon Islands, Thailand, Tokelau and Vanuatu in 2018, contributing between 43.0% (the Philippines) and 96.9% (Vanuatu) of total tax revenue. Taxes on goods and services also contributed the largest share of revenues for the LAC and African regions, on average, amounting to more than 50% of total tax revenue. In most of the economies in which revenue from taxes on goods and services are the main source of revenues, taxes on goods and services other than VAT, such as excises and import duties, contributed typically a larger share than VAT revenues to total tax revenues. Seven economies recorded higher revenues from other taxes on goods and services, ranging from 31.1% of total tax revenues in Kazakhstan to 73.2% in the Solomon Islands, while three economies received a larger share of revenue from VAT: Mongolia (28.2%), Samoa (40.1%) and the Cook Islands (44.6%).

As discussed earlier, social security contributions played a small role in revenues for most Asian and Pacific economies, with a few exceptions. Japan derived the largest share of total tax revenues from social security contributions, at 39.9% in 2017. Social security contributions also played a significant role in revenues in Mongolia (20.1%) and Korea (25.4%), with shares that are close to the OECD average (26.0% in 2017).

Figure 1.8. Tax structures as a percentage of total taxation (2018)

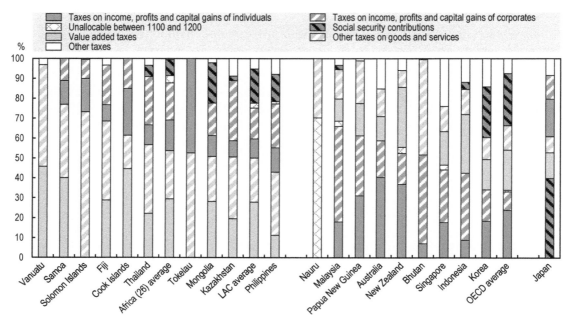

Notes: The figures do not include sub-national tax revenue for the Cook Islands, Fiji, Malaysia, Papua New Guinea, Samoa and the Solomon Islands.

The averages for Africa (26 countries), for LAC (25 Latin American and Caribbean countries) and the OECD (36 countries) are unweighted.

Australia, Japan, Korea and New Zealand are part of the OECD (36) group. Data for Australia, Japan, Korea, New Zealand and the OECD average are taken from *Revenue Statistics 2019* [(OECD, 2019[1])

2017 data are used for the Africa (26) average, Australia, Japan and the OECD average.

Data for China are not included in this graph as detailed data on revenue from social security contributions were not available.

Source: (OECD, 2020[29]), "Revenue Statistics - Asian and Pacific Economies: Comparative tables", *OECD Tax Statistics* (database).

StatLink 🖳📊 https://stat.link/xk7s1j

Across most economies in this publication, VAT is an important and increasing source of revenues, particularly in the Pacific (Figure 1.9). Excluding Nauru, Bhutan, Tokelau and the Solomon Islands, which do not have value added taxes, VAT revenue ranged from 11.3% of total tax revenue in the Philippines to 45.8% of total tax revenue in Vanuatu in 2018. In addition, VAT revenues as a share of total taxes are typically higher in Pacific than in Asian economies. In the Asian countries in this publication, VAT revenue ranged from 11.3% of total tax revenue in the Philippines to 29.5% of total tax revenue in Indonesia. Besides Indonesia, Mongolia was the only other Asian country in which VAT revenues accounted for more than 25% of total tax revenue in 2018. In the Pacific economies that apply a VAT system, only Australia and Papua New Guinea had shares of VAT of less than 25% (12.2% [2017 figure] and 16.2%, respectively), while the Cook Islands and Vanuatu had the largest shares (44.6% and 45.8% of total tax revenues, respectively).

Figure 1.9. Revenue from value added tax and other taxes on goods and services as a percentage of total tax revenue (2018)

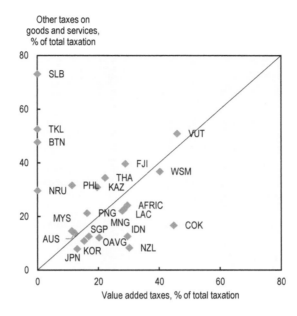

Notes: The figures do not include sub-national tax revenue for the Cook Islands, Fiji, Malaysia, Papua New Guinea, Samoa and the Solomon Islands.

The averages for Africa (26 countries), for LAC (25 Latin American and Caribbean countries) and the OECD (36 countries) are unweighted.

Australia, Japan, Korea and New Zealand are part of the OECD (36) group. Data for Australia, Japan, Korea, New Zealand and the OECD average are taken from *Revenue Statistics 2019* (OECD, 2019[24]).

2017 data are used for the Africa (26) average, Australia, Japan and the OECD average.

Bhutan, Nauru, the Solomon Islands and Tokelau do not levy value added tax.

Data for China are not included in this graph as detailed data on revenue from social security contributions were not available.

Source: (OECD, 2020[29]), "Revenue Statistics - Asian and Pacific Economies: Comparative tables", *OECD Tax Statistics* (database).

StatLink 🔗 https://stat.link/khirng

Revenues from other goods and services contributed between 8.0% of total tax revenue in Japan (2017 figure) and 73.2% in the Solomon Islands in 2018. The high share in the Solomon Islands is derived from general taxes on goods and services, such as the goods tax and the sales tax and export duties on various products, particularly logging (the Solomon Islands do not apply a VAT). Shares of non-VAT taxes in total revenue are also comparatively high in Bhutan, Fiji, Samoa, Tokelau and Vanuatu, where they are larger than 35% of total tax revenues.

In 2018, revenue from other taxes on goods and services played a more prominent role in the Pacific economies than in the Asian countries covered in this publication. Seven of the ten Pacific economies generated more revenue from other taxes on goods and services than from VAT, whereas six of the eleven Asian countries received more revenue from VAT. For the Africa, LAC and OECD averages, revenue from VAT contributed a larger share to total tax revenue than other goods and services.

The share of revenue from VAT increased most in Mongolia (9.3 p.p.) and New Zealand (6.6 p.p.) between 2007 and 2018. Three economies increased their VAT rate between 2007 and 2018: New Zealand, with an increase from 12.5% to 15% in 2010 (OECD, 2012[40]); Japan, from 5% to 8% in 2014 (OECD, 2014[41]); and the Cook Islands, from 12.5% to 15% in 2014 (Cook Islands News, 2013[42]).

Malaysia replaced its sales tax with a VAT at 10% in 2015 (Bloomberg, 2015[43]), and VAT revenues increased from 15.8% of total tax revenues in 2015 to 24.1% in 2017, but decreased to 11.2% in 2018 following the government's decision to return to the sales tax and abolish the VAT (ASEAN, 2018[30]). Mongolia has passed VAT reforms to broaden the tax base or to increase the efficiency of the VAT administration (Bloomberg, 2018[44]); (World Bank, 2018[45]).

Six economies experienced a decline in the share of VAT revenues over this period: Australia, Fiji, Korea, the Philippines, Singapore and Vanuatu. In Fiji, the share of VAT revenue declined by 7.4 p.p. in 2018 to 28.8% of total tax revenue, following a decrease of the VAT rate from 15% to 9% in 2016. Similarly, the share of VAT revenue in Vanuatu declined by 11.2 p.p. in 2018 to 42.5% of total tax revenue due to higher revenue from excises and other taxes on goods and services. Decreases in Australia, Korea and Singapore were less than 1 p.p., while the share decreased by 1.6 p.p. in the Philippines over the same period.

The composition of income taxes between corporate and personal income taxes also varied in Asian and Pacific economies (Figure 1.10). In 2018, all Asian countries except Japan and Korea had a greater share of CIT revenues relative to PIT. In contrast, all Pacific economies covered in this publication except Fiji had a greater share of PIT than CIT.

In 2018, revenues from CIT contributed between 28.1% of total income tax revenue in New Zealand and 86.3% of total income tax revenue in Bhutan. In nine economies, the share of CIT revenues in total income tax revenue was larger than 60% and many of these economies receive a significant share of CIT from companies in the oil and mining sector (Mongolia, Malaysia, Kazakhstan, Indonesia and Bhutan). By contrast, revenue from PIT as a percentage of total income tax ranged from 13.7% in Bhutan to 100% in Tokelau (the latter does not have a CIT).

Between 2007 and 2018, revenues from CIT and PIT were relatively variable as a share of total tax revenues in all economies covered in this publication. The share of CIT revenues was lower in 2018 than in 2007 in nine economies, by between 3.1 p.p. of total tax revenues in the Philippines and 25.7 p.p. in Papua New Guinea.

The share of revenues from PIT decreased for ten Asian and Pacific economies between 2007 and 2018, and the scale of the decreases ranged from 0.4 p.p. of total tax revenues in the Philippines to 7.9 p.p. in Fiji. Revenue from PIT increased as a share of total taxation for eight economies (excluding China, Nauru and Vanuatu) in this period, from 0.3 p.p. in Bhutan to 14.0 p.p. in Papua New Guinea.

Figure 1.10. Revenue from corporate income tax and personal income tax (2018)

Percentage of total income tax revenue

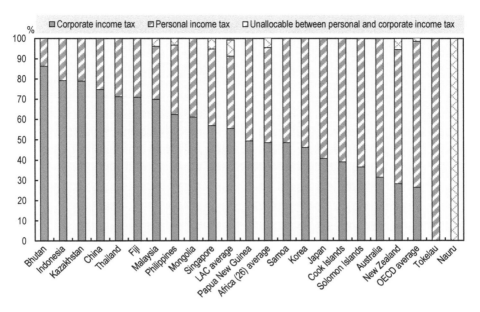

Notes: The figures do not include sub-national tax revenue for the Cook Islands, Fiji, Malaysia, Papua New Guinea, Samoa and the Solomon Islands.

The averages for Africa (26 countries), for LAC (25 Latin American and Caribbean countries) and the OECD (36 countries) are unweighted.

Australia, Japan, Korea and New Zealand are part of the OECD (36) group. Data for Australia, Japan, Korea, New Zealand and the OECD average are taken from *Revenue Statistics 2019* (OECD, 2019[24]).

Vanuatu does not levy personal or corporate income tax, and Tokelau does not levy corporate income tax.

The distinction between revenue from personal and corporate income taxes was not possible in Nauru.

Source: Authors' calculations based on (OECD, 2020[38]), "Revenue Statistics - Asian and Pacific Economies: Comparative tables", *OECD Tax Statistics* (database).

StatLink https://stat.link/82o6zr

Box 1.2. VAT revenue ratios in Asian countries

The VAT revenue ratio (VRR) measures the difference between the VAT revenue collected and what would theoretically be raised if VAT was applied at the standard rate to the entire potential tax base in a "pure" VAT regime and all revenue was collected. A VRR of 1 suggests no loss of VAT revenue as a consequence of exemptions, reduced rates, fraud, evasion or tax planning. This box describes the VRR levels in the Asian countries in this publication.

There was a wide disparity of VRRs in Asian countries in 2018 (Figure 1.11). The Philippines had the lowest VRR at 0.2 and Mongolia and China had the highest at 0.96 (2017 figure for Mongolia). Of the countries in this publication, Japan, Korea and Singapore have relatively high VRRs (exceeding 0.6), above the OECD average of 0.56 (2016 figure). This is partially because of the relatively broad-based VAT in each country: Japan does not have any reduced rates while in Singapore, only international services are zero-rated, with the only exemptions applying to the sales and leases of residential properties and to most financial services (Ministry of Finance of Singapore, 2020[46]). Korea has a reduced rate on a number of goods and services. In comparison, many OECD countries have one or more reduced rates (OECD, 2016[47]), which partly explains the lower average VRR in the OECD region.

The VRR needs to be interpreted with caution and can be affected by several factors that inflate it. One reason can be where exemptions on products and services relating to intermediate consumption can lead to a cascading effect that increases VAT revenue (IMF, 2017[48]). For example, in Thailand, a large amount of exemptions on a variety of products may cause "cascading", which artificially increases the VRR. Another reason the VRR may be inflated is if refund processes do not work correctly, which may discourage taxpayers from claiming their VAT refunds, resulting in artificially higher VAT revenue and VRR.

On the other hand, the VRR can be deflated by the absence of rules and mechanisms for the collection of VAT on inbound business-to-consumer (B2C) supplies of services resulting from the ever-growing digital trade. To date, over 60 countries in the world have adopted the rules for the application of VAT to such supplies and 40 of them have implemented simplified registration and collection regimes for the actual collection of VAT according to the OECD standards. Japan and Korea collect VAT on these supplies since 2015; and Singapore, Indonesia and Malaysia should implement similar measures in 2020.

Figure 1.11. VAT revenue ratios (VRRs) in Asian countries (2018)

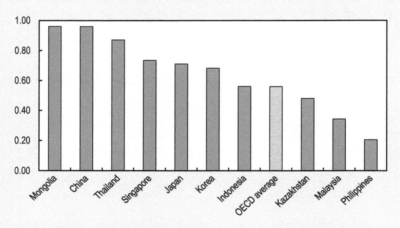

Notes: Data for Japan and the OECD average are taken from (OECD, 2018[49]) and therefore show data for 2016.
Philippines: The VRR measure is currently underestimated as the VAT revenue collected at customs is not accounted for in total VAT revenue in this publication (this revenue could not be distinguished from revenue from other import duties and is currently classified under heading 5120 (taxes on specific goods and services).
Mongolia: 2017 data are used because the VAT data for 2018 is artificially high due to a large reimbursement requested in December 2018 which was processed in 2019.
Sources: Countries, Trading Economics and KPMG websites and (OECD, 2018[49]) for VAT rates; World Economic Outlook April 2020 (IMF, 2020[17]) and OECD Annual National Accounts (OECD, 2020[50]) for final expenditure consumption figures; and country tables in Chapter 4 for VAT revenues.

StatLink 🖳 https://stat.link/2smd5r

Environmental taxes in Asia and the Pacific

Environmentally related taxes,[5] and price-based policy instruments more generally, play an increasingly significant role in many countries to support a transition to a sustainable and low-carbon economic growth. By incorporating a price signal into consumer and producer decisions, these taxes give effect to the polluter-pays principle and encourage businesses and households to consider the environmental costs of their behaviour. Although environmentally related tax revenues (OECD, 2017[61])[6] are not separately identified in the standard OECD tax classification, they can be identified through the detailed list of specific taxes included for most countries within this overarching classification. It is on this basis that they are included in the *OECD Policy Instruments for the Environment* (PINE) database (OECD, 2017[61]).[7]

A detailed examination of country-specific taxes for the Asian and Pacific economies for which information is available demonstrates that revenue from environmentally related taxes in 2018 ranged from less than 0.05% of GDP in Papua New Guinea to 8.0% of GDP in the Solomon Islands.[8] The case of the Solomon Islands is notable as their environmentally related tax revenue is particularly high compared to the levels in other Asian and Pacific economies or even to the OECD average, due in large part to higher export duties, particularly on timber. The second highest revenues from environmental related taxes in the region are levied by Korea and Nauru, amounting to over 2.0% of GDP in 2018, a similar level to the OECD average (2.3% of GDP, estimated 2018 figure (OECD, 2019[24])).

Figure 1.12. Environmentally related tax revenue in Asian and Pacific economies, by main tax base (2018)

Percentage of GDP

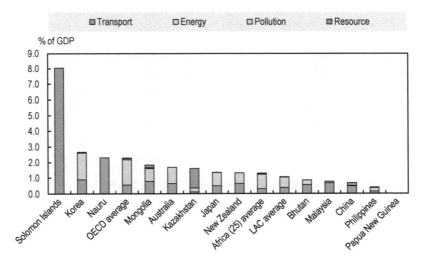

Notes: It has not been possible to identify environmentally related tax revenue for Thailand and Samoa due to data availability issues. 2016 data are used for Australia and 2014 data for Korea as these are the latest years available in the PINE database.
Sources: PINE database for Australia, Japan, Korea and New Zealand; (OECD, 2020[51]) and authors' calculations based on (OECD, 2020[38]), "Revenue Statistics - Asian and Pacific Economies: Comparative tables", *OECD Tax Statistics* (database).

StatLink ᵐᵗˢᴸ https://stat.link/f97o5p

The Asian and Pacific economies in this report rely on different environmentally related tax revenue (ERTR) bases:

- In the Solomon Islands and Kazakhstan, the majority of environmentally related tax revenues are from resource taxes (timber for the Solomon Islands through export taxes, and minerals for Kazakhstan through an excise tax). They represent 78% of total environmentally related tax revenue in Kazakhstan and the totality for the Solomon Islands.

- In other Asian and Pacific economies, environmentally related tax revenues are principally levied either from taxes on energy (five countries, most commonly from diesel and petrol) and from transport taxes (six countries, registration or road use of motor vehicles or departure taxes). In almost all countries, a combination of these two types of taxes is used; Nauru is the exception as it resorts entirely to transport taxes, sourcing 99% of ERTRs from departure taxes and passenger taxes.

- Only 6 countries (China, Japan, Korea, Kazakhstan, Mongolia, and the Philippines) out of the 13 for which data are available collect environmentally related tax revenues from three different bases or more, whereas other countries rely mainly on one base (Nauru, Papua New Guinea and the Solomon Islands) or two bases (Australia, New Zealand, Bhutan and Malaysia).

- The composition of environmentally related tax revenues varies more in Asian and Pacific economies than in African (25), LAC and OECD countries, where transport taxes are more dominant (70% in Africa and the OECD, and 60% in LAC).

In comparison to OECD countries, the use of taxation to address environmental issues is low in the region and there is a significant scope to resort more to this type of taxation. The underutilisation of environmental taxes in the Asia-Pacific region needs also to be understood in the context of the extensive use of fossil fuels subsidies. Reforming energy subsidies is considered by ADB (2016[52]) as "one of the most important policy challenges for developing Asian economies". UN ESCAP (2016[53]) recommends that governments should gradually phase out energy subsidies while implementing measures to compensate vulnerable groups and to ensure international competitiveness in a sustainable way. Reforming energy subsidies while at the same time implementing environmental taxation has the potential to mobilise significant government revenues and help to meet the Sustainable Development Goals (SDGs). Singapore has recently introduced significant green tax reforms:

- In 2019, Singapore became the only country in Southeast Asia to impose a carbon tax. Its payment would be first levied in 2020, based on emissions in 2019. The tax is applied on the total direct emissions of facilities that emit 25 000 tCO_2e or more annually, and covers six greenhouse gases (NCCS, 2020[54]). This tax complements the carbon emissions-based vehicle scheme (CEVS) introduced in January 2013, which levies a tax on all new cars, taxis and newly-imported used cars, based on their CO_2/km performance.

Taxes by level of government

This section discusses the relative share of tax revenues attributed to different levels of government in 2018: central government, regional or provincial government (including state government, where relevant), and local government as well as social security funds.

In many economies included in this publication, the share of sub-national taxes was comparatively small as a share of total tax revenues in 2018 (Table 1.1). Shares of sub-national government tax revenue in the Asian countries ranged from 0.2% of total revenues in Bhutan to 23.9% (2017 figure) in Japan and 22.1% in Kazakhstan. In Indonesia, revenues attributed to sub-national governments rose to over 10% in 2018, following the shift of property taxation to the local level in 2014. Revenue collected by sub-national governments accounted for 16.9% of total taxes in 2018 in Mongolia. In New Zealand, sub-national government revenues were 6.6% and in Australia, subnational revenues (including both state and local tax revenues) amounted to 20.5% of total tax revenues (2017 figure).

The types of taxes levied by local governments vary between countries. Local governments in the Philippines have a narrow range of taxes under their jurisdiction, relying on property taxes and taxes on income and profits. Sub-national governments in Japan and Korea raised revenue from taxes on income and profits, property taxes, taxes on goods and services, payroll (Korea only) and other taxes. The share of sub-national government revenue also depends on the range of services which local governments are expected to provide: for example, local revenues are higher in Japan since local governments finance a wide range of goods and services including public welfare and are responsible for financing some education and debt servicing (Beshho, 2016[55]).

Between 2000 and 2018, the share of revenues collected by sub-national governments was stable, with the exception of Indonesia and Kazakhstan. In Indonesia, the share of revenues attributed to sub-national governments increased by 7.0 p.p., whereas in Kazakhstan it decreased by 27.6 p.p.

As social security contributions play a smaller role in total revenues in Asia and the Pacific than in other regions, the share of revenues attributed to social security funds was also low. Australia, Bhutan, New Zealand and Singapore do not have social security funds and the proportion of total tax revenues collected by social security funds therefore was zero in 2018, and was under 6% of total revenues in Indonesia, Kazakhstan, Malaysia and Thailand. By contrast, countries that source a greater share of their revenues from social security contributions also had higher shares of revenues attributed to social security funds: at 40.4% of tax revenues in Japan in 2017 and 25.7% in Korea and 21.0% in Mongolia in 2018. The share of tax revenues attributed to social security funds has increased in Japan (by 5.2 p.p.) and Korea (by 9.0 p.p.) since 2000, and in Mongolia since 2006 (by 10.8 p.p.).

Table 1.1. Attribution of tax revenues to sub-sectors of general government

Percentage of total tax revenue (2000-18)

	Federal or central government				Sub-national government				Social security funds			
	2000	2010	2015	2018	2000	2010	2015	2018	2000	2010	2015	2018
Australia	81.8	80.2	79.3	79.5	18.2	19.8	20.7	20.5	0.0	0.0	0.0	0.0
Bhutan	..	99.9	99.6	99.8	..	0.1	0.4	0.2	..	0.0	0.0	0.0
Indonesia	96.1	92.8	88.8	85.7	3.9	7.2	10.6	10.8	..	..	0.6	3.5
Japan	38.7	33.0	36.7	35.7	26.1	25.9	23.9	23.9	35.2	41.1	39.4	40.4
Kazakhstan	50.3	81.3	72.2	74.6	49.7	16.2	24.0	22.1	..	2.5	3.8	3.2
Korea	68.2	60.0	55.4	57.0	15.1	16.6	18.0	17.3	16.7	23.3	26.6	25.7
Mongolia	..	75.5	61.5	62.1	..	11.4	16.5	16.9	..	13.1	22.0	21.0
Malaysia	98.0	98.2	98.3	98.1	..	..	..	..	2.0	1.8	1.7	1.9
New Zealand	94.3	92.8	93.2	93.4	5.7	7.2	6.8	6.6	0.0	0.0	0.0	0.0
Philippines	81.5	82.2	80.5	81.3	5.3	5.2	5.4	5.3	13.1	12.7	14.1	13.4
Singapore	100.0	100.0	100.0	100.0	..	..	..	..	0.0	0.0	0.0	0.0
Thailand	88.9	86.3	86.4	85.6	7.5	6.6	8.0	8.6	3.7	7.1	5.6	5.7

Notes: Australia, Japan, Korea and New Zealand are part of the OECD (36) group. Data for Australia, Japan, Korea and New Zealand are taken from (OECD, 2019[1]).

The figures do not include sub-national tax revenue for the Cook Islands, Fiji, Malaysia, Papua New Guinea, Samoa and the Solomon Islands. 2017 data are used for Australia and Japan.

Australia: Sub-national figures include data of state and local government.

Data for China are not included in this table as detailed data on revenue from social security contributions were not available.

Source: (OECD, 2020[29]), "Revenue Statistics - Asian and Pacific Economies: Comparative tables", *OECD Tax Statistics* (database).

StatLink ᴍᴍᴤ📊 https://stat.link/xuiayr

Non-tax revenues in selected economies

This publication also includes information on non-tax revenues for selected economies for which data are available. Non-tax revenues are defined as all revenues received by general government that do not meet the OECD definition of taxes, as set out in the Interpretative Guide (Annex A). They are further divided into five categories according to the definitions set out in Annex B: grants; property income; sales of goods and services; fines, penalties and forfeits; and miscellaneous and unidentified revenues.

Non-tax revenues as a percentage of GDP

Non-tax revenues were equivalent to a significant share of GDP in 2018 for five economies for which data are available. Non-tax revenues were around 12.9% of GDP in 2018 in Bhutan and the Cook Islands, and around 18.2% of GDP in Vanuatu, whereas they amounted to 92.7% of GDP for Nauru and to 236.4% of GDP for Tokelau. The very high level of non-tax revenues in Tokelau, measured as a share of GDP, is due to the fact that non-tax revenues are derived primarily from payments by foreign vessels for access to Tokelau's fishing waters. In the 2008 System of National Accounts, these revenues are recorded as part of GNI, but they do not add to GDP. By contrast, non-tax revenues are below 6.5% of GDP in the remaining economies (see Table 1.2).

Further, non-tax revenues have been increasing since 2007 (or earliest available year) for the majority of the economies, whereas they have been declining as a share of GDP for Bhutan (since 2008), Mongolia, Papua New Guinea and Samoa. The upward trend for Tokelau has been driven by the increase in revenues from property income, which is entirely sourced from fishery income. Tokelau receives support from New Zealand to strengthen the management of its Exclusive Economic Zone to maximise Tokelau's revenue collection from its international fisheries (New Zealand Foreign Affairs & Trade, 2018[56]). Fisheries income also increased after Tokelau became a partner to the Nauru Agreement, which administers the fishing vessel-day scheme (VSD). The VSD is the system to sustainably manage the world's largest tuna fishery in the Western and Central Pacific Ocean, and has increased revenue to participating islands by over 500% in the past six years (Parties to the Nauru Agreement, 2016[57]).

The increase in non-tax revenue for the Cook Islands has been predominantly driven by an increase in grant revenues from New Zealand, Australia and the European Union. This support contributes to upgrading infrastructure, growing sustainable tourism, and supporting initiatives that strengthen the public sector and improve education, health and social services. Increases in non-tax revenues in Vanuatu can be explained by increases in grant revenue in response to Cyclone Pam in 2015 (causing losses to the economy of over 60% of GDP (IMF, 2016[58])) and volcano eruptions in 2017 (causing the evacuation of 11 000 people (MEAE France, 2017[59])). Besides higher grant revenue relative to 2007, the success of the government citizenship programme in Vanuatu also contributed the most to increases in non-tax revenue in 2018 (Department of Finance and Treasury of Vanuatu, 2018[60]).

Structure of non-tax revenues

Non-tax revenues are divided into different categories: grants; property income; sales of goods and services; fines, penalties and forfeits; and miscellaneous and unidentified revenues.

In 2018, the shares of each of these categories in total non-tax revenues varied across the 12 economies for which data are available (Figure 1.13). Notable trends include:

- Grants were an important source of revenues for half of the economies in 2018, exceeding 30% of total non-tax revenues in six economies: Vanuatu (33.6%), Samoa (33.8%), Tokelau (36.3%), Bhutan (46.2%), the Cook Islands (46.7%) and Papua New Guinea (62.6%). In 2018, they were the main source of non-tax revenues for the Cook Islands, Papua New Guinea and Bhutan.

- Property income accounted for over 40% of total non-tax revenue in three-quarters of the economies for which non-tax revenue data are available. The only exceptions are Vanuatu, which does not have revenues from property income, Samoa (16.0%) and Papua New Guinea (36.3%).

Property income in Tokelau and Nauru was derived predominantly from fisheries income (i.e. fishing rents, fishing days, support vessels, etc.), which represented more than 80% of total property income in both economies. Rents and royalties accounted for 78.1% of total non-tax revenue in Kazakhstan, mainly from oil revenues in 2018.

Table 1.2. Non-tax revenue of main headings as a percentage of GDP in selected Pacific economies (2007-18)

	2007	2008	2009	2010	2011	2012	2013	2014	2015	2016	2017	2018
Bhutan		25.53	26.46	21.85	21.54	16.56	20.61	14.83	17.74	14.99	16.44	12.87
Cook Islands	5.59	5.19	9.21	13.54	8.20	8.40	14.29	16.19	13.89	16.39	14.32	12.91
Fiji				2.64	3.31	2.76	2.67	2.94	2.88	3.21	3.50	3.59
Kazakhstan	1.71	1.64	1.25	1.22	1.58	2.18	1.28	0.68	0.49	1.35	1.24	1.73
Mongolia	9.53	6.41	7.86	6.55	7.42	6.93	7.17	7.76	6.30	5.07	4.33	4.59
Nauru								28.63	65.16	63.74	70.79	92.67
Philippines								1.89	2.17	1.90	1.81	1.95
Papua New Guinea	4.00	4.08	3.51	4.71	3.27	3.09	2.41	3.10	3.24	3.17	3.18	3.56
Thailand	2.60	2.90	2.87	3.27	2.72	2.79	2.92	3.11	3.53	3.63	3.55	3.70
Tokelau	149.26	157.58	165.20	154.60	196.37	192.57	246.59	173.40	252.49	236.47	177.95	236.43
Vanuatu	1.44	6.49	7.00	8.27	5.89	5.23	4.22	5.83	14.79	9.56	14.20	18.18
Samoa	7.09	9.66	3.45	9.01	6.02	4.84	6.97	4.81	4.76	4.74	5.61	6.07

Note: Tokelau receives significant revenues from foreign vessels for access to Tokelau fishing waters. In the 2008 SNA, these revenues are recorded as part of GNI, but they do not add to GDP.
Source: (OECD, 2020[29]), "Revenue Statistics - Asian and Pacific Economies: Comparative tables", *OECD Tax Statistics* (database).

StatLink https://stat.link/9cv68e

Figure 1.13. Structure of non-tax revenue (2018)

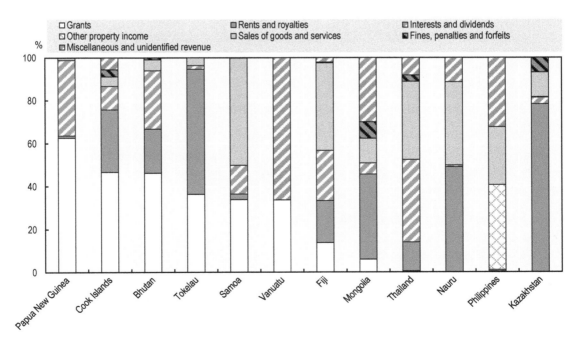

Source: (OECD, 2020[29]), "Revenue Statistics - Asian and Pacific Economies: Comparative tables", *OECD Tax Statistics* (database).

StatLink https://stat.link/9hijs4

References

ADB (2016), *Fossil Fuel Subsidies in Asia: Trends, Impacts, and Reforms*, https://www.adb.org/sites/default/files/publication/182255/fossil-fuel-subsidies-asia.pdf (accessed on 25 June 2020).   [52]

Aizenman, E. (2015), "Tax revenue trends in Asia and Latin America: A comparative analysis", *NBER Working Paper* No.217555, Cambridge, http://www.nber.org/papers/w21755.   [10]

ASEAN (2018), *Malaysia to re-introduce sales and services tax from September 1*, https://www.aseanbriefing.com/news/malaysia-to-re-introduce-sales-and-services-tax-from-sept-1/.   [30]

Beshho, S. (2016), "Case Study of Central and Local Government Finance in Japan", *ADBI Working Paper No.599*, https://www.adb.org /publications/case-study-centraland-centraland-and-local-government-finance-japan/.   [55]

Bhutanese, T. (2017), *Government slashes Petrol by Nu 10.29 a liter and diesel by Nu 7.75 from 11th Nov*, https://thebhutanese.bt/govt-slashes-petrol-by-nu-10-29-a-liter-and-diesel-by-nu-7-75-from-11th-nov.   [32]

Bloomberg (2018), "Mongolia's Tax Collectors are the Real Winner in National Lotto - Bloomberg", https://www.bloomberg.com/news/articles/2018-12-25/mongolia-s-tax-collectors-are-the-real-winner-in-national-lotto (accessed on 29 May 2020).   [44]

Bloomberg (2015), "Malaysia's New GST: A Brief Comparison with its Former Sales Tax and Service Tax Regime", https://www.bna.com/malaysias-new-gst-b17179925799.   [43]

Business Times (2018), *Singapore budget revenue and spending breakdown 2018*, https://www.businesstimes.com.sg/specials/singapore-budget-2018/singapore-budget-revenue-and-spending-breakdown-2018/index.html (accessed on 20 April 2020).   [31]

Cook Islands News (2013), *Changes to the Cook Islands System*, http://www.cookislandsnews.com/item/42583-changes-to-the-cook-islands-tax-system/.   [42]

Cullen, R. (2017), *E-government in Pacific Island countries*, Springer, http://dx.doi.org/10.1007/978-3-319-50972-3_1.   [35]

Department of Finance and Treasury of Vanuatu (2018), *Treasury Monthly Budget Report-November 2018*, https://doft.gov.vu/images/2019/November_Monthly_Report_FINAL.pdf (accessed on 10 June 2020).   [60]

IMF (2020), *Republic of Nauru : 2019 Article IV Consultation*, https://www.imf.org/en/Publications/CR/Issues/2020/01/29/Republic-of-Nauru-2019-Article-IV-Consultation-Press-Release-Staff-Report-and-Statement-by-49001 (accessed on 30 June 2020).   [28]

IMF (2020), *Solomon Islands : 2019 Article IV Consultation*, https://www.imf.org/en/Publications/CR/Issues/2020/02/18/Solomon-Islands-2019-Article-IV-Consultation-Press-Release-Staff-Report-and-Statement-by-the-49060. (accessed on 28 May 2020).   [37]

IMF (2020), *World Economic Outlook, April 2020 : The Great Lockdown*, [17]
http://dx.doi.org/10.5089/9781513539744.081 (accessed on 15 June 2020).

IMF (2019), *World Economic Outlook - Frequently Asked Questions*, [15]
https://www.imf.org/external/pubs/ft/weo/faq.htm#q4d (accessed on 6 September 2019).

IMF (2018), *2018 Article IV Consultation-Press Release; Staff Report; and Statement by the* [36]
Executive Director for the Solomon Islands; Country Report No. 18/309; November 2018,
http://www.imf.org.

IMF (2018), *Samoa : 2018 Article IV Consultation-Press Release; Staff Report; Staff Statement;* [34]
and Statement by the Executive Director for Samoa,
https://www.imf.org/en/Publications/CR/Issues/2018/06/04/Samoa-2018-Article-IV-
Consultation-Press-Release-Staff-Report-Staff-Statement-and-Statement-45934 (accessed
on 24 June 2020).

IMF (2017), *Indonesia : Selected Issues*, [48]
https://www.imf.org/en/Publications/CR/Issues/2017/02/11/Indonesia-Selected-Issues-44654
(accessed on 24 June 2020).

IMF (2016), *Resilience and Growth in the Small States of the Pacific*, [58]
http://dx.doi.org/10.5089/9781513507521.071.

Inland Revenue Board of Malaysia (2016), "Agriculture allowances public ruling no. 1/2016", [7]
http://www.hasil.gov.my/pdf/pdfam/PR_01_2016.pdf.

MEAE France (2017), *Vanuatu – Volcanic eruption on the island of Ambae – French assistance* [59]
(03.10.17) - France-Diplomatie - Ministère de l'Europe et des Affaires étrangères,
https://www.diplomatie.gouv.fr/en/country-files/vanuatu/events/article/vanuatu-volcanic-
eruption-on-the-island-of-ambae-french-assistance-03-10-17 (accessed on 31 May 2019).

Ministry of Finance of Singapore (2020), *MOF | Goods and Services Tax*, [46]
https://www.mof.gov.sg/Policies/Tax-Policies/Goods-and-Services-Tax (accessed on
24 June 2020).

Ministry of International Trade and Industry of Malaysia (2016), [8]
http://www.miti.gov.my/index.php/pages/view/content5235.html.

MOHRSS (2020), *Statistics Reports (series)*, Ministry of Human Resources and Social Security [5]
of China, http://www.mohrss.gov.cn/SYrlzyhshbzb/zwgk/szrs/tjgb/.

MOHRSS (2017), *Annual Report on China's Social Insurance Development in 2016*, Social [4]
Insurance Administration, Ministry of Human Resources and Social Security of China.

MOHRSS (2016), *Annual Report on China's Social Insurance Development in 2015*, Social [3]
Insurance Administration, Ministry of Human Resources and Social Security of China.

MOHRSS (2015), *Annual Report on China's Social Insurance Development in 2014*, Social [2]
Insurance Administration, Ministry of Human Resources and Social Security of China.

Nauru, G. (2019), *NRO Tax rates*, [27]
http://www.naurugov.nr/media/118293/nro_tax_rates_as_at_1_july_2019.pdf.

NCCS (2020), *Carbon Tax*, https://www.nccs.gov.sg/faqs/carbon-tax/ (accessed on 22 June 2020). [54]

New Zealand Foreign Affairs & Trade (2018), "Aid partnership with Tokelau", https://www.mfat.govt.nz/en/aid-and-development/our-work-in-the-pacific/tokelau/. [56]

news.mn (2018), *Mongolia's tax revenue increases*, https://news.mn/en/785771/ (accessed on 15 April 2020). [25]

OECD (2020), *"Revenue Statistics in Asian and Pacific Economies: Comparative tables"*, OECD *Tax statistics (database)*. [29]

OECD (2020), *Annual national accounts (database)*, https://stats.oecd.org/Index.aspx?DataSetCode=SNA_TABLE1. [50]

OECD (2020), *Database on Policy Instruments for the Environment*, https://pinedatabase.oecd.org/ (accessed on 15 June 2020). [51]

OECD (2020), *Global Revenue Statistics Database*, OECD Publishing, http://www.oecd.org/tax/tax-policy/global-revenue-statistics-database.htm. [20]

OECD (2020), *Revenue Statistics - Asian and Pacific Economies: Country tables*, OECD *Tax statistics (database)*. [38]

OECD (2019), *Revenue Statistics 2019*, OECD Publishing, Paris, https://dx.doi.org/10.1787/0bbc27da-en. [1]

OECD (2019), *"Revenue Statistics 2019: Tax Revenue Trends in the OECD"*, *Www.Oe.Cd/Global-Rev-Stats-Database*, http://dx.doi.org/10.1021/ja02021a006. [24]

OECD (2019), *Social Protection System Review of Indonesia*, OECD Development Pathways, OECD Publishing, Paris, https://dx.doi.org/10.1787/788e9d71-en. [11]

OECD (2018), *Consumption tax trends 2018 : VAT/GST and excise rates, trends and policy issues.*, OECD Publishing, https://doi.org/10.1787/19990979. [49]

OECD (2018), *Making Development Co-operation Work for Small Island Developing States*, OECD Publishing, Paris, https://dx.doi.org/10.1787/9789264287648-en. [23]

OECD (2018), *OECD Economic Surveys: Indonesia 2018*, OECD Publishing, Paris, http://dx.doi.org/10.1787/eco_surveys-idn-2018-en. [12]

OECD (2017), *Policy INstruments Environment*, http://oe.cd/pine (accessed on 15 June 2020). [61]

OECD (2016), *Consumption Tax Trends 2016: VAT/GST and excise rates, trends and policy issues*, OECD Publishing, Paris, https://dx.doi.org/10.1787/ctt-2016-en. [47]

OECD (2014), *Consumption tax trends 2014 : VAT/GST and excise rates, trends and policy issues*, OECD Publishing, Paris. [41]

OECD (2014), *Development Co-operation Report 2014 : Mobilising Resources for Sustainable Development.*, OECD Publishing, Paris. [9]

OECD (2012), *Consumption Tax Trends 2012.*, OECD Publishing, Paris. [40]

OECD/ATAF/AUC (2019), *Revenue Statistics in Africa 2019: 1990-2017*, OECD Publishing, Paris, https://dx.doi.org/10.1787/5daa24c1-en-fr. [21]

OECD et al. (2020), *Revenue Statistics in Latin America and the Caribbean 2020*, OECD Publishing, Paris, https://dx.doi.org/10.1787/68739b9b-en-es. [22]

Parties to the Nauru Agreement (2016), "PNA members confirm: Vessel Day Scheme is here to stay", https://www.pnatuna.com/node/340. [57]

PEAKS, E. (2013), *Taxation and Developing Countries*, Overseas Development Institute training notes. [6]

The United States Social Security Administration (2018), *Indonesia Old Age, Disability, and Survivors Regulatory Framework*, https://www.bpjsketenagakerjaan.go.id/ (accessed on 28 May 2019). [39]

Tokelau (2017), *Tokelau wins prestigious 2017 WHO Tobacco Free global award*, http://(https://www.tokelau.org.nz/Bulletin/Sept+2017/Tokelau+wins+prestigious+2017+WHO+Tobacco+Free+global+award.html) (accessed on 18 April 2020). [26]

UNCTAD (2012), *World Investment Report 2012, Towards a new Generation of Investment Policies, New York*, http://unctad.org/en/PublicationsLibrary/wir2012_embargoed_en.pdf. [13]

UNESCAP (2016), *Environmental Tax Reform in Asia and the Pacific*, https://www.unescap.org/sites/default/files/S2_Environmental-Tax-Reform.pdf (accessed on 25 June 2020). [53]

UNESCAP (2014), *Economic and Social Survey of Asia and the Pacific 2014, Regional Connectivity for Shared Prosperity*, UN, https://www.unescap.org/sites/default/files/Economic20and%20Social%20Survey%20of%20Asia%20and%20the%20Pacific%202014.pdf. [14]

WHO (2015), *Purchasing Power Parity 2005*, http://www.who.int/choice/costs/ppp/en/. [16]

World Bank (2020), *"Central government debt, total (% of GDP)", World Development Indicators (database)*, https://data.worldbank.org/indicator/GC.DOD.TOTL.GD.ZS. [19]

World Bank (2020), *"Expense (% of GDP)", World Development Indicators (database)*, https://data.worldbank.org/indicator/GC.XPN.TOTL.GD.ZS. [18]

World Bank (2018), *Mongolia Distributional impact of taxes and transfers*, http://documents.worldbank.org/curated/en/234971541520019289/pdf/131852-POV180-PRWP8639.pdf (accessed on 29 May 2020). [45]

World Bank (2011), *Mongolia Quarterly Economic Update*, https://www.mongolbank.mn/documents/moneypolicy/mongolia_quarterly42010_full.pdf (accessed on 28 May 2020). [33]

Notes

[1] This information was provided by the Ministry of Finance of Mongolia during exchanges with the OECD Secretariat in preparation of this publication.

[2] This information was provided by the Tokelau Statistical Office during exchanges with the OECD Secretariat in preparation of this publication.

[3] Data for Bhutan and Fiji are only available from 2008, so the data used for both economies in this section are from 2008-18. Data for the Africa (26) average cover 2008 to 2017. In addition, 2018 data for Australia, Japan and the OECD average are not available, so 2017 data are used instead. Nauru is excluded from this analysis as data are only available from 2014 onwards.

[4] Detailed data on SSCs for China were not available, but the OECD Secretariat estimates SSCs to be approximately 4.0% of GDP in 2018 based on publicly available data from China's Ministry of Human Resources and Social Security.

[5] An environmentally related tax is a tax whose base is a physical unit (or a proxy of a physical unit) of something that has a proven, specific harmful impact on the environment regardless of whether the tax is intended to change behaviours or is levied for another purpose .

[6] The figures in this report do not include revenues (that may be significant) from other policies addressing environmental issues such as fees and charges or revenues from emissions trading schemes. However the PINE database provides additional data on fees and charges, subsidies, voluntary approaches, tradable permits, deposit-refund systems for more than 80 countries.

[7] Data on environmentally related tax revenue are presented for four tax-base categories: energy (including all CO_2 related taxes); transport (mostly motor vehicle taxes); pollution (e.g. discharges of waste or pollutants, taxes on waste or packaging); and resources (e.g. water extraction, hunting and fishing, mining).

[8] These figures need to be treated with caution as some environmentally related taxes may not be captured if the data are not sufficiently disaggregated.

2 Tax policy and administration responses to COVID-19

Chapter 2 is a special chapter summarising a discussion on tax policy and tax administration responses to COVID-19 in the Asia-Pacific region, which took place during an ADB-CATA-OECD-PITAA-SGATAR virtual meeting held in May 2020.

Introduction

COVID-19 is an infectious disease which first emerged in late 2019-early 2020. Although COVID-19 initially affected Asia-Pacific economies, it has rapidly spread to all corners of the world. The World Health Organization (WHO) declared COVID-19 a pandemic on 11 March 2020. The pandemic has exacted a heavy toll on global public health, infecting more than 8 million people and causing more than 425 000 deaths worldwide by 16 June 2020. The trajectory of the pandemic remains subject to a great deal of uncertainty. [1]

Asia has been hard hit by COVID-19, with all sub-regions and countries of the continent affected, as well as several Pacific countries. The Asia-Pacific region is already responding to the COVID-19 outbreak in various ways, with many governments establishing inter-agency task forces and other co-ordinating mechanisms to ensure a harmonised public health response.

At the same time, the lockdowns, travel bans, community quarantines, and other restrictions due to COVID-19 have derailed the world economy, with the OECD projecting global output to decline by between -6% and -7.6% in 2020 (OECD, 2020[1]). The economies of the Asia-Pacific region will also suffer a sharp downturn. The evolution of the outbreak, and hence Asia-Pacific's outlook, remain highly uncertain but the Asian Development Bank's (ADB) baseline forecast is that regional growth will slow steeply from 5.2% in 2019 to 2.2% in 2020, before recovering to 6.2% in 2021. Excluding the newly industrialised economies, growth is seen to slow from 5.7% in 2019 to 2.4% in 2020, and then to pick up to 6.7% in 2021, according to (ADB, 2020[2]).

Growth will weaken in all of Asia-Pacific's sub-regions in 2020. Lower global demand will weigh on the 2020 outlook, particularly in the more open sub-regions and tourism-dependent economies such as those in the Pacific. (ADB, 2020[2]) forecasts that growth in East Asia will dip from 5.4% in 2019 to 2.0% in 2020, before accelerating to 6.5% in 2021. Southeast Asia is forecast to slow to 2.8% in 2020, before recovering to 4.4% in 2021. Growth in Central Asia will also slow to 2.9% this year due in part to lower oil prices, and the Pacific will contract by 0.3% due to declining tourism, before rebounding in 2021. South Asia's growth rate is forecast to slow from 5.0% in the 2019 fiscal year to 4.7% in 2020, before accelerating to 6.2% in 2021, largely tracking the recovery in India.

Across Asia and the Pacific, governments have introduced fiscal stimulus packages and eased monetary policy to support economic activity. In addition, to support economic growth and help the most vulnerable population groups, the region's governments are ramping up spending. In the immediate future, tax revenues will suffer as corporate revenues and household incomes fall due to the economic downturn. Given the magnitude of the economic shock, the drop in tax revenues is likely to be substantial. As the pandemic eventually recedes, higher government spending to boost health care, economy and society in the aftermath of COVID-19 will not be sustainable without adequate fiscal revenues. The need to balance economic stimulus with mobilising fiscal revenues brings into sharp relief the importance of tax administration and tax policy in Asia and the Pacific.[2]

This chapter, and the virtual meeting from which it is drawn, provide an overview of government responses to the challenges posed by the COVID-19 crisis. Section 2.2 below considers the impact of the crisis on tax revenues, including the channels of impact and the changes seen in the global financial crisis. Sections 2.3 and 2.4 consider the responses of tax administrations and policy makers to the challenges posed by different phases of the COVID-19 crisis, respectively, while Section 2.5 discusses policy and administrative considerations for low-income governments facing this shock.

The impact of COVID-19 on revenues

With the slowdown of growth estimated by the ADB in the Asia-Pacific region, public revenues will most likely decline in 2020 as a result of COVID-19. However, the pandemic will affect public revenues in different economies differently and the timing of the impact may also vary. In addition to the nature and extent of the COVID-19 impact, and of confinement measures to address it, the structure of a country's economy, exposure to international flows including trade and tourism, sources of government revenues, and the measures it takes to cushion firms and households from the economic impact of the pandemic, will all be significant.

Revenue data for the first months of calendar 2020 give some indication of the impact. For example, initial reports from Japan indicate a fall in revenues of 9.2% in the year ending March 2020 (Reuters, 2020[3]), and in Korea, revenues for Q1 2020 declined by KRW 8.5 trillion relative to Q1 2019 (a fall of approximately 11%) (Eun-joo, 2020[4]). However, given that the pandemic and its economic impact are still evolving, it is difficult to extrapolate from these initial indications. In addition, it is difficult to disentangle the causes of revenue declines (and their respective magnitudes): the direct impact on tax receipts associated with declining economic activity and emergency fiscal response measures may be augmented by the deferral of tax payments. Finally, the nature and depth of the crisis is unprecedented, limiting the ability to predict revenue impacts on the basis of already available information and estimates based on historical data.

While it is difficult to predict the impact of COVID-19 on government revenues at this stage, certain economies are likely to be more vulnerable than others. South Asia's revenues are particularly vulnerable to the current slowdown in global trade, which (according to the World Trade Organization [WTO]) will be more severe than during the global financial crisis (GFC): revenues from trade taxes in the sub-region averaged nearly 15% of total revenues in 2015-17. Meanwhile, travel restrictions have taken a massive toll on tourism in the Pacific Islands (a number of which have no recorded cases of Covid-19), where tourism receipts represented more than 40% of exports on average over 2008-17 and are a key source of public revenues.[3] Sharp declines in commodity prices will affect producer countries. Countries such as Brunei, Indonesia, Kazakhstan, Malaysia, Singapore, Thailand and Viet Nam, which generate significant public revenues from the production or refinery of oil, will likely experience a sharp drop in revenues as a result.

The economic changes associated with Covid-19 will also affect tax types in different ways, even before taking into account the measures to mitigate the consequences of the crisis. Corporate income tax (CIT) revenues, which are typically most responsive to economic cycles, are likely to decrease by more than the fall in economic activity. A reduction in employment and in wages will likely translate into lower personal income tax (PIT) revenues and social security contributions. Revenues from consumption taxes, especially from valued-added taxes (VAT), are also likely to fall due to the impact of lockdowns and lower consumer confidence, as well as a potential shift towards the consumption of staple goods, which are often taxed at reduced or zero rates. The structure of tax revenues in Asian and Pacific economies may render them more vulnerable due to their high reliance on CIT, that accounted for 19.0% of total tax revenues in 2017 in the countries included in this publication, on average, compared to 9.3% for OECD countries (OECD, 2020[5]).

One indication of the potential impact of Covid-19 is to analyse how a previous crisis – the global financial crisis from 2007 to 2009 – affected tax revenues in the region, although this is likely to be a lower bound estimate. Over that period, the tax-to-GDP ratio in Asian and Pacific economies declined by 1.0 percentage point on average, with almost all countries in the region experiencing a decrease (Figure 2.1). CIT was most affected, declining from 4.9% of GDP in 2007[4] to 4.1% of GDP in 2009. Some countries were more affected than others: those dependent on revenues from natural resources, such as Kazakhstan and Papua New Guinea, experienced the largest losses in revenue due in large part to the fall of commodity prices. On average, it was not until 2012 that the tax-to-GDP ratios of Asian and Pacific economies exceeded their pre-crisis levels.

Figure 2.1. Changes of tax-to-GDP ratios in Asian and Pacific economies during the global financial crisis (2007 and 2009)

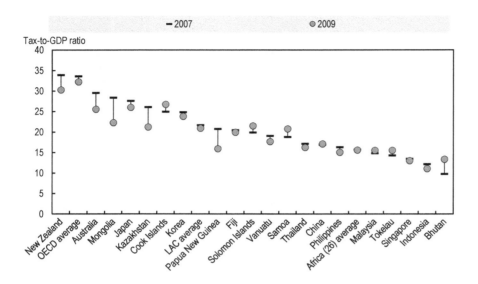

Note: 2008-09 changes are shown for Bhutan, Fiji and the Africa (26) average as 2007 data are not available.
Source: Authors' calculations based on Table 3.1 in Chapter 3.

StatLink https://stat.link/kh28e4

Responses of tax administrations to COVID-19

Tax administrations across the globe have played a critical role in supporting citizens and the economy at a time of crisis, including by helping to mitigate cash flow difficulties and minimise compliance burdens and, in many cases, by working with other parts of government in providing assistance to businesses and citizens, including through grants or loans (Suzuki, 2020[12]).[5]

Slower economic growth during COVID-19 will have a significant impact on tax policy across the region. Countries in Asia and the Pacific can take specific steps that will benefit their economies both during the pandemic and over the longer term. Throughout the region, countries must optimise tax policy to take into account shrinking economic growth during the pandemic and increased economic activity in the years that follow.

During the pandemic, tax agencies have focused on maintaining the operation of essential business processes, including taxpayer registration, taxpayer services, tax return and payment processing. The need to ensure the safety of staff to be deployed in the core business processes is an important part of this response, including strict compliance with policies on health and hygiene. Data and cyber security are also of critical importance.

In the immediate response phase, tax-related policies have been implemented in many countries to assist businesses and other taxpayers during the crisis. These included a holistic approach to tax relief measures that will help stabilise the economy, with some countries deferring or waiving taxes. Box 2.1 provides an overview of the combined tax policy and administrative responses to COVID-19 in Malaysia.

These measures need to be considered against the specific legal and regulatory operational framework, as well as the existing tax policies and incentives that vary from country to country. This should be done following the "Three Ts" Principle: the most effective immediate measures are those that are timely, targeted and temporary (Summers, 2008[6]). These policies have often been combined with other financing/liquidity measures to stabilise the economy, in particular, with those targeting small and medium-sized enterprises.

To ease the burden caused by the pandemic-induced state of uncertainty, delivering public services has also been a vital part of the response. Tax administration can aid this by being flexible in the use of staff to manage peaks in service demand and curtailing discretionary programmes where necessary, such as field audits. To ease the business cash-flow situation of taxpayers, policy options that have been implemented include tax debt payment plans and the prioritisation of value added tax refunds to ensure quick payouts.

The global economic impact of the pandemic could expand the informal economy, particularly among small businesses. It may also have a negative impact on tax compliance. These changes could trigger increases in value-added tax fraud or missing trader fraud, to which tax agencies need to be alert. Tax administrators should seek to strike the right balance between service demands and tax compliance.

According to ADB research, as economies open back up, economic growth in the region could rebound to 6.2% in 2021 (ADB, 2020[2]). In terms of debt sustainability and revenue mobilisation, tax policy makers and administrators should consider what tax reforms are needed in the aftermath of the pandemic. Digital transformation will help tax administrations and it will promote effective, timely, and corruption-free delivery of public services to support greater accountability.

Countries that innovate more tend to have faster economic growth, according to ADB research. Middle-income economies in Asia and the Pacific have increased spending on innovation, which is vital for productivity growth. Investment in research and development in these economies are three times bigger than their peers. In addition, innovations contribute to more inclusive and environmentally sustainable growth in the region. Tax policy should be part of this focus on innovation. New ideas and strategies will be needed for tax agencies working in the post-pandemic environment.

In the recovery period, governments will need to address several tax administration considerations: business restoration governance; scenario planning; analysis and monitoring; business restoration planning; opening of offices; staff welfare; reputation management and communication; working methods; and longer-term implications for tax administrations. As in the crisis period, it is important to keep to the forefront the various factors which distinguish the Covid-19 pandemic from one-off events or events hitting particular sectors or locations. These are: the continued risks to health, including from possible further outbreaks; the impacts on staff, taxpayers and administration systems from the need for continuing and careful adjustments; and the potential length and volatility of the recovery period given the depth and scale of the economic shock.

There are a number of overarching objectives which administrations might wish to consider adopting in the recovery period, notably:

- **Maintaining the decision-making processes of the crisis stage into the recovery phase.** As in the crisis period, at times the environment will be fast moving, complex and involve all parts of the administration. The planning assumptions during the recovery phase should take into account the possibility of set-backs (and potentially major set-backs) in the containment of the virus, the possible volatility of the economy, different recovery speeds for different households and sectors, and potential new demands on tax administrations.

- **Effective joining-up with other parts of government.** As well as taking supportive measures under existing powers, many tax administrations have also played a crucial role in delivering wider government support to affected taxpayers, such as the payment of grants and other financial reliefs. During the recovery period, the role of tax administrations within the wider government response will continue to be critical, including in ensuring that conflicting approaches are not taken. It will be important to join-up on both decision-making and information sharing.

- **Developing a dedicated communication strategy to support recovery.** Most tax administrations have put in place COVID-19 crisis communication strategies. These have been both internal strategies to support staff and the effective operation of administration functions, and external strategies to provide timely information and support to taxpayers. During the recovery period, it would be sensible to refresh these strategies to take account of the move from a crisis to a prolonged and potentially difficult recovery period. In particular, consideration should be given as to how to best maintain the dual emphasis on a supportive relationship with taxpayers as well as bringing in tax revenue to fund public services.

- **Maintaining the safety of staff and taxpayers.** Consideration will need to be given to how to maintain staff and taxpayer safety during the recovery period in light of continuing health risks, including the potential for further waves of the virus. There will need to be detailed plans for ongoing safety precautions as offices start to reopen. Engagement and consultation with staff and staff representatives will also be important to ensure clarity and transparency as to requirements and expectations.

- **Planning and prioritisation of the steps towards normalisation of administration functions.** Administrations may also wish to ask those responsible for separate tax administration functions to draw up strategies for a return to normalisation, for example as regards compliance activities, debt recovery, dealing with backlogs, critical IT maintenance, etc. Ideally such strategies would reflect the different considerations which might arise under different recovery scenarios. The production of such strategies will help in taking decisions on relative priorities, in ensuring that decisions are taken and communicated in a holistic manner, and will make it easier to make rapid adjustments where necessary.

- **Logging lessons learned and updating business continuity plans.** Logging of actions taken during both the crisis and recovery period, including their rationale and impact, will be important both for transparency purposes (for example independent reviews) and for the updating of business continuity plans in case of a recurrence of Covid-19 or a similar crisis. Tax administrations may wish to do this on a systematic and consistent basis, to ensure that full information is captured, issues identified, and early remedial actions are taken where appropriate.

- **Learning lessons.** Many administrations have adopted different ways of working during the crisis, including remote working, remote auditing, more automated procedures and adjustments to risk parameters. It would be sensible for administrations to look at the way these different procedures and approaches have worked during the crisis and consider if they remain valid during the recovery period and, possibly, on a permanent basis to improve the efficiency of tax administration and to lower burdens.

Box 2.1. Tax policy and administrative responses to COVID-19 in Malaysia

The Malaysian government responded to COVID-19 with three stimulus packages worth a total of USD 60 billion across the period from 27 February to 6 April 2020 to mitigate the impact oCOVID-19, strengthen the economy and assist low- and middle-income households and individuals. As of 10 May 2020, around 10.6 million households and individuals have received financial aid from the government. The Inland Revenue Board of Malaysia (IRBM) has assumed responsibility of disbursement of this financial aid.

To supplement these policies, temporary tax incentives have been introduced and include: (i) tax deductions or capital allowance on expenses incurred in providing personal protective equipment to employees; (ii) a further tax deduction for owners of building or business space who reduced or waived rents for small and medium-sized enterprise (SME) tenants; and (iii) an accelerated capital allowance for machinery and equipment, including ICT equipment, applying from 1 March to 31 December 2020.

With respect to tax administration, IRBM has supported taxpayers through: (i) extending deadlines for tax filing; (ii) allowing for the revision of income tax estimates and deferral of payments; (iii) supporting debt payment plans; (iv) suspending debt recovery until 31 May 2020; (v) providing quicker refunds; (vi) changing the audit policy; and (vii) enhancing taxpayer communication initiatives.

Recognising its core role in responding to the crisis, IRBM has strengthened its business continuity. IRBM was well better prepared to evaluate the current and pending scenarios and to take appropriate action due to actions taken to improve governance arrangements before the crisis struck. It has also produced a Policy and Manual of Business Continuity System, which has been reviewed from time to time.

Source: Summary of presentation by Inland Revenue Board of Malaysia (2020[7]) on "Inland Revenue Board of Malaysia (IRBM) responses to COVID-19 outbreaks" at the virtual meeting on 14 May 2020.

Tax policy responses to Covid-19

Alongside the measures undertaken by tax administrations, tax policy makers are also considering a range of responses to the Covid-19 crisis. Policy responses to the Covid-19 crisis need to evolve as the crisis evolves across different phases: the emergency response, exit from confinement (for countries that have gone into some degree of lockdown), recovery and, over the long term, putting public finances on a sustainable footing (OECD, 2020[10]) (OECD, 2020[8]).[6]

The OECD is tracking measures taken by governments within and beyond the OECD membership in the emergency response phase. In this phase, fiscal packages have been put in place by many governments, with the size of such packages varying across countries. So far, policy measures introduced by emerging and developing countries have not been fundamentally different to those taken by OECD and G20 countries, but they have been more modest as the fiscal space in these economies is often smaller. Overall, policy measures taken in the emergency response phase can be grouped into four categories: support to businesses; support to households; support to investment and consumption; and support to the healthcare sector.

Support to business

A key priority from a tax perspective has been to support business cash flow. Measures to achieve this include: increased lending to firms; providing subsidies to non-wage business costs and support measures targeted at specific business sectors such as tourism, transport, airlines (e.g. Australia); providing subsidies to the self-employed; and allowing tax deferrals (and more rarely, tax waivers and tax rate reductions). For instance, tax payment deferrals have been introduced by three quarters of OECD and G20 countries, and correspond to 45% of the total number of measures reported by countries outside the OECD and the G20. Several countries have also adopted tax filing extensions and more flexible tax debt repayment plans (e.g. Australia and New Zealand). Only a few countries introduced tax waivers, which were particularly targeted at the tourism sector [e.g. Indonesia and Korea (OECD, 2020[8])].

Specific measures to boost business cash flows have been observed. These have included: deferral of taxes and social security contribution (SSC) payments (80% of OECD and G20 countries have changed due dates and/or reduced or waived advance payments, including Australia, Cambodia [see also Box 2.2], Japan and Indonesia), and the provision of enhanced tax refunds (e.g. Australia and Indonesia), in particular for VAT (30% of OECD and G20 countries). Tax loss provisions were also enhanced (carry forward or carry backward) (e.g. New Zealand).

Many governments have introduced measures to ensure that the connection between employers and employees is maintained through the emergency response phase. These include short-time work schemes or wage subsidies paid by governments to the employer (e.g. Australia, New Zealand and Thailand), under the condition that the employer does not fire its employees. These measures have been more common among OECD and G20 countries, which may be explained by their high cost and by the limited experience across emerging and developing countries with this type of measure.

Support to households

Governments have also moved very quickly to protect households via tax and expenditure measures, including payments delivered through the tax system. Measures to support households include: partial unemployment schemes for workers that continue to be employed (e.g. wage subsidies paid to the employee); increased eligibility of cash transfers (e.g. extending the availability of unemployment benefits to the self-employed [e.g. Australia]); increased access to benefits (e.g. eliminating waiting period before sickness or unemployment benefits can be received); and higher benefits. Decisions over the type of support have generally been driven by the need to deliver support quickly, leading to a preference for the use of existing systems and mechanisms over new ones. Some emerging and developing countries beyond the OECD and the G20 have reported introducing cash transfers for households, in particular to reach households not engaged in the formal sector, which might be excluded under other policy measures. Emerging and developing countries have not reported any expansions in sick leave or unemployment benefits, which may be a reflection of weaker social protection systems.

Support to investment and consumption

There have been very few tax measures so far to support investment and consumption, as these may conflict with measures to contain the pandemic, such as lockdown and social distancing. Some examples include increases in thresholds for low-value asset write-offs (e.g. Australia and New Zealand), and reductions in corporate taxes for manufacturing companies in a variety of sectors in Indonesia. Countries outside the OECD and the G20 have made greater use of tax measures with the goal of supporting investment and consumption. For example, Kazakhstan lowered the standard or reduced VAT rates. Policy measures to support investments and consumption are likely to take a more prominent role during the recovery phase to stimulate the economy.

Support to the healthcare sector

Tax policy measures to support the healthcare sector have been more common in countries outside the OECD and the G20. For instance, in some countries healthcare workers may benefit from a reduction in PIT or SSCs (e.g. Kazakhstan and Malaysia), and retired healthcare workers are able to resume work without losing pension and benefit entitlements. In Malaysia, healthcare and immigration workers receive a special allowance.

Businesses producing health equipment, goods and services may benefit from reduced tax rates or accelerated tax depreciation (e.g. Thailand). Further, some countries have introduced VAT exemptions or reductions for medicine, equipment and services directly involved in the containment and fight against COVID-19 (e.g. Indonesia and the Philippines). Other measures include expediting customs clearance for goods necessary in fighting COVID-19.

Box 2.2. Tax policy and tax administration responses to the COVID-19 crisis in Cambodia

Cambodia has implemented three rounds of emergency policy measures to support businesses, families and the economy since the outbreak of COVID-19.

The first round of measures provided tax relief to businesses in vulnerable sectors such as tourism, real estate, garment, footwear, textile and others. For example, hotels and guesthouses in the province of Siem Reap were exempted from paying corporate income taxes for four months from February to May 2020, while comprehensive tax audits for these businesses were deferred for the entire year of 2020. The transfer tax was waived for any real estate purchases below USD 70 000 from licensed property developers in Cambodia for one year starting from February. Tax on salary (TOS) was waived for seniority indemnity payments (which function as an extended severance pay) made to Cambodian employees who worked in the garment, footwear, textile and other sectors in 2019 or earlier. For seniority indemnity payments made in 2020 and after, the TOS exemption will only apply to those who earn less than KHR 4 million per year. Tax exemptions were also given to companies that recruit, train, send and supervise Cambodian workers to work abroad.

The second round of emergency policies included income support for Cambodian workers, as well as more tax relief to businesses. In terms of support for workers, the government will contribute 20% to minimum wages paid to workers and employees of hotels, guesthouses, restaurants and travel agencies operating in Phnom Penh, Siem Reap, Sihanouk, Kep, Kampot, Bavet and Poipet. For businesses, the corporate income tax exemption implemented in the first round was extended to cover hotels, guesthouses, restaurants and travel agencies operating in the same areas. These businesses must file tax returns for 2019 by the end of March, but can make payments by monthly instalments until November 2020. Airline companies in Cambodia received a three-month exemption from paying the annual Minimum Tax between March and May 2020, while aviation fees were deferred for a period of six months and made payable by instalments.

Tax policies were not included in the third set of emergency policies. These measures mostly consisted of measures to combat COVID-19 and stimulate the Cambodian economy, such as the extension of travel restrictions, enhanced lockdown measures, establishment of a task force to control supply and prices of strategic goods, and improved budget financing and social assistance during the pandemic, as well as a co-financing scheme for SMEs.

At the time of writing, the government is planning a fourth round of policy measures that could be implemented in the near future.

Source: Summary of presentation by the General Department of Taxation of Cambodia (2020[9]) on "Tax policy and tax administration responses to the COVID-19 crisis by the Royal Government of Cambodia" at the virtual meeting on 14 May 2020.

Considerations for tax officials in low income Asian and Pacific economies

The coronavirus (COVID-19) pandemic has affected many low-income countries in the Asia-Pacific region and around the world. Additional support for consumers and businesses may be required both from internal and external sources to allow these countries to respond to the crisis and to support an economic recovery. Tax policy makers and tax administrations will play an important role in supporting the wider government response to coronavirus across the crisis and recovery stages (Steel, I., Phillips, 2020[11]).[7]

There are three important considerations that Ministries of Finance and revenue administrations in low-income countries need to keep in mind in responding to COVID-19: (1) assessing revenue impacts and potentially take measures to shore up the fiscal position; (2) developing, appraising and implementing tax policy responses to different phases of the crisis and recovery; and (3) facilitating the use of tax data for economic, social and public health monitoring purposes.

1. Assessing revenue impacts in relation to global and domestic economic shocks is an important foundation for shoring up the fiscal position for responding to COVID-19. It will be important that governments closely monitor the fluctuating situations and update revenue impacts as the crisis unfolds, which will be essential to support cash and debt management operations, determine external financing requirements, and identify space available for additional health and fiscal support measures. Importantly, the revenue impacts are more likely to be acute in low-income countries because of their more limited access to capital markets and lesser scope for temporary central bank financing of government debts, as well as widespread and simultaneous calls on external finance.

2. The role of tax policy approach is likely to evolve alongside the different phases of the crisis:

   o Phase 1: Support — Immediate support to businesses is the priority during this phase, to help them survive the economic fallout from the crisis. In this phase, support to households is also critically important. The measures taken during this phase include tax payment deferrals, expedited refunds, and targeted help for affected sectors. Targeted support rather than broad-based stimulus is more appropriate while social distancing measures prevent normal economic activity and where fiscal situations are tight.

   o Phase 2: Stimulus — In this phase, the goal of tax policy is to boost demand to support the economic recovery once social distancing measures have been eased or lifted. Governments may wish to consider using a different range of tax policy options to deliver support in this phase, such as temporary VAT reductions or increases in capital allowances.

   o Phase 3: Consolidation — Once the economic recovery is underway, tax measures to restore fiscal sustainability, building on existing strategies and domestic resource mobilisation plans, will be increasingly important.

In each phase, country contexts are a key factor to consider in understanding the impact of the crisis and the effectiveness of measures to support the economy and households. Elements of the country context which are significant include: *(i)* administrative and policy evaluation capacity; *(ii)* fiscal capacity and government liquidity; *(iii)* the economic structure, including sectoral composition; and *(iv)* the other measures taken by the government to address the crisis (e.g. social distancing and lockdown).

During the support phase, the immediate focus of the response has been to support business cash-flow and to maintain formal sector employee-employer relationships, while avoiding new administrative and compliance burdens. A broader set of considerations than national tax policy has applied (e.g. social protection, funding for local government, and financial sector policies) – not least in countries with large informal sectors that are hard to reach directly through tax measures – and tax measures to support social distancing have also been implemented in some countries.

During this phase, general reductions in CIT and PIT rates have been rarely utilised, in view of maintaining tax revenue from taxpayers less affected by the crisis.

While moving into the "stimulus" phase of the recovery, weak domestic and global demand may warrant fiscal stimulus measures, subject to fiscal capacity. Under this situation, explicit and temporary investment and consumption tax incentives could be considered in order to encourage businesses and consumers to bring forward investments and purchases. Given the high level of uncertainty, however, direct government investment may be more effective than tax incentives. At the same time, governments will need to give careful consideration as to how to unwind and modify the measures that were implemented during the "support" phase.

In the "consolidation" phase, there may be a chance to realise long-run reform agendas, while taking into account the post-crisis economic reality. The crisis can provide an impetus to implement difficult, but ultimately beneficial, reforms to the tax system. These could include measures to make the tax system greener and more consistent with climate change objectives. Also, this provides an opportunity to reconsider and rationalise tax expenditures and incentives.

3. Tax administrations can support the response to COVID-19 by facilitating the use of tax data for economic and public health monitoring purposes. Often, official economic statistics are too slow to inform policy, and economic data lag events in the real world. Tax administrations may have access to data that become available earlier, particularly from taxes collected frequently and with a closer link to economic activity (e.g. VAT or goods and services taxes [GST], withholding on salaries, customs duties). To the extent possible under confidentiality rules, anonymised (and aggregated) tax data can be shared within government, and with academics and researchers, to help them undertake analysis and inform policy.

Tax administrations can also make use of existing data-sharing protocols and agreements, or introduce them when necessary. These are a number of potential uses of tax data, for example:

o securing supplies of essentials – using customs data to anticipate shortfalls in essentials and identify trade dependencies;

o dealing with health impacts – falling receipts could be an indication of whether social distancing is effective or not;

o monitoring economic situations – getting a snapshot of how the economy is developing by comparing weekly or monthly data with an equivalent period in previous years;

o developing targeted responses – identifying the worst-affected sectors or regions, and targeting policy responses accordingly; and

o preparing for recovery – using tax data to identify early signs of recovery and potential bottlenecks.

References

ADB (2020), *Asian Development Outlook 2020*, Asian Development Bank, http://dx.doi.org/10.22617/FLS200119-3. [2]

Eun-joo, L. (2020), "S. Korea's Q1 tax revenue shrinks $6.9 bn, fiscal deficit hits record high by March", *Pulse by Maeil Business News Korea & mk.co.kr*, https://pulsenews.co.kr/view.php?year=2020&no=466629 (accessed on 7 May 2020). [4]

Inland Revenue Board of Malaysia (2020), *Responses to COVID-19 outbreaks*, https://static1.squarespace.com/static/5c6aa605ca525b3b56a7e512/t/5ec7bb8414b2283a6e347f6a/1590147984395/Malaysia_IRBM+Responses+to+COVID-19+Outbreaks+_Dr+Sabin.pdf (accessed on 26 June 2020). [7]

OECD (2020), *Global Revenue Statistics Database*, http://www.oecd.org/tax/tax-policy/global-revenue-statistics-database.htm. [5]

OECD (2020), *OECD Database of Tax Policy Responses to COVID-19*, https://www.oecd.org/tax/tax-policy/tax-database/. [10]

OECD (2020), *OECD Economic Outlook, Volume 2020 Issue 1: Preliminary version*, OECD Publishing, Paris, https://dx.doi.org/10.1787/0d1d1e2e-en. [1]

OECD (2020), *Tax and Fiscal Policy in Response to the Coronavirus Crisis: Strengthening Confidence and Resilience - OECD*, http://www.oecd.org/ctp/tax-policy/tax-and-fiscal-policy-in-response-to-the-coronavirus-crisis-strengthening-confidence-and-resilience.htm (accessed on 22 June 2020). [8]

Reuters (2020), "Japan tax collections fall most since June, more drops seen as virus bites", *Reuters*, https://www.reuters.com/article/us-health-coronavirus-japan-tax/japan-tax-collections-fall-most-since-june-more-drops-seen-as-virus-bites-idUSKBN22J1JX (accessed on 7 May 2020). [3]

Royal Government of Cambodia (2020), *Tax Policy and Tax Administration Responses to COVID-19 By the Royal Government of Cambodia General Department of Taxation*, https://static1.squarespace.com/static/5c6aa605ca525b3b56a7e512/t/5ec7bac883adba6fbbb27ba2/1590147787570/Cambodia_OECD_Meeting.pdf (accessed on 26 June 2020). [9]

Steel, I., Phillips, D. (2020), *How tax officials in lower-income countries can respond to the coronavirus pandemic*, Overseas Development Institute (ODI), https://www.odi.org/publications/16816-how-tax-officials-lower-income-countries-can-respond-coronavirus-pandemic (accessed on 22 June 2020). [11]

Summers, L. (2008), *Fiscal Stimulus Issues: Testimony before the Joint Economic Committee*, http://larrysummers.com/wp-content/uploads/2012/10/1-16-08_Fiscal_Stimulus_Issues.pdf. [6]

Suzuki, Y. (2020), *How can tax agencies tackle the impact of COVID-19?*, https://blogs.adb.org/blog/how-can-tax-agencies-tackle-impact-covid-19 (accessed on 22 June 2020). [12]

Notes

[1] This chapter is the summary of an ADB-CATA-OECD-PITAA-SGATAR virtual meeting that was held on 14 May 2020. The meeting discussed tax policy and tax administration responses to COVID-19 and had over 90 participants from 29 economies in Asia and the Pacific. This chapter draws on the presentations and underlying reports of the speakers at the meeting, who included: Donghyun Park (ADB), Yasushi Suzuki (ADB), Duncan Onduru (CATA), Peter Green (OECD), David Bradbury (OECD), Ben Dickinson (OECD), Varsha Singh (OECD), Koni Ravono (PITAA), John Hutagaol (SGATAR), Dr Sabin Samitah (Malaysia), Dr Lamy Mong (Cambodia), Ian Steel (ODI) and David Phillips (IFS). Presentations from this meeting are available at the following webpage: http://www.oecd.org/tax/tax-global/meeting-tax-policy-and-tax-administration-responses-to-covid-19-for-asia-pacific-may-2020.htm.

[2] To help developing Asian countries cope with the devastating impact of the pandemic, ADB has scaled up the size of assistance to USD 20 billion (find the latest information here). ADB's support will address the mid- to long-term economic impact of COVID-19 transmitted through various channels, including sharp declines in consumption and investment (information on the ADB COVID-19 Policy Measures can be accessed here). In terms of tax policy and administration, at a corporate strategic level, ADB is elevating domestic resource mobilisation (DRM) and international tax co-operation as one of the priorities under the new president's direction. ADB will strengthen its effort in DRM and international tax co-operation in conjunction with ADB's Strategy 2030.

[3] Figure taken from the presentation of Iain Steel (ODI) and David Phillips (IFS) on "How tax officials can respond to the coronavirus pandemic" at the virtual meeting on 14 May 2020.

[4] 2008 data were used for Bhutan and Fiji as 2007 data are not available.

[5] This section draws on the presentations given by Peter Green (OECD) on "Tax Administration Responses to Covid-19" and by Yasushi Suzuki (ADB) on "ADB response" at the seminar virtual meeting on 14 May 2020, as well as on https://blogs.adb.org/blog/how-can-tax-agencies-tackle-impact-COVID-19.

In order to support these efforts the OECD Forum on Tax Administration (FTA) has published a number of reference documents. These cover measures taken to support taxpayers, business continuity considerations and, most recently, a reference document on the issues which tax administrations may wish to take into account in their planning for the recovery from COVID-19 (https://www.oecd.org/tax/forum-on-tax-administration).

[6] This section draws on the presentation given by David Bradbury on "Tax policy responses to the Covid-19 crisis" at the virtual meeting on 14 May 2020, as well as on the *OECD Database of Tax Policy Responses to Covid-19* and on *Tax and Fiscal Policy in Response to the Coronavirus Crisis: Strengthening Confidence and Resilience*. The policy measures outlined in this section have been collected on the basis of questionnaires and ongoing engagement with governments from countries participating in the Inclusive Framework on Base Erosion and Profit Shifting, the Working Party No. 2 on Tax Policy and Statistics and the Working Party No. 9 on Consumption Taxes of the Committee of Fiscal Affairs.

[7] This section draws on the presentation given by Iain Steel (ODI) and David Phillips (IFS) on "How tax officials can respond to the coronavirus pandemic" at the virtual meeting on 14 May 2020.

3 Tax levels and tax structure, 1990-2018

Comparative tables, 1990-2018

In all of the following tables a ("..") indicates not available. The main series in this volume cover the years 1990 to 2018.

Figures referring to 1991-99 in Table 3.1 and Table 3.2 and figures relating to 1998-99, 2001-06, 2008-09 and 2011-12 in Tables 3.5 to 3.20 have been omitted because of lack of space. Complete series are, however, available on line at OECD (2020), "Revenue Statistics - Asian and Pacific Economies: Comparative tables", OECD Tax statistics (database).

The OECD average is taken from *Revenue Statistics (2019)*. Colombia was not an OECD Member at the time of preparation of this publication. Accordingly, Colombia does not appear in the list of OECD Members and is not included in the zone aggregates.

Table 3.1. Total tax revenue as percentage of GDP, 1990-2018

	1990	2000	2001	2002	2003	2004	2005	2006	2007	2008
Australia[1]	28.1	30.5	28.9	29.8	30.0	30.3	30.0	29.4	29.5	26.8
Bhutan	..	..	..	..	..	..	..	..	..	9.8
China[2]	..	..	..	..	..	..	..	..	16.9	17.0
Cook Islands	..	..	..	..	..	..	..	25.9	24.9	24.0
Fiji	..	..	..	..	..	..	..	..	..	20.5
Indonesia[3]	..	7.9	10.9	11.3	11.8	12.1	12.4	11.9	12.2	13.0
Japan[1]	28.2	25.8	25.9	24.9	24.5	25.2	26.2	27.0	27.5	27.4
Kazakhstan	..	19.9	22.2	20.5	22.7	21.7	25.5	26.1	26.1	27.6
Korea[1]	18.8	21.5	21.8	22.0	22.7	22.0	22.5	23.6	24.8	24.6
Malaysia[4]	18.5	14.1	18.3	18.3	16.3	15.9	15.5	15.1	14.8	15.1
Mongolia	..	..	..	..	..	..	..	26.8	28.4	26.7
Nauru	..	..	..	..	..	..	..	..	..	..
New Zealand[1]	36.2	32.5	31.9	33.3	33.2	34.2	36.1	35.3	33.9	32.9
Papua New Guinea[5]	..	..	..	20.0	20.2	24.2	25.6	20.0	20.8	18.6
Philippines	..	15.8	15.6	15.0	15.0	14.6	15.2	16.5	16.3	16.2
Samoa	..	..	..	..	..	..	22.5	22.4	18.8	18.7
Singapore	..	15.5	15.0	13.0	12.6	12.2	12.1	12.2	13.4	13.8
Solomon Islands	..	..	..	..	..	..	..	..	19.9	21.5
Thailand	..	14.6	14.8	15.2	16.5	17.1	18.4	17.6	17.1	17.2
Tokelau	..	..	..	..	..	..	..	13.3	14.3	16.1
Vanuatu	..	16.2	16.3	16.4	16.3	16.9	17.1	17.5	19.0	19.2
Africa (26) average[6]	..	..	..	..	..	..	..	..	..	15.7
LAC average[7]	15.9	18.7	18.8	18.8	19.2	19.6	20.4	21.2	21.6	21.7
OECD average[1,8,9]	31.9	33.8	33.2	33.0	32.9	32.9	33.4	33.5	33.6	32.9
	2009	2010	2011	2012	2013	2014	2015	2016	2017	2018
Australia[1]	25.5	25.3	25.9	26.9	27.1	27.3	27.9	27.6	28.5	..
Bhutan	13.3	13.9	15.1	14.2	13.4	13.7	13.5	12.8	13.7	12.3
China[2]	17.1	17.8	18.4	18.7	18.6	18.5	18.1	17.5	17.4	17.0
Cook Islands	26.7	26.9	24.7	27.5	25.1	22.1	26.7	27.1	28.3	29.8
Fiji	19.9	20.0	21.0	22.0	21.9	22.7	23.6	23.1	24.2	23.7
Indonesia[3]	11.0	11.4	12.2	12.5	12.5	12.2	12.1	12.0	11.5	11.9
Japan[1]	26.0	26.5	27.5	28.2	28.9	30.3	30.7	30.7	31.4	..
Kazakhstan	21.2	23.8	25.5	23.9	22.6	21.1	15.5	14.9	16.0	16.8
Korea[1]	23.8	23.4	24.2	24.8	24.3	24.6	25.2	26.2	26.9	28.4
Malaysia[4]	15.5	13.8	15.3	16.1	15.8	15.3	14.5	14.0	13.4	12.5
Mongolia	22.3	25.3	24.5	22.2	23.5	20.2	19.1	19.1	21.5	24.0
Nauru	..	..	..	..	..	8.3	23.1	15.6	29.0	35.4
New Zealand[1]	30.2	30.3	30.1	31.6	30.5	31.3	31.7	31.7	32.1	32.7
Papua New Guinea[5]	15.9	17.0	20.0	18.9	18.4	18.2	15.2	13.2	11.9	12.1
Philippines	15.0	14.8	15.1	15.8	16.2	16.7	17.0	17.0	17.6	18.2
Samoa	20.8	19.6	20.5	23.1	23.8	22.9	24.0	24.4	24.5	25.8
Singapore	13.0	12.8	13.1	13.6	13.3	13.6	13.1	13.3	14.1	13.2
Solomon Islands	21.5	24.5	28.8	30.4	29.5	29.4	29.4	27.2	28.7	30.4
Thailand	16.2	17.3	18.6	17.6	19.2	18.2	18.7	17.8	17.3	17.5
Tokelau	15.5	17.7	15.6	15.3	16.2	17.1	15.1	14.7	14.2	18.1
Africa (26) average[6]	15.5	15.3	16.0	16.3	16.7	16.8	17.2	17.2	17.2	..
LAC average[7]	20.9	21.2	21.6	21.9	22.0	22.2	22.6	22.6	22.7	23.1
OECD average[1,8,9]	32.2	32.3	32.6	33.1	33.4	33.6	33.7	34.4	34.2	34.3

.. Not available

1. Australia, Japan, Korea and New Zealand are part of the OECD(36) group. Data for Australia, Japan, Korea, New Zealand and the OECD average are taken from OECD (2019), *Revenue Statistics 2019*.
2. The tax-to-GDP ratio for China does not include revenue from social security contributions (SSCs) as detailed data were not available. The Secretariat estimates SSCs to be approximately 4.0% of GDP in 2018 based on publicly available data from China's Ministry of Human Resources and Social Security.
3. Social security contributions data for Indonesia are only available for 2015-18 and are deemed negligible in earlier years.
4. Figures do not include tax revenues from local governments (Quit Rent and Assessment tax), which are unavailable.
5. Total revenues are not calculated for 2000 and 2001 as the data are incomplete and do not include customs revenues for these two years.
6. Represents an unweighted average for the 26 African countries included in the publication *Revenue Statistics in Africa 2019*.
7. Represents an unweighted average for the 25 Latin American and Caribbean (LAC) countries included in the publication *Revenue Statistics in Latin America and the Caribbean 2020*.
8. 1990 to 2017: represents an unweighted average for the 36 OECD member countries included in the publication *Revenue Statistics 2019*. The OECD average in 2016 excludes the one-off revenues from stability contributions in Iceland.
9. 2018: calculated by applying the unweighted average percentage change for 2017 in the 34 countries providing data for that year to the overall average tax-to-GDP ratio in 2017.

StatLink ᐧᒥᔅᐦ https://stat.link/6xzq2i

Table 3.2. Total tax revenue (excluding social security contributions) as percentage of GDP, 1990-2018

	1990	2000	2001	2002	2003	2004	2005	2006	2007	2008
Australia[1]	28.1	30.5	28.9	29.8	30.0	30.3	30.0	29.4	29.5	26.8
Bhutan	..	..	..	..	..	..	..	..	..	9.8
China	..	..	..	..	..	..	..	..	16.9	17.0
Cook Islands	..	..	..	..	..	..	..	25.9	24.9	24.0
Fiji	..	..	..	..	..	..	..	..	..	20.5
Indonesia[2]	..	..	..	..	..	..	..	..	..	
Japan[1]	20.7	16.7	16.5	15.4	15.1	15.7	16.6	17.1	17.5	16.8
Kazakhstan	..	19.9	22.2	20.5	22.7	21.7	25.4	25.9	25.7	27.2
Korea[1]	16.9	17.9	17.8	17.8	18.2	17.4	17.8	18.6	19.6	19.3
Malaysia[3]	18.5	13.8	18.0	18.0	16.0	15.7	15.2	14.8	14.6	14.9
Mongolia	..	..	..	..	..	..	..	24.1	25.1	23.2
Nauru	..	..	..	..	..	..	..	..	..	
New Zealand[1]	36.2	32.5	31.9	33.3	33.2	34.2	36.1	35.3	33.9	32.9
Papua New Guinea[4]	..	..	..	20.0	20.2	24.2	25.6	20.0	20.8	18.6
Philippines	..	13.7	13.5	12.8	13.0	12.6	13.3	14.6	14.4	14.4
Samoa	..	..	..	..	..	..	22.5	22.4	18.8	18.7
Singapore	..	15.5	15.0	13.0	12.6	12.2	12.1	12.2	13.4	13.8
Solomon Islands	..	..	..	..	..	..	..	..	19.9	21.5
Thailand	..	14.1	14.3	14.7	15.8	16.3	17.5	16.8	16.2	16.3
Tokelau	..	..	..	..	..	..	..	13.3	14.3	16.1
Vanuatu	..	16.2	16.3	16.4	16.3	16.9	17.1	17.5	19.0	19.2
Africa (26) average[5]	..	..	..	..	..	..	..	..	..	
LAC average[6]	13.7	15.8	15.9	15.9	16.3	16.7	17.4	18.2	18.6	18.6
OECD average[1, 7, 8]	24.6	25.2	24.6	24.3	24.2	24.3	24.9	25.1	25.1	24.4
	2009	**2010**	**2011**	**2012**	**2013**	**2014**	**2015**	**2016**	**2017**	**2018**
Australia[1]	25.5	25.3	25.9	26.9	27.1	27.3	27.9	27.6	28.5	..
Bhutan	13.3	13.9	15.1	14.2	13.4	13.7	13.5	12.8	13.7	12.3
China	17.1	17.8	18.4	18.7	18.6	18.5	18.1	17.5	17.4	17.0
Cook Islands	26.7	26.9	24.7	27.5	25.1	22.1	26.7	27.1	28.3	29.8
Fiji	19.9	20.0	21.0	22.0	21.9	22.7	23.6	23.1	24.2	23.7
Indonesia[2]	..	..	..	..	..	..	12.0	11.6	11.1	11.5
Japan[1]	15.3	15.6	16.1	16.5	17.1	18.3	18.6	18.3	18.8	..
Kazakhstan	20.7	23.2	25.0	23.3	22.0	20.5	15.0	14.4	15.5	16.4
Korea[1]	18.2	17.9	18.4	18.7	17.9	18.0	18.5	19.4	20.0	21.2
Malaysia[3]	15.2	13.6	15.0	15.9	15.6	15.1	14.3	13.8	13.1	12.2
Mongolia	18.4	22.0	21.0	18.2	19.2	16.2	14.9	14.7	17.0	19.2
Nauru	..	..	..	..	..	8.3	23.1	15.6	29.0	35.4
New Zealand[1]	30.2	30.3	30.1	31.6	30.5	31.3	31.7	31.7	32.1	32.7
Papua New Guinea[4]	15.9	17.0	20.0	18.9	18.4	18.2	15.2	13.2	11.9	12.1
Philippines	13.1	12.9	13.2	13.8	14.1	14.5	14.6	14.6	15.2	15.7
Samoa	20.8	19.6	20.5	23.1	23.8	22.9	24.0	24.4	24.5	25.8
Singapore	13.0	12.8	13.1	13.6	13.3	13.6	13.1	13.3	14.1	13.2
Solomon Islands	21.5	24.5	28.8	30.4	29.5	29.4	29.4	27.2	28.7	30.4
Thailand	15.3	16.1	17.7	16.8	18.4	17.3	17.6	16.8	16.3	16.5
Tokelau	15.5	17.7	15.6	15.3	16.2	17.1	15.1	14.7	14.2	18.1
Africa (26) average[5]	..	14.2	14.9	15.2	15.5	15.6	16.0	15.9	15.9	
LAC average[6]	17.5	17.8	18.1	18.3	18.3	18.5	18.7	18.7	18.7	19.1
OECD average[1, 7, 8]	23.3	23.5	23.7	24.1	24.3	24.6	24.7	25.3	25.1	24.9

.. Not available

1. Australia, Japan, Korea and New Zealand are part of the OECD (36) group. Data for Australia, Japan, Korea, New Zealand and the OECD average are taken from OECD (2019), *Revenue Statistics 2019*.
2. Social security contributions data for Indonesia are only available for 2015 to 2018 and are deemed negligible in earlier years.
3. Figures do not include tax revenues from local governments (Quit Rent and Assessment tax), which are unavailable.
4. Total revenues are not calculated for 2000 and 2001 as the data are incomplete and do not include customs revenues for these two years.
5. Represents an unweighted average for the 26 African countries included in the publication *Revenue Statistics in Africa 2019*.
6. Represents an unweighted average for the 25 Latin American and Caribbean (LAC) countries included in the publication *Revenue Statistics in Latin America and the Caribbean 2020*.
7. 1990 to 2017: represents an unweighted average for the 36 OECD member countries included in the publication *Revenue Statistics 2019*. The OECD average in 2016 excludes the one-off revenues from stability contributions in Iceland.
8. 2018: calculated by applying the unweighted average percentage change for 2017 in the 34 countries providing data for that year to the overall average tax-to-GDP ratio in 2017.

StatLink 🔗 https://stat.link/d45bm8

Table 3.3. Tax revenue of main headings as percentage of GDP, 2018

	1000 Income & profits	2000 Social security	3000 Payroll	4000 Property	5000 Goods & services	6000 Other
Australia[1,2]	16.8	0.0	1.4	3.0	7.4	0.0
Bhutan	6.4	0.0	0.0	0.0	5.9	0.0
China[3]	6.0	..	0.0	1.4	9.6	0.0
Cook Islands	11.5	0.0	0.0	0.0	18.3	0.0
Fiji	6.7	0.0	0.0	0.8	16.3	0.0
Indonesia	5.1	0.4	0.0	0.2	5.0	1.2
Japan[1,2]	9.6	12.5	0.0	2.6	6.6	0.1
Kazakhstan	6.4	0.4	1.0	0.5	8.5	0.0
Korea[2]	9.7	7.2	0.1	3.3	7.5	0.6
Malaysia[4]	8.6	0.3	0.0	0.0	3.2	0.4
Mongolia	6.5	4.8	0.0	0.5	12.2	0.0
Nauru	24.8	0.0	0.0	0.0	10.5	0.0
New Zealand[2]	18.2	0.0	0.0	2.0	12.6	0.0
Papua New Guinea	7.4	0.0	0.0	0.1	4.6	0.0
Philippines	6.5	2.5	..	0.5	7.8	1.0
Samoa	5.9	0.0	0.0	0.0	19.8	0.0
Singapore	6.1	0.0	0.0	1.8	3.9	1.3
Solomon Islands[5]	8.0	0.0	0.0	0.2	22.3	0.0
Thailand	6.0	1.0	0.0	0.5	9.9	0.1
Tokelau	8.6	0.0	0.0	0.0	9.5	0.0
Vanuatu	0.0	0.0	0.0	0.6	17.4	0.0
Africa (26) average[1,6]	5.9	1.6	0.2	0.3	9.4	0.1
LAC average[7]	6.3	4.0	0.2	0.8	11.5	0.4
OECD average[1,2,8]	11.6	9.1	0.4	1.9	10.9	0.1

.. Not available

1. Data for Australia, Japan, the Africa (26) average and the OECD average are for 2017.
2. Australia, Japan, Korea and New Zealand are part of the OECD (36) group. Data for Australia, Japan, Korea, New Zealand and the OECD average are taken from OECD (2019), *Revenue Statistics 2019*.
3. The tax-to-GDP figures for China do not include revenue from social security contributions as detailed data were not available.
4. Heading 2000: Data are estimated for 2018.
5. The social security contributions in the Solomon Islands are zero as they do not meet the social security criteria of the OECD classifications set in Annex A of the Interpretative Guide.
6. Represents an unweighted average for the 26 African countries included in the publication *Revenue Statistics in Africa 2019*.
7. Represents an unweighted average for the 25 Latin American and Caribbean (LAC) countries included in the publication *Revenue Statistics in Latin America and the Caribbean 2020*.
8. Represents an unweighted average for the 36 OECD member countries included in the publication *Revenue Statistics 2019*. Data for 2017 are used.

StatLink 🔗 https://stat.link/lnwtvh

Table 3.4. Tax revenue of main headings as percentage of total taxation, 2018

	1000 Income & profits	2000 Social security	3000 Payroll	4000 Property	5000 Goods & services	6000 Other
Australia[1,2]	58.8	0.0	4.8	10.3	26.0	0.0
Bhutan	51.7	0.0	0.3	0.2	47.8	0.0
China[3]	..	..	..	..	..	..
Cook Islands	38.6	0.0	0.0	0.0	61.4	0.0
Fiji	28.1	0.0	0.0	3.3	68.6	0.0
Indonesia	42.5	3.5	0.0	1.4	42.1	10.5
Japan[1,2]	30.7	39.9	0.0	8.2	21.0	0.2
Kazakhstan	38.3	2.2	6.0	2.9	50.6	0.0
Korea[2]	34.1	25.4	0.3	11.6	26.3	2.3
Malaysia[4]	68.6	2.2	0.0	0.0	25.9	3.4
Mongolia	26.8	20.1	0.0	2.2	50.8	0.0
Nauru	70.2	0.0	0.0	0.0	29.8	0.0
New Zealand[2]	55.6	0.0	0.0	6.0	38.5	0.0
Papua New Guinea	61.3	0.0	0.1	1.0	37.6	0.0
Philippines	35.4	13.7	..	2.6	43.0	5.3
Samoa	23.0	0.0	0.0	0.0	77.0	0.0
Singapore	46.6	0.0	0.0	14.0	29.5	10.0
Solomon Islands[5]	26.3	0.0	0.0	0.5	73.2	0.0
Thailand	34.1	5.7	0.0	2.7	56.7	0.7
Tokelau	47.3	0.0	0.0	0.0	52.7	0.0
Vanuatu	0.0	0.0	0.0	3.1	96.9	0.0
Africa (26) average[1,6]	36.2	8.1	1.0	1.6	53.7	0.8
LAC average[7]	27.8	17.1	0.7	3.6	50.1	1.5
OECD average[1,2,8]	34.0	26.0	1.1	5.8	32.4	0.4

.. Not available

1. Data for Australia, Japan, the Africa (26) average and the OECD average are for 2017.
2. Australia, Japan, Korea and New Zealand are part of the OECD (36) group. Data for Australia, Japan, Korea, New Zealand and the OECD average are taken from OECD (2019), *Revenue Statistics 2019*.
3. Data for China are not included in this table as detailed data on revenue from social security contributions were not available.
4. Heading 2000: Data are estimated for 2018.
5. The social security contributions in the Solomon Islands are zero as they do not meet the social security criteria of the OECD classifications set in Annex A of the Interpretative Guide.
6. Represents an unweighted average for the 26 African countries included in the publication *Revenue Statistics in Africa 2019*.
7. Represents an unweighted average for the 25 Latin American and Caribbean (LAC) countries included in the publication *Revenue Statistics in Latin America and the Caribbean 2020*.
8. Represents an unweighted average for the 36 OECD member countries included in the publication *Revenue Statistics 2019*. Data for 2017 are used.

StatLink ⧉ https://stat.link/oegv2f

Table 3.5. Taxes on income and profits (1000) as percentage of GDP

	1997	2000	2007	2010	2013	2014	2015	2016	2017	2018
Australia[1]	16.2	17.6	17.5	14.3	15.4	15.8	15.8	15.8	16.8	..
Bhutan	..	..	..	8.9	8.4	7.8	7.6	6.8	6.8	6.4
China	..	..	4.6	4.6	5.4	5.6	5.7	5.8	5.9	6.0
Cook Islands	..	..	9.8	10.6	8.1	5.7	9.4	9.1	10.3	11.5
Fiji	..	..	..	6.5	5.3	5.6	6.1	7.1	7.6	6.7
Indonesia	3.6	3.8	5.5	5.2	5.3	5.2	5.2	5.4	4.8	5.1
Japan[1]	9.7	9.0	10.0	8.0	9.4	9.6	9.6	9.4	9.6	10.1
Kazakhstan	..	8.3	14.0	9.5	8.1	7.8	6.0	5.6	5.8	6.4
Korea[1]	5.1	6.2	7.9	6.6	7.1	7.2	7.6	8.2	8.6	9.7
Malaysia	9.8	7.7	9.9	9.1	11.2	10.9	9.0	8.3	8.0	8.6
Mongolia	..	..	13.1	10.0	5.8	5.0	5.1	4.4	5.8	6.5
Nauru	..	..	..	..	..	0.0	12.1	9.2	18.8	24.8
New Zealand[1]	20.3	19.5	21.3	16.3	16.7	17.1	17.4	17.6	17.8	18.2
Papua New Guinea	..	9.6	15.1	11.8	12.3	12.2	9.9	8.1	7.2	7.4
Philippines	6.1	6.1	6.6	5.8	6.7	6.7	6.8	6.9	7.0	6.5
Samoa	..	..	4.4	4.8	5.8	5.6	5.5	5.6	5.4	5.9
Singapore	..	8.2	6.1	5.7	5.7	6.0	5.9	6.0	6.8	6.1
Solomon Islands	..	..	4.6	7.4	8.7	8.1	8.8	7.9	8.5	8.0
Thailand	..	4.6	6.8	6.3	7.3	6.7	6.5	6.1	5.8	6.0
Tokelau	..	..	6.8	9.0	9.4	8.2	7.7	8.0	7.9	8.6
Vanuatu	..	0.0	0.0	0.0	0.0	0.0	0.0	0.0	0.0	0.0
Africa (26) average[2]	..	..	..	5.3	6.2	6.1	6.1	5.9	5.9	..
LAC average[3]	3.9	4.4	6.0	5.8	6.1	6.2	6.2	6.0	6.0	6.3
OECD average[1,4]	11.5	11.9	12.1	10.6	11.1	11.2	11.3	11.3	11.6	..

.. Not available

1. Australia, Japan, Korea and New Zealand are part of the OECD (36) group. Data for Australia, Japan, Korea, New Zealand and the OECD average are taken from OECD (2019), *Revenue Statistics 2019*.
2. Represents an unweighted average for the 26 African countries included in the publication *Revenue Statistics in Africa 2019*.
3. Represents an unweighted average for the 25 Latin American and Caribbean (LAC) countries included in the publication *Revenue Statistics in Latin America and the Caribbean 2020*.
4. Represents an unweighted average for the 36 OECD member countries included in the publication *Revenue Statistics 2019*.

StatLink ￼ https://stat.link/k96ebw

Table 3.6. Taxes on income and profits (1000) as percentage of total taxation

	1997	2000	2007	2010	2013	2014	2015	2016	2017	2018
Australia[1]	56.6	57.9	59.3	56.5	56.8	57.8	56.6	57.2	58.8	..
Bhutan	..	..	..	64.0	62.5	57.5	56.1	53.0	49.8	51.7
China[2]	..	..	..	..	..	..	..	..	..	..
Cook Islands	..	..	39.2	39.4	32.3	25.6	35.0	33.5	36.6	38.6
Fiji	..	..	..	32.6	24.0	24.7	25.8	30.6	31.5	28.1
Indonesia	47.2	47.7	45.3	45.8	42.5	42.5	43.1	44.7	41.3	42.5
Japan[1]	37.0	34.8	36.4	30.2	32.5	31.8	31.2	30.6	30.7	..
Kazakhstan	..	41.4	53.7	40.0	36.0	37.2	38.8	37.3	36.0	38.3
Korea[1]	26.2	28.8	31.8	28.0	29.3	29.1	30.3	31.2	32.1	34.1
Malaysia	49.8	54.6	66.6	66.1	70.9	71.0	61.9	59.3	60.1	68.6
Mongolia	..	..	46.1	39.5	24.6	24.6	26.5	22.8	26.9	26.8
Nauru	..	..	..	..	..	0.0	52.2	58.7	64.9	70.2
New Zealand[1]	59.8	60.0	62.9	53.8	54.6	54.6	54.9	55.6	55.6	55.6
Papua New Guinea	..	..	73.0	69.4	67.0	67.3	65.2	61.4	60.9	61.3
Philippines	36.6	38.6	40.4	39.2	41.1	39.8	40.3	40.4	39.8	35.4
Samoa	..	..	23.6	24.7	24.2	24.4	23.1	22.8	22.1	23.0
Singapore	..	52.8	45.4	44.7	43.1	44.2	44.7	44.9	48.3	46.6
Solomon Islands	..	..	23.1	30.3	29.3	27.4	30.1	29.1	29.6	26.3
Thailand	..	31.8	39.6	36.5	38.0	36.6	34.9	34.4	33.4	34.1
Tokelau	..	..	47.8	51.1	57.7	48.1	51.1	54.6	55.8	47.3
Vanuatu	..	0.0	0.0	0.0	0.0	0.0	0.0	0.0	0.0	0.0
Africa (26) average[3]	..	..	..	36.0	39.0	37.9	36.8	36.1	36.2	..
LAC average[4]	21.9	22.7	27.4	26.9	27.9	28.0	27.4	27.2	27.2	27.8
OECD average[1,5]	34.0	34.8	35.9	32.8	33.4	33.3	33.6	33.2	34.0	..

.. Not available

1. Australia, Japan, Korea and New Zealand are part of the OECD (36) group. Data for Australia, Japan, Korea, New Zealand and the OECD average are taken from OECD (2019), *Revenue Statistics 2019*.
2. Data for China are not included in this table as detailed data on revenue from social security contributions were not available.
3. Represents an unweighted average for the 26 African countries included in the publication *Revenue Statistics in Africa 2019*.
4. Represents an unweighted average for the 25 Latin American and Caribbean (LAC) countries included in the publication *Revenue Statistics in Latin America and the Caribbean 2020*.
5. Represents an unweighted average for the 36 OECD member countries included in the publication *Revenue Statistics 2019*.

StatLink ᵐˢᴸ https://stat.link/31xwgi

Table 3.7. Social security contributions (2000) as percentage of GDP

	1997	2000	2007	2010	2013	2014	2015	2016	2017	2018
Australia[1]	0.0	0.0	0.0	0.0	0.0	0.0	0.0	0.0	0.0	..
Bhutan	..	..	..	0.0	0.0	0.0	0.0	0.0	0.0	0.0
China[2]	..	..	..	..	..	..	..	..	..	..
Cook Islands	..	..	0.0	0.0	0.0	0.0	0.0	0.0	0.0	0.0
Fiji	..	..	..	0.0	0.0	0.0	0.0	0.0	0.0	0.0
Indonesia[3,4]	..	..	..	..	..	..	0.1	0.4	0.4	0.4
Japan[1]	9.0	9.1	10.0	10.9	11.8	12.0	12.1	12.4	12.5	..
Kazakhstan	..	0.0	0.4	0.6	0.6	0.6	0.6	0.6	0.5	0.4
Korea[1]	2.8	3.6	5.1	5.5	6.4	6.6	6.7	6.9	6.9	7.2
Malaysia[5]	0.0	0.3	0.3	0.2	0.2	0.2	0.2	0.3	0.3	0.3
Mongolia	..	..	3.2	3.3	4.3	3.9	4.2	4.4	4.5	4.8
Nauru	..	..	..	..	..	0.0	0.0	0.0	0.0	0.0
New Zealand[1]	0.0	0.0	0.0	0.0	0.0	0.0	0.0	0.0	0.0	0.0
Papua New Guinea	..	0.0	0.0	0.0	0.0	0.0	0.0	0.0	0.0	0.0
Philippines	1.4	2.1	1.9	1.9	2.1	2.3	2.4	2.4	2.4	2.5
Samoa	..	..	0.0	0.0	0.0	0.0	0.0	0.0	0.0	0.0
Singapore	..	0.0	0.0	0.0	0.0	0.0	0.0	0.0	0.0	0.0
Solomon Islands[6]	..	..	0.0	0.0	0.0	0.0	0.0	0.0	0.0	0.0
Thailand	..	0.5	0.9	1.2	0.8	1.0	1.1	1.0	1.0	1.0
Tokelau	..	..	0.0	0.0	0.0	0.0	0.0	0.0	0.0	0.0
Vanuatu	..	0.0	0.0	0.0	0.0	0.0	0.0	0.0	0.0	0.0
Africa (26) average[7]	..	..	..	1.3	1.4	1.5	1.5	1.5	1.6	
LAC average[8]	2.6	2.9	3.0	3.4	3.7	3.7	3.9	3.9	4.0	4.0
OECD average[1,9]	8.7	8.6	8.4	8.8	9.0	9.0	9.0	9.1	9.1	..

.. Not available

1. Australia, Japan, Korea and New Zealand are part of the OECD (36) group. Data for Australia, Japan, Korea, New Zealand and the OECD average are taken from OECD (2019), *Revenue Statistics 2019*.
2. Data for China are not included in this table as detailed data on revenue from social security contributions were not available.
3. Social security contributions data for Indonesia are only available for 2015 to 2018 and are deemed negligible in earlier years.
4. Heading 2400: Includes Pension Insurance (JP), and mandatory contributions from BPJS Health for formal workers. Data in 2015 only include Pension Insurance (JP). Contributions from the BPJS Health for 2018 have been estimated.
5. Heading 2000: Data are estimated for 2018.
6. The social security contributions in the Solomon Islands are zero as they do not meet the social security criteria of the OECD classifications set in Annex A of the Interpretative Guide.
7. Represents an unweighted average for the 26 African countries included in the publication *Revenue Statistics in Africa 2019*.
8. Represents an unweighted average for the 25 Latin American and Caribbean (LAC) countries included in the publication *Revenue Statistics in Latin America and the Caribbean 2020*.
9. Represents an unweighted average for the 36 OECD member countries included in the publication *Revenue Statistics 2019*.

StatLink 🔗 https://stat.link/utvy05

Table 3.8. Social security contributions (2000) as percentage of total taxation

	1997	2000	2007	2010	2013	2014	2015	2016	2017	2018
Australia[1]	0.0	0.0	0.0	0.0	0.0	0.0	0.0	0.0	0.0	..
Bhutan	..	..	..	0.0	0.0	0.0	0.0	0.0	0.0	0.0
China[2]	..	..	..	..	..	..	..	..	..	..
Cook Islands	..	..	0.0	0.0	0.0	0.0	0.0	0.0	0.0	0.0
Fiji	..	..	..	0.0	0.0	0.0	0.0	0.0	0.0	0.0
Indonesia[3]	..	..	..	..	..	..	0.6	3.2	3.5	3.5
Japan[1]	34.3	35.2	36.5	41.1	40.8	39.7	39.4	40.4	39.9	..
Kazakhstan	..	0.0	1.5	2.5	2.5	2.7	3.8	3.8	3.2	2.2
Korea[1]	14.2	16.7	20.7	23.3	26.4	26.9	26.6	26.2	25.7	25.4
Malaysia[4]	0.0	2.0	1.7	1.8	1.6	1.6	1.7	1.8	1.9	2.2
Mongolia	..	..	11.4	13.1	18.2	19.4	22.0	23.2	21.0	20.1
Nauru	..	..	..	..	..	0.0	0.0	0.0	0.0	0.0
New Zealand[1]	0.0	0.0	0.0	0.0	0.0	0.0	0.0	0.0	0.0	0.0
Papua New Guinea	..	..	0.0	0.0	0.0	0.0	0.0	0.0	0.0	0.0
Philippines	8.1	13.1	11.8	12.7	12.7	13.5	14.1	14.0	13.4	13.7
Samoa	..	..	0.0	0.0	0.0	0.0	0.0	0.0	0.0	0.0
Singapore	..	0.0	0.0	0.0	0.0	0.0	0.0	0.0	0.0	0.0
Solomon Islands[5]	..	..	0.0	0.0	0.0	0.0	0.0	0.0	0.0	0.0
Thailand	..	3.7	5.1	7.1	4.2	5.3	5.6	5.6	5.7	5.7
Tokelau	..	..	0.0	0.0	0.0	0.0	0.0	0.0	0.0	0.0
Vanuatu	..	0.0	0.0	0.0	0.0	0.0	0.0	0.0	0.0	0.0
Africa (26) average[6]	..	..	..	7.3	7.4	7.8	7.8	7.9	8.1	
LAC average[7]	14.3	15.4	14.4	16.1	16.8	16.7	16.9	17.0	17.3	17.1
OECD average[1,8]	25.1	25.0	24.8	26.8	26.5	26.3	26.2	26.1	26.0	..

.. Not available

1. Australia, Japan, Korea and New Zealand are part of the OECD (36) group. Data for Australia, Japan, Korea, New Zealand and the OECD average are taken from OECD (2019), *Revenue Statistics 2019*.
2. Data for China are not included in this table as detailed data on revenue from social security contributions were not available.
3. Heading 2400: Includes Pension Insurance (JP), and mandatory contributions from BPJS Health for formal workers. Data in 2015 only include Pension Insurance (JP). Contributions from the BPJS Health for 2018 have been estimated.
4. Heading 2000: Data are estimated for 2018.
5. The social security contributions in the Solomon Islands are zero as they do not meet the social security criteria of the OECD classifications set in Annex A of the Interpretative Guide.
6. Represents an unweighted average for the 26 African countries included in the publication *Revenue Statistics in Africa 2019*.
7. Represents an unweighted average for the 25 Latin American and Caribbean (LAC) countries included in the publication *Revenue Statistics in Latin America and the Caribbean 2020*.
8. Represents an unweighted average for the 36 OECD member countries included in the publication *Revenue Statistics 2019*.

StatLink https://stat.link/4ue81j

Table 3.9. Taxes on property (4000) as percentage of GDP

	1997	2000	2007	2010	2013	2014	2015	2016	2017	2018
Australia[1]	2.6	2.7	2.6	2.4	2.6	2.8	3.0	3.0	3.0	..
Bhutan	..	..	..	0.0	0.0	0.0	0.0	0.0	0.0	0.0
China	..	..	1.6	1.3	1.4	1.5	1.7	1.5	1.5	1.4
Cook Islands	..	..	0.0	0.0	0.0	0.0	0.0	0.0	0.0	0.0
Fiji	..	..	..	0.0	0.5	0.7	0.7	0.8	0.7	0.8
Indonesia	0.3	0.3	0.7	0.6	0.3	0.3	0.3	0.2	0.2	0.2
Japan[1]	2.9	2.7	2.5	2.6	2.6	2.6	2.5	2.6	2.6	2.6
Kazakhstan	..	0.8	0.6	0.6	0.4	0.5	0.6	0.5	0.5	0.5
Korea[1]	2.5	2.7	3.2	2.6	2.5	2.7	3.1	3.0	3.1	3.3
Malaysia[2]	0.0	0.0	..	..	0.0	0.0	0.0	0.0	0.0	0.0
Mongolia	..	..	0.6	0.5	0.6	0.5	0.5	0.5	0.6	0.5
Nauru	..	..	..	..	..	0.0	0.0	0.0	0.0	0.0
New Zealand[1]	1.8	1.7	1.8	2.0	1.9	2.0	2.0	1.9	1.9	2.0
Papua New Guinea	..	0.5	0.3	0.2	0.1	0.2	0.1	0.1	0.1	0.1
Philippines	0.2	0.5	0.5	0.4	0.5	0.5	0.5	0.5	0.5	0.5
Samoa	..	..	0.1	0.0	0.0	0.0	0.0	0.0	0.0	0.0
Singapore	..	1.7	2.3	1.9	2.1	1.8	1.7	1.7	2.0	1.8
Solomon Islands	..	..	0.2	0.1	0.1	0.2	0.2	0.2	0.2	0.2
Thailand	..	0.3	0.2	0.2	0.4	0.5	0.5	0.4	0.5	0.5
Tokelau	..	..	0.0	0.0	0.0	0.0	0.0	0.0	0.0	0.0
Vanuatu	..	0.5	0.8	0.7	0.5	0.5	0.5	0.4	0.5	0.6
Africa (26) average[3]	..	..	..	0.4	0.3	0.4	0.4	0.4	0.3	..
LAC average[4]	0.7	0.7	1.0	0.8	0.8	0.9	0.9	0.8	0.8	0.8
OECD average[1,5]	1.7	1.8	1.8	1.7	1.8	1.9	1.9	2.3	1.9	..

.. Not available

1. Australia, Japan, Korea and New Zealand are part of the OECD (36) group. Data for Australia, Japan, Korea, New Zealand and the OECD average are taken from OECD (2019), *Revenue Statistics 2019*.
2. Figures do not include tax revenues from local governments (Quit Rent and Assessment tax), which are unavailable.
3. Represents an unweighted average for the 26 African countries included in the publication *Revenue Statistics in Africa 2019*.
4. Represents an unweighted average for the 25 Latin American and Caribbean (LAC) countries included in the publication *Revenue Statistics in Latin America and the Caribbean 2020*.
5. Represents an unweighted average for the 36 OECD member countries included in the publication *Revenue Statistics 2019*.

StatLink 📊 https://stat.link/4azm62

Table 3.10. Taxes on property (4000) as percentage of total taxation

	1997	2000	2007	2010	2013	2014	2015	2016	2017	2018
Australia[1]	9.2	8.8	9.0	9.4	9.5	10.2	10.7	10.8	10.3	..
Bhutan	..	..	..	0.1	0.0	0.1	0.4	0.3	0.2	0.2
China[2]	..	..	..	..	..	..	..	..	..	..
Cook Islands	..	..	0.0	0.0	0.0	0.0	0.0	0.0	0.0	0.0
Fiji	..	..	..	0.0	2.4	3.3	3.1	3.3	2.9	3.3
Indonesia	4.2	3.7	5.6	5.2	2.5	2.2	2.4	1.6	1.4	1.4
Japan[1]	11.2	10.5	9.0	9.7	8.8	8.5	8.2	8.3	8.2	..
Kazakhstan	..	4.1	2.2	2.4	2.0	2.3	3.6	3.3	3.0	2.9
Korea[1]	12.7	12.4	12.8	11.3	10.3	11.0	12.4	11.6	11.7	11.6
Malaysia[3]	0.0	0.0		..	0.0	0.0	0.0	0.0	0.0	0.0
Mongolia	..	..	2.0	1.9	2.5	2.6	2.6	2.7	2.6	2.2
Nauru	..	..	..	..	..	0.0	0.0	0.0	0.0	0.0
New Zealand[1]	5.4	5.3	5.3	6.6	6.4	6.3	6.2	6.1	6.0	6.0
Papua New Guinea	..	..	1.4	1.0	0.8	1.3	0.6	0.9	0.5	1.0
Philippines	0.9	3.1	2.9	2.9	3.0	2.8	2.8	2.7	2.8	2.6
Samoa	..	..	0.5	0.0	0.0	0.0	0.0	0.0	0.0	0.0
Singapore	..	11.2	17.1	14.5	15.9	13.2	13.0	13.0	14.1	14.0
Solomon Islands	..	..	1.1	0.6	0.5	0.6	0.8	0.7	0.5	0.5
Thailand	..	2.2	1.2	1.3	2.3	2.6	2.7	2.3	2.8	2.7
Tokelau	..	..	0.0	0.0	0.0	0.0	0.0	0.0	0.0	0.0
Vanuatu	..	3.2	4.4	4.4	2.8	3.1	3.0	2.9	3.0	3.1
Africa (26) average[4]	..	..	..	1.8	1.6	1.7	1.7	1.7	1.6	..
LAC average[5]	3.8	3.7	4.8	3.9	4.0	3.9	3.9	3.7	3.6	3.6
OECD average[1, 6]	5.3	5.4	5.5	5.4	5.5	5.6	5.7	6.5	5.8	..

.. Not available

1. Australia, Japan, Korea and New Zealand are part of the OECD (36) group. Data for Australia, Japan, Korea, New Zealand and the OECD average are taken from OECD (2019), *Revenue Statistics 2019*.
2. Data for China are not included in this table as detailed data on revenue from social security contributions were not available.
3. Figures do not include tax revenues from local governments (Quit Rent and Assessment tax), which are unavailable.
4. Represents an unweighted average for the 26 African countries included in the publication *Revenue Statistics in Africa 2019*.
5. Represents an unweighted average for the 25 Latin American and Caribbean (LAC) countries included in the publication *Revenue Statistics in Latin America and the Caribbean 2020*.
6. Represents an unweighted average for the 36 OECD member countries included in the publication *Revenue Statistics 2019*.

StatLink 🔗 https://stat.link/i2l6ga

Table 3.11. Taxes on goods and services (5000) as percentage of GDP

	1997	2000	2007	2010	2013	2014	2015	2016	2017	2018
Australia[1]	7.9	8.8	8.0	7.3	7.8	7.3	7.7	7.5	7.4	..
Bhutan	..	..	..	4.8	4.9	5.8	5.8	6.0	6.9	5.9
China	..	..	10.7	11.9	11.8	11.5	10.7	10.2	10.0	9.6
Cook Islands	..	..	15.1	16.3	17.0	16.5	17.4	18.0	17.9	18.3
Fiji	..	..	..	13.5	16.1	16.3	16.8	15.3	15.9	16.3
Indonesia	3.6	3.5	5.1	4.7	5.7	5.4	5.2	4.8	5.0	5.0
Japan[1]	4.5	5.0	4.9	5.0	5.1	6.0	6.4	6.3	6.6	6.2
Kazakhstan	..	6.9	8.8	11.9	12.4	11.1	7.2	7.2	8.2	8.5
Korea[1]	8.3	8.2	7.8	7.9	7.5	7.4	7.1	7.4	7.5	7.5
Malaysia	8.9	5.6	4.1	3.9	3.7	3.6	4.8	5.0	4.7	3.2
Mongolia	..	..	11.5	11.5	12.9	10.8	9.3	9.8	10.7	12.2
Nauru	..	..	..	..	..	8.3	11.0	6.5	10.2	10.5
New Zealand[1]	11.8	11.3	10.7	12.0	11.9	12.3	12.3	12.1	12.3	12.6
Papua New Guinea	..	3.3	5.3	5.0	5.9	5.7	5.2	5.0	4.6	4.6
Philippines	8.4	6.6	6.6	6.1	6.4	6.7	6.6	6.6	7.1	7.8
Samoa	..	..	14.3	14.7	18.1	17.3	18.5	18.8	19.1	19.8
Singapore	..	4.8	4.4	4.4	4.1	4.2	4.2	4.2	4.0	3.9
Solomon Islands	..	..	15.1	16.9	20.7	21.2	20.3	19.1	20.0	22.3
Thailand	..	9.0	9.1	9.4	10.6	10.0	10.5	10.1	9.9	9.9
Tokelau	..	..	7.4	8.6	6.9	8.8	7.4	6.7	6.3	9.5
Vanuatu	..	15.7	18.2	15.6	16.7	16.8	15.8	14.8	16.6	17.4
Africa (26) average[2]	..	..	..	8.3	8.7	8.8	9.2	9.4	9.4	..
LAC average[3]	9.9	10.3	11.1	10.6	10.8	10.9	11.2	11.3	11.4	11.5
OECD average[1, 4]	11.0	10.9	10.6	10.6	10.8	10.8	10.9	11.0	10.9	..

.. Not available

1. Australia, Japan, Korea and New Zealand are part of the OECD (36) group. Data for Australia, Japan, Korea, New Zealand and the OECD average are taken from OECD (2019), *Revenue Statistics 2019*.
2. Represents an unweighted average for the 26 African countries included in the publication *Revenue Statistics in Africa 2019*.
3. Represents an unweighted average for the 25 Latin American and Caribbean (LAC) countries included in the publication *Revenue Statistics in Latin America and the Caribbean 2020*.
4. Represents an unweighted average for the 36 OECD member countries included in the publication *Revenue Statistics 2019*.

StatLink 🔗 https://stat.link/zjgb1w

Table 3.12. Taxes on goods and services (5000) as percentage of total taxation

	1997	2000	2007	2010	2013	2014	2015	2016	2017	2018
Australia[1]	27.5	28.8	27.0	29.0	28.6	26.9	27.6	27.1	26.0	..
Bhutan	..	..	..	34.8	36.3	42.2	43.2	47.1	50.0	47.8
China[2]	..	..	..	..	..	..	..	..	..	..
Cook Islands	..	..	60.8	60.6	67.7	74.4	65.0	66.5	63.4	61.4
Fiji	..	..	..	67.4	73.6	72.0	71.2	66.2	65.6	68.6
Indonesia	47.6	44.7	41.9	41.8	45.4	44.4	43.3	39.8	43.0	42.1
Japan[1]	17.2	19.3	18.0	18.7	17.6	19.8	21.0	20.4	21.0	..
Kazakhstan	..	34.7	33.8	50.2	54.8	52.7	46.5	48.1	51.1	50.6
Korea[1]	42.7	38.4	31.3	33.7	30.7	30.0	28.0	28.1	27.7	26.3
Malaysia	45.2	39.8	27.9	28.4	23.5	23.6	33.0	35.6	34.8	25.9
Mongolia	..	..	40.4	45.5	54.7	53.4	48.9	51.3	49.6	50.8
Nauru	..	..	..	..	..	100.0	47.8	41.3	35.1	29.8
New Zealand[1]	34.8	34.7	31.7	39.6	39.0	39.2	38.9	38.3	38.4	38.5
Papua New Guinea	..	..	25.5	29.6	32.2	31.2	34.3	37.5	38.5	37.6
Philippines	50.2	42.0	40.7	41.3	39.4	40.0	39.0	39.1	40.3	43.0
Samoa	..	..	76.0	75.3	75.8	75.6	76.9	77.2	77.9	77.0
Singapore	..	31.1	32.9	34.4	30.8	31.3	31.7	31.8	28.5	29.5
Solomon Islands	..	..	75.8	69.1	70.2	72.0	69.1	70.1	69.8	73.2
Thailand	..	61.9	53.4	54.4	54.9	54.9	56.2	56.9	57.4	56.7
Tokelau	..	..	52.2	48.9	42.3	51.9	48.9	45.4	44.2	52.7
Vanuatu	..	96.8	95.6	95.6	97.2	96.9	97.0	97.1	97.0	96.9
Africa (26) average[3]	..	..	..	54.4	51.3	51.8	53.0	53.9	53.7	
LAC average[4]	57.4	56.0	51.4	51.0	49.7	49.7	50.2	50.4	50.5	50.1
OECD average[1,5]	33.6	33.0	32.0	33.2	32.7	32.7	32.7	32.5	32.4	..

.. Not available

1. Australia, Japan, Korea and New Zealand are part of the OECD (36) group. Data for Australia, Japan, Korea, New Zealand and the OECD average are taken from OECD (2019), *Revenue Statistics 2019*.
2. Data for China are not included in this table as detailed data on revenue from social security contributions were not available.
3. Represents an unweighted average for the 26 African countries included in the publication *Revenue Statistics in Africa 2019*.
4. Represents an unweighted average for the 25 Latin American and Caribbean (LAC) countries included in the publication *Revenue Statistics in Latin America and the Caribbean 2020*.
5. Represents an unweighted average for the 36 OECD member countries included in the publication *Revenue Statistics 2019*.

StatLink https://stat.link/054kos

Table 3.13. Taxes on general consumption (5110) as percentage of GDP

	1997	2000	2007	2010	2013	2014	2015	2016	2017	2018
Australia[1]	2.4	3.7	3.9	3.5	3.6	3.6	3.7	3.6	3.6	..
Bhutan	..	..	..	2.1	2.0	2.5	2.6	2.5	2.6	2.7
China[2]	..	..	8.8	9.1	8.9	8.6	7.8	7.6	7.6	7.3
Cook Islands	..	..	10.8	11.0	11.3	11.6	12.5	12.5	12.6	13.3
Fiji	..	..	..	8.1	9.6	9.3	9.8	7.5	7.8	7.6
Indonesia	2.7	2.3	3.6	3.4	4.0	3.9	3.7	3.3	3.5	3.6
Japan[1]	1.9	2.3	2.4	2.5	2.7	3.7	4.2	4.1	4.1	4.1
Kazakhstan	..	4.4	4.9	3.1	3.7	3.0	2.3	3.2	3.1	3.3
Korea[1]	3.7	3.7	3.9	4.1	4.1	4.2	3.8	4.2	4.3	4.3
Malaysia	2.2	1.7	1.0	1.0	1.0	1.0	2.7	3.3	3.2	1.7
Mongolia	..	..	5.3	5.9	7.5	6.2	4.5	4.8	5.8	6.8
Nauru	..	..	..	..	..	0.0	0.0	0.0	0.0	0.0
New Zealand[1]	8.3	8.1	8.0	9.3	9.3	9.5	9.6	9.5	9.7	9.8
Papua New Guinea	..	3.3	2.3	2.3	2.9	2.9	2.7	2.5	2.1	2.0
Philippines[3]	1.8	1.5	2.1	1.9	2.2	2.2	2.2	2.3	2.3	2.1
Samoa	..	..	7.2	6.9	9.5	9.2	9.7	9.4	9.8	10.3
Singapore	..	1.3	2.3	2.5	2.5	2.6	2.4	2.5	2.3	2.2
Solomon Islands	..	..	15.1	8.2	9.9	9.7	8.9	7.9	8.4	8.7
Thailand	..	3.4	3.5	3.6	3.9	4.0	3.9	3.8	3.8	3.9
Tokelau	..	..	0.0	0.0	0.0	0.0	0.0	0.0	0.0	0.0
Vanuatu	..	9.1	10.9	6.3	7.2	7.3	7.0	6.4	7.3	8.3
Africa (26) average[4]			..	4.7	5.0	5.1	5.2	5.2	5.2	..
LAC average[5]	5.7	5.8	6.9	6.5	7.0	7.1	7.2	7.3	7.2	7.3
OECD average[1, 6]	6.7	6.7	6.8	6.7	6.8	6.9	6.9	7.0	7.0	..

.. Not available

1. Australia, Japan, Korea and New Zealand are part of the OECD (36) group. Data for Australia, Japan, Korea, New Zealand and the OECD average are taken from OECD (2019), *Revenue Statistics 2019*.
2. Revenues from import VAT and import excises, urban maintenance and construction tax and refunds on export VAT and export excises are taxes levied on both VAT and excises, however it is not possible to distinguish revenues between the two sources. Therefore all revenues have been allocated to heading 5111 as VAT represents the majority of these revenues.
3. The data exclude revenue from VAT on imports. This revenue could not be distinguished from revenue from other import duties and is currently classified under heading 5120 (taxes on specific goods and services).
4. Represents an unweighted average for the 26 African countries included in the publication *Revenue Statistics in Africa 2019*.
5. Represents an unweighted average for the 25 Latin American and Caribbean (LAC) countries included in the publication *Revenue Statistics in Latin America and the Caribbean 2020*.
6. Represents an unweighted average for the 36 OECD member countries included in the publication *Revenue Statistics 2019*.

StatLink ᵐˢˡ https://stat.link/wqtcev

Table 3.14. Taxes on general consumption (5110) as percentage of total taxation

	1997	2000	2007	2010	2013	2014	2015	2016	2017	2018
Australia[1]	8.4	12.0	13.1	13.8	13.1	13.1	13.3	13.2	12.5	..
Bhutan	..	..	..	15.1	14.7	18.3	19.4	19.4	19.1	21.7
China[2]	..	..	..	..	..	..	..	..	..	..
Cook Islands	..	..	43.4	41.1	45.1	52.4	46.6	46.1	44.4	44.6
Fiji	..	..	..	40.4	43.9	41.0	41.3	32.4	32.3	32.2
Indonesia	35.5	29.4	29.4	29.6	32.3	31.9	30.4	27.8	30.7	30.5
Japan[1]	7.2	9.1	8.8	9.6	9.2	12.2	13.7	13.3	13.0	..
Kazakhstan	..	22.2	18.8	13.1	16.3	14.3	14.8	21.3	19.2	19.6
Korea[1]	18.9	17.0	15.8	17.5	17.0	17.2	15.3	15.8	16.0	15.3
Malaysia	11.1	11.9	6.7	7.2	6.3	6.5	18.9	23.6	24.2	13.4
Mongolia	..	..	18.9	23.4	31.9	30.6	23.7	25.0	27.0	28.2
Nauru	..	..	..	..	..	0.0	0.0	0.0	0.0	0.0
New Zealand[1]	24.5	24.9	23.5	30.7	30.6	30.4	30.2	29.8	30.2	30.1
Papua New Guinea	..	..	11.1	13.3	15.8	15.8	17.9	19.1	18.0	16.4
Philippines[3]	10.6	9.5	12.9	13.0	13.4	13.2	13.0	13.5	13.1	11.3
Samoa	..	..	38.2	35.0	39.8	40.3	40.4	38.5	40.0	40.1
Singapore	..	8.3	16.8	19.6	18.6	18.9	18.6	18.9	16.5	16.8
Solomon Islands	..	..	75.8	33.3	33.5	32.9	30.1	28.8	29.4	28.6
Thailand	..	23.1	20.6	20.8	20.5	21.9	20.8	21.5	21.9	22.2
Tokelau	..	..	..	0.0	0.0	0.0	0.0	0.0	0.0	0.0
Vanuatu	..	56.4	57.1	38.8	41.8	42.2	42.8	41.6	42.5	45.8
Africa (26) average[4]	..	..	..	30.8	29.6	29.7	29.7	29.6	29.9	..
LAC average[5]	30.9	30.0	30.6	30.4	31.1	31.1	31.3	31.8	31.5	31.5
OECD average[1, 6]	20.3	20.1	20.4	21.0	20.8	21.0	20.9	20.7	20.8	..

.. Not available

1. Australia, Japan, Korea and New Zealand are part of the OECD (36) group. Data for Australia, Japan, Korea, New Zealand and the OECD average are taken from OECD (2019), *Revenue Statistics 2019*.
2. Data for China are not included in this table as detailed data on revenue from social security contributions were not available.
3. The data exclude revenue from VAT on imports. This revenue could not be distinguished from revenue from other import duties and is currently classified under heading 5120 (taxes on specific goods and services).
4. Represents an unweighted average for the 26 African countries included in the publication *Revenue Statistics in Africa 2019*.
5. Represents an unweighted average for the 25 Latin American and Caribbean (LAC) countries included in the publication *Revenue Statistics in Latin America and the Caribbean 2020*.
6. Represents an unweighted average for the 36 OECD member countries included in the publication *Revenue Statistics 2019*.

StatLink https://stat.link/xc0z1i

Table 3.15. Taxes on specific goods and services (5120) as percentage of GDP

	1997	2000	2007	2010	2013	2014	2015	2016	2017	2018
Australia[1]	4.0	4.3	3.3	3.0	2.9	2.9	2.9	2.8	2.8	..
Bhutan	..	..	..	2.7	2.9	3.3	3.0	3.3	4.0	3.0
China[2]	..	..	1.8	2.5	2.5	2.5	2.5	2.2	2.2	2.0
Cook Islands	..	..	4.1	5.0	5.4	4.6	4.7	5.3	5.1	4.8
Fiji	..	..	..	5.4	6.5	7.0	7.0	7.8	8.0	8.6
Indonesia	0.9	1.2	1.5	1.4	1.6	1.5	1.6	1.4	1.4	1.4
Japan[1]	2.1	2.0	2.0	1.9	1.9	1.8	1.8	1.7	2.1	1.7
Kazakhstan	..	2.1	3.1	8.3	8.3	7.7	4.6	3.7	4.8	4.9
Korea[1]	4.2	4.2	3.6	3.5	2.9	2.7	2.8	2.8	2.7	2.7
Malaysia	5.4	2.9	2.5	2.4	2.2	2.2	1.6	1.3	1.0	1.2
Mongolia	..	..	4.9	4.8	4.4	3.8	4.1	4.1	3.8	4.6
Nauru	..	..	..	..	..	7.6	10.3	6.0	9.6	9.8
New Zealand[1]	2.8	2.5	2.0	1.9	1.8	1.9	1.9	1.9	1.8	1.9
Papua New Guinea	..	..	3.0	2.8	3.0	2.8	2.5	2.4	2.4	2.6
Philippines[3]	6.5	5.0	4.4	4.1	4.1	4.4	4.3	4.3	4.7	5.7
Samoa	..	..	7.1	7.9	8.6	8.1	8.8	9.4	9.3	9.5
Singapore	..	2.0	1.4	1.3	1.2	1.3	1.3	1.2	1.2	1.1
Solomon Islands	..	..	8.1	8.7	10.7	11.3	11.3	11.1	11.4	13.4
Thailand	..	5.4	5.4	5.6	5.6	4.9	5.3	5.2	5.2	5.0
Tokelau	..	..	7.4	8.6	6.9	8.8	7.4	6.7	6.3	9.5
Vanuatu	..	6.5	7.3	6.7	6.0	5.9	6.2	5.9	6.4	6.5
Africa (26) average[4]	..	..	..	3.4	3.5	3.6	3.8	4.0	4.0	..
LAC average[5]	4.0	4.1	3.8	3.7	3.4	3.5	3.6	3.7	3.8	3.8
OECD average[1, 6]	3.7	3.6	3.2	3.3	3.3	3.2	3.2	3.3	3.2	..

.. Not available

1. Australia, Japan, Korea and New Zealand are part of the OECD (36) group. Data for Australia, Japan, Korea, New Zealand and the OECD average are taken from OECD (2019), *Revenue Statistics 2019*.
2. Revenues from import VAT and import excises, urban maintenance and construction tax and refunds on export VAT and export excises are taxes levied on both VAT and excises, however it is not possible to distinguish revenues between the two sources. Therefore all revenues have been allocated to heading 5111 as VAT represents the majority of these revenues.
3. The data include revenues from VAT on imports, usually classified under heading 5110 (taxes on general consumption). This revenue could not be distinguished from revenue from other import duties.
4. Represents an unweighted average for the 26 African countries included in the publication *Revenue Statistics in Africa 2019*.
5. Represents an unweighted average for the 25 Latin American and Caribbean (LAC) countries included in the publication *Revenue Statistics in Latin America and the Caribbean 2020*.
6. Represents an unweighted average for the 36 OECD member countries included in the publication *Revenue Statistics 2019*.

StatLink 🖳 https://stat.link/dpuny8

Table 3.16. Taxes on specific goods and services (5120) as percentage of total taxation

	1997	2000	2007	2010	2013	2014	2015	2016	2017	2018
Australia[1]	13.8	14.1	11.3	11.9	10.8	10.5	10.4	10.0	9.8	..
Bhutan	..	..	..	19.6	21.6	23.9	22.2	25.9	29.2	24.2
China[2]	..	..	..	..	..	..	..	..	..	
Cook Islands	..	..	16.3	18.6	21.5	20.6	17.7	19.5	18.1	16.1
Fiji	..	..	..	26.9	29.6	30.9	29.8	33.7	33.2	36.3
Indonesia	12.1	15.3	12.5	12.2	13.1	12.6	12.9	12.0	12.3	11.6
Japan[1]	7.9	7.9	7.1	7.2	6.7	6.0	5.8	5.7	6.6	..
Kazakhstan	..	10.3	12.1	35.1	36.6	36.3	29.5	24.9	30.2	29.3
Korea[1]	21.6	19.7	14.5	15.1	11.8	10.8	10.9	10.5	10.1	9.4
Malaysia	27.5	20.5	17.1	17.3	14.1	14.1	11.0	9.0	7.8	9.4
Mongolia	..	..	17.3	19.0	18.9	18.6	21.3	21.6	17.8	18.9
Nauru	..	..	..	..	..	91.6	44.6	38.2	33.3	27.8
New Zealand[1]	8.2	7.5	5.9	6.4	5.9	6.1	6.1	5.9	5.7	5.7
Papua New Guinea	..	..	14.4	16.3	16.3	15.4	16.4	18.4	20.5	21.2
Philippines[3]	39.1	32.0	27.0	27.6	25.4	26.2	25.5	25.1	26.6	31.2
Samoa	..	..	37.8	40.2	36.1	35.3	36.5	38.7	38.0	36.9
Singapore	..	13.0	10.1	10.3	8.9	9.5	10.0	9.2	8.8	8.7
Solomon Islands	..	..	40.7	35.3	36.2	38.4	38.4	40.6	39.8	44.1
Thailand	..	37.0	31.5	32.1	29.1	27.1	28.3	29.0	30.0	28.8
Tokelau	..	..	52.2	48.9	42.3	51.9	48.9	45.4	44.2	52.7
Vanuatu	..	40.4	38.6	40.8	34.8	33.7	38.1	38.7	37.6	36.0
Africa (26) average[4]	..	..	..	22.1	20.7	21.2	22.2	23.1	22.7	
LAC average[5]	25.0	24.4	19.2	18.7	16.7	16.6	16.9	16.7	17.1	16.7
OECD average[1, 6]	11.4	11.1	9.8	10.3	9.9	9.7	9.8	9.8	9.6	..

.. Not available

1. Australia, Japan, Korea and New Zealand are part of the OECD (36) group. Data for Australia, Japan, Korea, New Zealand and the OECD average are taken from OECD (2019), *Revenue Statistics 2019*.
2. Data for China are not included in this table as detailed data on revenue from social security contributions were not available.
3. The data include revenues from VAT on imports, usually classified under heading 5110 (taxes on general consumption). This revenue could not be distinguished from revenue from other import duties.
4. Represents an unweighted average for the 26 African countries included in the publication *Revenue Statistics in Africa 2019*.
5. Represents an unweighted average for the 25 Latin American and Caribbean (LAC) countries included in the publication *Revenue Statistics in Latin America and the Caribbean 2020*.
6. Represents an unweighted average for the 36 OECD member countries included in the publication *Revenue Statistics 2019*.

StatLink https://stat.link/7fte3r

Table 3.17. Gross domestic product for tax reporting years at market prices, in national currency

	1997	2000	2007	2010	2013	2014	2015	2016	2017	2018
Australia[1,2]	588	705	1 177	1 417	1 599	1 624	1 662	1 765	1 848	1 939
Bhutan	..	..	..	77 717	109 649	122 462	136 804	152 322	163 449	176 719
China	7 972	10 028	27 009	41 212	59 296	64 356	68 886	74 640	83 204	91 928
Cook Islands[2]	..	..	314 585	339 219	368 867	409 195	439 214	465 766	504 258	548 693
Fiji[3]	3 275	..	5 940	6 526	8 358	9 167	9 822	10 327	11 065	11 557
Indonesia	754 614	1 520 683	4 323 057	6 864 133	9 546 134	10 569 705	11 526 333	12 401 729	13 587 213	14 837 358
Japan[1]	533 393	528 447	530 923	499 429	507 255	518 235	532 983	536 808	547 496	550 099
Kazakhstan	1 672	2 600	12 850	21 816	35 999	39 676	40 884	46 971	54 379	61 820
Korea	530 347	635 185	1 043 258	1 265 308	1 429 445	1 486 079	1 564 124	1 641 786	1 730 399	1 782 269
Malaysia	282	356	665	821	1 019	1 106	1 177	1 250	1 372	1 447
Mongolia	933	1 224	4 957	9 757	19 174	22 227	23 150	23 943	27 876	32 411
Nauru	..	..	29 090	53 762	96 046	114 454	104 318	137 494	145 347	159 999
New Zealand[1,2]	105	122	189	206	237	245	257	273	289	300
Papua New Guinea	10 701	9 736	28 304	38 752	47 721	57 131	60 139	65 038	75 626	82 341
Philippines	2 689	3 581	6 893	9 003	11 538	12 634	13 322	14 480	15 808	17 426
Samoa[2,4]	733	796	1 758	1 742	1 793	1 918	2 061	2 107	2 131	2 218
Singapore[5]	149	166	273	327	385	399	423	440	472	503
Solomon Islands	1 833	..	4 123	5 613	7 410	7 720	8 130	8 686	9 173	9 854
Thailand	4 710	5 070	9 076	10 808	12 915	13 230	13 743	14 593	15 487	16 366
Tokelau[2]	..	..	8 399	9 597	11 501	12 355	14 222	14 838	17 706	15 739
Vanuatu	31 606	37 627	53 926	67 912	75 803	79 109	82 798	87 250	94 887	99 818

.. Not available

Note: All units are in billions except for Bhutan, Cook Islands, Fiji, Nauru, Papua New Guinea, Samoa, Solomon Islands, Tokelau and Vanuatu. Due to the size of their economies, the GDP figures for Cook Islands, Nauru and Tokelau are expressed in thousands while they are in millions for Bhutan, Fiji, Papua New Guinea, Samoa, Solomon Islands and Vanuatu.

1. The year Y is calculated (at annual rate) as the average of: Q2(Y) to Q1(Y+1) for Japan; and Q3(Y) to Q2(Y+1) for Australia and New Zealand.
2. Data are reported on a fiscal year basis beginning 1st July. For example, the data for 2018 represent the period from July 2018 to June 2019.
3. Fiji has recently rebased its GDP. As a result, tax-to-GDP ratios for Fiji are lower than the levels shown in previous editions. The difference in tax-to-GDP ratios for the year 2017 between the two publications amounted to 2.4 percentage points.
4. The year Y is calculated using the formula GDP(Y)/2+GDP(Y-1)/2. This is done in order to make the value of the GDP correspond more closely to a July(Y-1)-to-June(Y) fiscal year.
5. The year Y is calculated using the formula GDP(Y)*3/4+GDP(Y+1))/4 in order to make it correspond more closely to an April(Y)-to-March(Y+1) fiscal year.
Source: OECD National Accounts data for Australia, Indonesia, Japan, Korea and New Zealand; National statistical offices for Cook Islands and Tokelau; National Statistical Offices for Bhutan, China, Malaysia, Mongolia, Philippines, Singapore and Thailand; Asian Development Bank's Key Indicators Database for Fiji, Papua New Guinea, Samoa, Solomon Islands and Vanuatu. Data for 2018 were estimated for 2018 for Fiji and Vanuatu, using the GDP growth rates of the IMF's *World Economic Outlook* (WEO) April 2020 edition; Data for 2017 and 2018 using the WEO growth rates for the Solomon Islands and for 2019 for Bhutan.

StatLink https://stat.link/x45iq2

Table 3.18. Gross domestic product for tax reporting years at market prices, in millions of US dollars at market exchange rates

	1997	2000	2007	2010	2013	2014	2015	2016	2017	2018
Australia[1,2]	436 263	408 375	985 048	1 299 443	1 542 380	1 464 150	1 249 051	1 311 576	1 415 970	1 448 282
Bhutan	..	..	..	1 666	1 999	1 992	2 205	2 297	2 477	2 719
China	961 601	1 211 331	3 550 327	6 087 192	9 570 470	10 475 625	11 061 573	11 233 315	12 310 490	13 894 907
Cook Islands[2]	..	..	232	245	303	340	308	325	358	380
Fiji	2 268	..	3 688	3 402	4 539	4 857	4 682	4 930	5 353	5 537
Indonesia	259 373	180 566	472 983	755 256	916 646	891 051	860 741	932 066	1 015 292	1 042 613
Japan[1]	4 408 334	4 900 526	4 508 703	5 690 809	5 197 390	4 896 054	4 404 734	4 933 774	4 880 376	4 981 073
Kazakhstan	22 166	18 292	104 850	148 047	236 635	221 416	184 388	137 289	166 806	179 340
Korea	557 962	561 792	1 122 446	1 095 096	1 305 518	1 411 196	1 382 579	1 414 614	1 530 466	1 619 970
Malaysia	100 169	93 790	193 614	255 024	323 276	338 066	301 355	301 255	318 955	358 579
Mongolia	1 181	1 137	4 235	7 185	12 582	12 227	11 750	11 159	11 426	13 138
Nauru	..	..	23	47	99	105	87	100	110	124
New Zealand[1,2]	69 287	55 432	138 908	148 338	193 973	203 009	179 294	190 304	205 228	207 499
Papua New Guinea	7 442	3 499	9 545	14 251	21 261	23 211	21 723	20 759	23 716	25 111
Philippines	91 234	81 023	149 360	199 591	271 836	284 585	292 774	304 898	313 620	330 910
Samoa[2,3]	286	256	649	686	785	826	850	806	841	880
Singapore[4]	100 124	96 077	180 942	239 808	307 576	314 864	307 999	318 642	341 858	373 199
Solomon Islands	493	..	539	696	1 015	1 048	1 031	1 095	1 143	1 232
Thailand	150 180	126 392	262 943	341 105	420 334	407 339	401 266	413 489	456 382	506 399
Tokelau[2]	..	..	6	7	9	10	10	10	13	11
Vanuatu	273	273	527	681	798	817	774	798	880	920

.. Not available

Note: This table is produced based on GDP data in national currency from Table 3.17 and exchange rate data from Table 3.20.

1. The year Y is calculated (at annual rate) as the average of: Q2(Y) to Q1(Y+1) for Japan; and Q3(Y) to Q2(Y+1) for Australia and New Zealand.
2. Data are reported on a fiscal year basis. The data for 2018 represent the period from July 2018 to June 2019.
3. The year Y is calculated using the formula GDP(Y)/2+GDP(Y-1)/2. This is done in order to make the value of the GDP correspond more closely to a July(Y-1)-to-June(Y) fiscal year.
4. The year Y is calculated using the formula GDP(Y)*3/4+GDP(Y+1))/4 in order to make it correspond more closely to an April(Y)-to-March(Y+1) fiscal year.

StatLink ᵐˢ˥ https://stat.link/0tqk94

Table 3.19. Total tax revenue in millions of US dollars at market exchange rates

	1997	2000	2007	2010	2013	2014	2015	2016	2017	2018
Australia	125 058	124 385	290 788	328 349	418 120	399 343	348 153	362 049	404 009	..
Bhutan	..	..	..	232	268	272	297	294	339	335
China[1]	..	..	599 678	1 081 331	1 783 962	1 939 874	2 005 974	1 961 814	2 135 982	2 364 024
Cook Islands	..	..	58	66	76	75	82	88	101	113
Fiji	..	..	..	680	994	1 102	1 105	1 140	1 296	1 312
Indonesia	19 709	14 213	57 546	85 766	114 437	108 382	104 245	111 934	117 072	124 067
Japan	1 153 894	1 263 376	1 241 967	1 509 609	1 500 082	1 482 193	1 351 487	1 516 166	1 530 992	..
Kazakhstan		3 643	27 329	35 169	53 446	46 682	28 652	20 478	26 658	30 124
Korea	108 274	120 547	278 198	256 154	317 220	347 014	347 879	371 149	411 689	460 420
Malaysia	19 726	13 180	28 684	35 260	51 071	51 794	43 777	42 264	42 679	44 783
Mongolia	..	..	1 201	1 819	2 955	2 465	2 244	2 129	2 461	3 157
Nauru	..	..	..	..	..	9	20	16	32	44
New Zealand	23 510	18 037	47 059	44 906	59 151	63 532	56 824	60 285	65 838	67 830
Papua New Guinea	..	..	1 981	2 417	3 909	4 214	3 302	2 747	2 818	3 045
Philippines	15 201	12 770	24 304	29 501	44 023	47 563	49 780	51 815	55 153	60 266
Samoa	..	..	122	134	187	189	204	197	206	227
Singapore	..	14 865	24 305	30 691	40 874	42 705	40 476	42 488	48 057	49 080
Solomon Islands	..	..	107	171	300	308	303	298	328	375
Thailand	..	18 452	44 995	59 031	80 862	74 215	74 982	73 553	78 784	88 430
Tokelau	..	..	1	1	2	2	2	2	2	2
Vanuatu	..	44	100	111	137	142	126	122	151	166

.. Not available
Note: This table is produced based on total tax revenues from Chapter 4 and exchange rate data from Table 3.20.
1. The figures for China do not include revenue from social security contributions as detailed data were not available.

StatLink https://stat.link/nx9ip4

Table 3.20. Exchange rates used, national currency per US dollar

	1997	2000	2007	2010	2013	2014	2015	2016	2017	2018
Australia	1.35	1.73	1.20	1.09	1.04	1.11	1.33	1.35	1.31	1.34
Bhutan	35.77	43.64	44.19	46.65	54.86	61.47	62.05	66.32	66.00	65.00
China	8.29	8.28	7.61	6.77	6.20	6.14	6.23	6.64	6.76	6.62
Cook Islands	1.51	2.19	1.36	1.39	1.22	1.20	1.43	1.44	1.41	1.44
Fiji	1.44	2.13	1.61	1.92	1.84	1.89	2.10	2.10	2.07	2.09
Indonesia	2 909.38	8 421.78	9 139.99	9 088.49	10 414.20	11 862.06	13 391.17	13 305.63	13 382.56	14 230.93
Japan	121.00	107.84	117.76	87.76	97.60	105.85	121.00	108.80	112.18	110.44
Kazakhstan	75.44	142.13	122.55	147.36	152.13	179.19	221.73	342.13	326.00	344.71
Korea	950.51	1 130.64	929.45	1 155.43	1 094.93	1 053.06	1 131.31	1 160.59	1 130.64	1 100.19
Malaysia	2.81	3.80	3.44	3.22	3.15	3.27	3.91	4.15	4.30	4.04
Mongolia	789.73	1 076.44	1 170.40	1 357.90	1 523.93	1 817.94	1 970.31	2 145.53	2 439.78	2 467.05
Nauru	..	..	1.27	1.14	0.98	1.09	1.20	1.37	1.33	1.29
New Zealand	1.51	2.21	1.36	1.39	1.22	1.21	1.43	1.44	1.41	1.45
Papua New Guinea	1.44	2.78	2.97	2.72	2.25	2.46	2.77	3.13	3.19	3.28
Philippines	29.47	44.19	46.15	45.11	42.45	44.40	45.50	47.49	50.40	52.66
Samoa	2.56	3.12	2.71	2.54	2.29	2.32	2.42	2.61	2.54	2.52
Singapore	1.49	1.72	1.51	1.36	1.25	1.27	1.38	1.38	1.38	1.35
Solomon Islands	3.72	5.09	7.65	8.07	7.30	7.36	7.89	7.93	8.03	8.00
Thailand	31.36	40.11	34.52	31.69	30.73	32.48	34.25	35.29	33.93	32.32
Tokelau	1.51	2.19	1.36	1.39	1.22	1.20	1.43	1.44	1.41	1.44
Vanuatu	115.87	137.87	102.33	99.70	95.00	96.86	107.00	109.31	107.77	108.53

.. Not available

Source: OECD National Accounts data for Australia, the Cook Islands, Indonesia, Japan, Korea, Nauru and New Zealand; IMF's *World Economic Outlook* (April 2020) for the Bhutan, China, Fiji, Kazakhstan, Mongolia, Malaysia, Nauru, Papua New Guinea, Philippines, Samoa, Singapore, Solomon Islands, Thailand and Vanuatu.

StatLink ᴍᴉsᴧ https://stat.link/yp9gvn

4 Country tables, tax revenues, 1997-2018

Country tax revenue tables, 1997-2018

In all of the following tables a ("..") indicates not available. The main series in this volume cover the years 1990 to 2018.

Figures referring to 1998-99, 2001-06, 2008-09 and 2011-12 in Tables 4.1 to 4.21 have been omitted because of lack of space. Full time series can be accessed at https://stats.oecd.org/ within the theme Public Sector, Taxation and Market Regulation/Taxation/Revenue Statistics Asian and Pacific Economies.

Table 4.1. Australia
Details of tax revenue
Million AUD

	1997	2000	2007	2010	2013	2014	2015	2016	2017	2018
Total tax revenue	**168 582**	**214 752**	**347 545**	**357 958**	**433 342**	**443 049**	**463 350**	**487 078**	**527 185**	..
1000 Taxes on income, profits and capital gains	**95 367**	**124 427**	**206 134**	**202 184**	**246 073**	**255 966**	**262 357**	**278 764**	**310 041**	..
1100 Of individuals	70 782	80 991	127 587	138 163	169 972	183 023	191 747	198 534	212 520	
1110 On income and profits	69 212	80 991	127 587	138 163	169 972	183 023	191 747	198 534	212 520	
1120 On capital gains	1 570	0	0	0	0	0	0	0	0	
1200 Corporate	24 585	43 436	78 547	64 021	76 101	72 943	70 610	80 230	97 521	
1210 On profits	22 253	43 436	78 547	64 021	76 101	72 943	70 610	80 230	97 521	
Income tax on companies	21 242	42 221	76 655	62 549	74 535	71 224	68 779	78 254	95 539	
Dividend and interest taxes	693	846	1 892	1 472	1 566	1 719	1 831	1 976	1 982	
Other withholding taxes	318	369	0	0	0	0	0	0	0	
1220 On capital gains	2 332	0	0	0	0	0	0	0	0	
1300 Unallocable between 1100 and 1200	0	0	0	0	0	0	0	0	0	
2000 Social security contributions	**0**	**0**	**0**	**0**	**0**	**0**	**0**	**0**	**0**	..
2100 Employees	0	0	0	0	0	0	0	0	0	
2110 On a payroll basis	..	..	..	..	..	..	..	..	..	
2120 On an income tax basis	..	..	..	..	..	..	..	..	..	
2200 Employers	0	0	0	0	0	0	0	0	0	
2210 On a payroll basis	..	..	..	..	..	..	..	..	..	
2220 On an income tax basis	..	..	..	..	..	..	..	..	..	
2300 Self-employed or non-employed	0	0	0	0	0	0	0	0	0	
2310 On a payroll basis	..	..	..	..	..	..	..	..	..	
2320 On an income tax basis	..	..	..	..	..	..	..	..	..	
2400 Unallocable between 2100, 2200 and 2300	0	0	0	0	0	0	0	0	0	
2410 On a payroll basis	..	..	..	..	..	..	..	..	..	
2420 On an income tax basis	..	..	..	..	..	..	..	..	..	
3000 Taxes on payroll and workforce	**11 277**	**9 624**	**16 407**	**18 492**	**22 210**	**22 776**	**23 354**	**23 799**	**25 520**	..
4000 Taxes on property	**15 505**	**18 825**	**31 156**	**33 526**	**40 963**	**45 293**	**49 641**	**52 585**	**54 533**	..
4100 Recurrent taxes on immovable property	7 739	9 067	15 615	19 907	23 603	25 062	27 093	29 232	30 344	
4110 Households	..	..	..	..	..	..	..	..	..	
4120 Others	..	..	..	..	..	..	..	..	..	
4200 Recurrent taxes on net wealth	0	0	0	0	0	0	0	0	0	
4210 Individual	..	..	..	..	..	..	..	..	..	
4220 Corporate	..	..	..	..	..	..	..	..	..	
4300 Estate, inheritance and gift taxes	0	0	0	0	0	0	0	0	0	
4310 Estate and inheritance taxes	..	..	..	..	..	..	..	..	..	
Estate duty central government	..	..	..	..	..	..	..	..	..	
St. and loc. estate probate and succession	..	..	..	..	..	..	..	..	..	
4320 Gift taxes	..	..	..	..	..	..	..	..	..	
4400 Taxes on financial and capital transactions	7 766	9 758	15 541	13 619	17 360	20 231	22 548	23 353	24 189	
4500 Non-recurrent taxes	0	0	0	0	0	0	0	0	0	
4510 On net wealth	..	..	..	..	..	..	..	..	..	
4520 Other non-recurrent taxes	..	..	..	..	..	..	..	..	..	
4600 Other recurrent taxes on property	0	0	0	0	0	0	0	0	0	
5000 Taxes on goods and services	**46 433**	**61 876**	**93 848**	**103 756**	**124 096**	**119 014**	**127 998**	**131 930**	**137 091**	..
5100 Taxes on production, sale, transfer, etc.	37 359	56 178	84 851	92 007	103 419	104 528	110 185	113 155	117 340	
5110 General taxes	14 085	25 830	45 486	49 329	56 819	57 830	61 815	64 251	65 700	
5111 Value added taxes	0	23 854	44 381	48 093	55 517	56 462	60 312	62 727	64 062	
5112 Sales tax	14 085	1 976	1 105	1 236	1 302	1 368	1 503	1 524	1 638	
5113 Other	0	0	0	0	0	0	0	0	0	
5120 Taxes on specific goods and services	23 274	30 348	39 365	42 678	46 600	46 698	48 370	48 904	51 640	
5121 Excise duties	14 449	19 768	24 357	26 689	26 472	24 506	22 541	22 773	23 673	
Excises central government	13 573	19 019	23 526	25 803	25 648	23 799	21 625	21 895	22 773	
Statutory corporate payments	258	295	231	452	343	209	405	335	346	
Primary production charges	618	454	600	434	481	498	511	543	564	
5122 Profits of fiscal monopolies	0	0	0	0	0	0	0	0	0	
5123 Customs and import duties	3 637	4 606	6 070	5 828	9 280	10 884	14 046	14 196	15 690	
Customs duties central government	3 637	4 606	6 070	5 828	9 280	10 884	14 046	14 196	15 690	
5124 Taxes on exports	6	0	10	11	10	12	11	11	0	
Customs duties on coal exports	0	..	0	0	0	0	0	0	0	
Other	6	..	10	11	10	12	11	11	0	
5125 Taxes on investment goods	0	0	0	0	0	0	0	0	0	
5126 Taxes on specific services	5 182	5 974	8 928	10 150	10 838	11 296	11 772	11 924	12 277	
Taxes race meetings	601	300	358	366	318	290	257	225	265	
Poker machines	1 760	2 074	3 009	3 125	3 238	3 480	3 684	3 717	3 881	
Lotteries	330	890	1 118	1 147	1 257	1 270	1 369	1 293	1 330	
Levies on fire insurance companies	521	574	937	1 232	740	739	786	803	812	
Other	1 970	2 136	3 506	4 280	5 285	5 517	5 676	5 886	5 989	

	1997	2000	2007	2010	2013	2014	2015	2016	2017	2018
5127 Other taxes on internat. trade and transactions	0	0	0	0	0	0	0	0	0	..
5128 Other taxes	0	0	0	0	0	0	0	0	0	..
5130 Unallocable between 5110 and 5120	0	0	0	0	0	0	0	0	0	..
5200 Taxes on use of goods and perform activities	9 074	5 698	8 997	11 749	20 677	14 486	17 813	18 775	19 751	..
5210 Recurrent taxes	8 956	5 698	8 997	11 749	20 677	14 486	17 813	18 775	19 751	..
5211 Paid by households: motor vehicles	2 188	3 908	6 196	7 229	8 591	9 155	9 586	9 930	7 695	..
5212 Paid by others: motor vehicles	1 350	125	189	232	301	308	318	344	3 108	..
Fees on motor vehicle registry	1 287	0	0	0	0	0	0	0	1 851	..
Drivers licences	0	0	0	0	0	0	0	0	0	..
Stamp duty on vehicle registry	63	125	189	232	301	308	318	344	1 257	..
5213 Paid in respect of other goods	5 418	1 665	2 611	4 288	11 786	5 022	7 910	8 501	8 947	..
Broadcasting tv licences	329	210	288	150	157	185	128	0	0	..
Business franchise lic. tobac. fuel	3 992	227	0	0	2	0	1	0	1	..
Other taxes	565	1 129	2 321	4 136	11 603	4 815	7 760	8 478	8 923	..
Liquor taxes	532	97	2	1	24	23	22	23	24	..
Dog licenses	0	0	0	0	0	0	0	0	0	..
5220 Non-recurrent taxes	118	0	0	0	0	0	0	0	0	..
5300 Unallocable between 5100 and 5200	0	0	0	0	0	0	0	0	0	..
6000 Other taxes	**0**	**0**	**0**	**0**	**0**	**0**	**0**	**0**	**0**	..
6100 Paid solely by business	..	..	..	..	..	..	..	..	..	..
6200 Other	..	..	..	..	..	..	..	..	..	..

Note: Data are on a fiscal year basis beginning 1st July.

From 1998 taxes are recorded on an accrual basis; prior to that they were on a cash basis.

Direct taxes paid by public trading enterprises are excluded from receipts.

The figures for total tax revenue do not match the published totals in Taxation Revenue Australia. The latter is based on an accrual IMF GFS methodology and there are some differences between that and the OECD equivalent.

Heading 5213 includes radio and television licenses fees, though these are usually not regarded as a tax revenue in the OECD list.

Headings for non-wastable tax credits 1110 and 1210 include the private health insurance tax offset, family benefit, baby bonus tax offsets (paid during the 2003-04 budget year), film tax offset, and research and development tax offsets. The estimation of non-wastable credits into the expenditure and transfer components is in accordance with the OECD guidelines on the treatment and the data for this memorandum item has been provided by the Australian Taxation Office.

Source: Australian Bureau of Statistics.

StatLink ᴍᴵSᴸ https://stat.link/fuv6jt

Table 4.2. Bhutan
Details of tax revenue
Million BTN

	1997	2000	2007	2010	2013	2014	2015	2016	2017	2018
Total tax revenue	..	..	..	**10 816**	**14 707**	**16 718**	**18 416**	**19 523**	**22 404**	**21 746**
1000 Taxes on income, profits and capital gains	..	..	..	**6 925**	**9 192**	**9 610**	**10 337**	**10 355**	**11 167**	**11 240**
1100 Of individuals	..	..	..	705	1 281	1 536	1 764	953	1 335	1 543
1110 On income and profits	..	..	..	705	1 281	1 536	1 764	953	1 335	1 543
Salary income	..	..	..	..	..	..	1 617	696	1 111	1 270
Rental income	..	..	..	..	..	..	32	34	37	43
Dividends and interest	..	..	..	..	..	..	92	125	106	122
Other income	..	..	..	..	..	..	23	97	81	108
1120 On capital gains	..	..	..	..	..	..	0	0	0	0
1200 Corporate	..	..	..	6 220	7 911	8 074	8 573	9 402	9 832	9 697
1210 On profits	..	..	..	6 220	7 911	8 074	8 573	9 402	9 832	9 697
Corporate income tax	..	..	..	5 110	6 127	6 489	7 430	8 149	9 014	9 022
Druk Holdings and Investments (DHI)	..	..	..	1 372	1 615	1 569	..	..	..	..
Druk Green Power Corporation Limited (DGPC)	..	..	..	1 953	2 312	2 134	..	..	..	..
Bhutan Power Corporation Limited (BPC)	..	..	..	346	336	415	..	..	..	..
Others	..	..	..	1 439	1 865	2 370	..	..	..	..
Business income tax	..	..	..	1 110	1 784	1 585	1 143	1 254	818	674
1220 On capital gains of corporates	..	..	..	0	0	0	0	0	0	0
1300 Unallocable between 1100 and 1200	..	..	..	0	0	0	0	0	0	0
2000 Social security contributions	..	..	..	**0**	**0**	**0**	**0**	**0**	**0**	**0**
2100 Employees	..	..	..	..	..	..	..	..	..	..
2110 On a payroll basis	..	..	..	..	..	..	..	..	..	..
2120 On an income tax basis	..	..	..	..	..	..	..	..	..	..
2200 Employers	..	..	..	..	..	..	..	..	..	..
2210 On a payroll basis	..	..	..	..	..	..	..	..	..	..
2220 On an income tax basis	..	..	..	..	..	..	..	..	..	..
2300 Self-employed or non-employed	..	..	..	..	..	..	..	..	..	..
2310 On a payroll basis	..	..	..	..	..	..	..	..	..	..
2320 On an income tax basis	..	..	..	..	..	..	..	..	..	..
2400 Unallocable between 2100, 2200 and 2300	..	..	..	..	..	..	..	..	..	..
2410 On a payroll basis	..	..	..	..	..	..	..	..	..	..
2420 On an income tax basis	..	..	..	..	..	..	..	..	..	..
3000 Taxes on payroll and workforce	..	..	..	**105**	**157**	**32**	**57**	**-80**	**-9**	**74**
Health contribution	..	..	..	105	157	32	57	-80	-9	74
4000 Taxes on property	..	..	..	**6**	**6**	**8**	**67**	**55**	**34**	**33**
4100 Recurrent taxes on immovable property	..	..	..	6	6	8	4	3	7	7
4110 Households	..	..	..	6	6	8	4	3	7	7
4120 Others	..	..	..	0	0	0	0	0	0	0
4200 Recurrent taxes on net wealth	..	..	..	0	0	0	0	0	0	0
4210 Individual	..	..	..	..	..	..	..	..	..	..
4220 Corporate	..	..	..	..	..	..	..	..	..	..
4300 Estate, inheritance and gift taxes	..	..	..	0	0	0	0	0	0	0
4310 Estate and inheritance taxes	..	..	..	..	..	..	..	..	..	..
4320 Gift taxes	..	..	..	..	..	..	..	..	..	..
4400 Taxes on financial and capital transactions	..	..	..	..	..	..	63	52	28	25
4500 Other non-reccurrent taxes on property	..	..	..	0	0	0	0	0	0	0
4510 On net wealth	..	..	..	..	..	..	..	..	..	..
4520 Other non-recurrent taxes	..	..	..	..	..	..	..	..	..	..
4600 Other recurrent taxes on property	..	..	..	0	0	0	0	0	0	0
5000 Taxes on goods and services	..	..	..	**3 760**	**5 335**	**7 048**	**7 954**	**9 192**	**11 212**	**10 399**
5100 Taxes on production, sale, transfer, etc	..	..	..	3 760	5 335	7 048	7 663	8 848	10 816	9 978
5110 General taxes on goods and services	..	..	..	1 636	2 163	3 060	3 575	3 796	4 270	4 714
5111 Value added taxes	..	..	..	0	0	0	0	0	0	0
5112 Sales tax	..	..	..	1 636	2 163	3 060	3 575	3 796	4 270	4 714
Goods and commodities	..	..	..	..	..	..	1 979	1 710	1 315	1 370
Beer	..	..	..	..	..	..	767	952	1 137	1 212
Vehicles	..	..	..	..	..	..	0	0	540	643
Petroleum products	..	..	..	..	..	..	234	434	414	522
Hotels and restaurants	..	..	..	..	..	..	318	393	448	500
Telecom services	..	..	..	..	..	..	178	179	223	252
Cement	..	..	..	..	..	..	50	70	92	97
Aerated water	..	..	..	..	..	..	26	35	76	94
Entertainment services	..	..	..	..	..	..	23	23	26	25
5113 Other	..	..	..	0	0	0	0	0	0	0
5120 Taxes on specific goods and services	..	..	..	2 124	3 172	3 987	4 088	5 052	6 546	5 264
5121 Excises	..	..	..	1 605	2 556	2 687	2 483	3 580	4 834	3 406
Distillery products	..	..	..	321	461	481	539	663	885	906

	1997	2000	2007	2010	2013	2014	2015	2016	2017	2018
Excise duty refund from India	..	..	..	1 284	2 096	2 206	1 944	2 917	3 949	2 500
5122 Profits of fiscal monopolies	..	..	..	0	0	0	0	0	0	0
5123 Customs and import duties	..	..	..	483	564	1 242	1 605	1 472	1 712	1 704
Customs duty on goods and commodities and customs service charge	..	..	..	..	..	..	597	563	773	678
Fuel	..	..	..	..	..	..	348	411	405	525
Motor vehicles	..	..	..	..	..	..	659	499	534	501
5124 Taxes on exports	..	..	..	0	0	0	0	0	0	0
5125 Taxes on investment goods	..	..	..	0	0	0	0	0	0	0
5126 Taxes on specific services	..	..	..	35	51	59	0	0	0	154
5127 Other taxes on internat. trade and transactions	..	..	..	0	0	0	0	0	0	0
5128 Other taxes	..	..	..	0	0	0	0	0	0	0
5130 Unallocable between 5110 and 5120	..	..	..	0	0	0	0	0	0	0
5200 Taxes on use of goods and to perform activities	..	..	..	0	0	0	291	344	395	422
5210 Recurrent taxes	..	..	..	..	..	..	259	303	323	351
5211 Paid by households: motor vehicles	..	..	..	..	..	..	172	198	214	238
5212 Paid by others: motor vehicles	..	..	..	..	..	..	0	0	0	0
5213 Paid in respect of other goods	..	..	..	..	..	..	87	105	110	114
5220 Non-recurrent taxes	..	..	..	..	..	..	32	41	72	70
5300 Unallocable between 5100 and 5200	..	..	..	..	..	..	0	0	0	0
6000 Other taxes	..	..	..	**20**	**17**	**20**	**0**	**0**	**0**	**0**
6100 Paid solely by business	..	..	..	..	..	..	..	..	..	..
6200 Other	..	..	..	..	..	..	..	..	..	..

Note: Data are reported on a fiscal year basis beginning 1st July. For example, the data for 2018 represent the period from July 2018 to June 2019.
The data are on a cash basis.
Source: Ministry of Finance, Bhutan.

StatLink ⬛⬛ https://stat.link/fhs5kp

Table 4.3. China
Details of tax revenue
Billion CNY

	1997	2000	2007	2010	2013	2014	2015	2016	2017	2018
Total tax revenue	..	..	**4 562**	**7 321**	**11 053**	**11 917**	**12 492**	**13 035**	**14 437**	**15 640**
1000 Taxes on income, profits and capital gains	..	..	**1 237**	**1 896**	**3 225**	**3 593**	**3 958**	**4 315**	**4 899**	**5 484**
1100 Of individuals	..	..	319	484	653	738	862	1 009	1 197	1 387
1110 On income and profits	..	..	..	..	..	..	..	..	..	..
1120 On capital gains	..	..	..	..	..	..	..	..	..	..
1200 Corporate	..	..	918	1 412	2 572	2 856	3 097	3 306	3 703	4 097
Enterprise income tax	..	..	878	1 284	2 243	2 464	2 713	2 885	3 212	3 532
Land appreciation tax	..	..	40	128	329	391	383	421	491	564
1210 On profits	..	..	..	..	..	..	..	..	..	..
1220 On capital gains of corporates	..	..	..	..	..	..	..	..	..	..
1300 Unallocable between 1100 and 1200	..	..	0	0	0	0	0	0	0	0
2000 Social security contributions	..	..	..	..	..	..	..	..	..	..
2100 Employees	..	..	..	..	..	..	..	..	..	..
2110 On a payroll basis	..	..	..	..	..	..	..	..	..	..
2120 On an income tax basis	..	..	..	..	..	..	..	..	..	..
2200 Employers	..	..	..	..	..	..	..	..	..	..
2210 On a payroll basis	..	..	..	..	..	..	..	..	..	..
2220 On an income tax basis	..	..	..	..	..	..	..	..	..	..
2300 Self-employed or non-employed	..	..	..	..	..	..	..	..	..	..
2310 On a payroll basis	..	..	..	..	..	..	..	..	..	..
2320 On an income tax basis	..	..	..	..	..	..	..	..	..	..
2400 Unallocable between 2100, 2200 and 2300	..	..	..	..	..	..	..	..	..	..
2410 On a payroll basis	..	..	..	..	..	..	..	..	..	..
2420 On an income tax basis	..	..	..	..	..	..	..	..	..	..
3000 Taxes on payroll and workforce	..	..	**0**	**0**	**0**	**0**	**0**	**0**	**0**	**0**
4000 Taxes on property	..	..	**443**	**540**	**839**	**938**	**1 153**	**1 099**	**1 208**	**1 321**
4100 Recurrent taxes on immovable property	..	..	96	190	330	384	419	448	496	528
4110 Households	..	..	0	0	0	0	0	0	0	0
4120 Others	..	..	96	190	330	384	419	448	496	528
House property tax	..	..	58	89	158	185	205	222	260	289
Urban and town land use tax	..	..	39	100	172	199	214	226	236	239
4200 Recurrent taxes on net wealth	..	..	0	0	0	0	0	0	0	0
4210 Individual	..	..	..	..	..	..	..	..	..	..
4220 Corporate	..	..	..	..	..	..	..	..	..	..
4300 Estate, inheritance and gift taxes	..	..	0	0	0	0	0	0	0	0
4310 Estate and inheritance taxes	..	..	..	..	..	..	..	..	..	..
4320 Gift taxes	..	..	..	..	..	..	..	..	..	..
4400 Taxes on financial and capital transactions	..	..	347	351	509	554	734	651	712	793
Stamp tax on securities transactions	..	..	201	54	47	67	255	125	107	98
Other stamp duties	..	..	26	50	77	87	89	96	114	122
Deed tax	..	..	121	246	384	400	390	430	491	573
4500 Other non-reccurrent taxes on property	..	..	0	0	0	0	0	0	0	0
4510 On net wealth	..	..	..	..	..	..	..	..	..	..
4520 Other non-recurrent taxes	..	..	..	..	..	..	..	..	..	..
4600 Other recurrent taxes on property	..	..	0	0	0	0	0	0	0	0
5000 Taxes on goods and services	..	..	**2 882**	**4 885**	**6 989**	**7 386**	**7 381**	**7 621**	**8 329**	**8 836**
5100 Taxes on production, sale, transfer, etc	..	..	2 855	4 769	6 756	7 121	7 105	7 345	8 081	8 601
5110 General taxes on goods and services	..	..	2 373	3 730	5 295	5 535	5 397	5 688	6 284	6 734
5111 Value added taxes	..	..	1 715	2 614	3 572	3 757	3 466	4 538	6 284	6 734
Domestic VAT	..	..	1 547	2 109	2 881	3 086	3 111	4 071	5 638	6 153
Import VAT & excise tax	..	..	615	1 049	1 400	1 443	1 253	1 278	1 597	1 688
Urban maintenance and construction tax	..	..	116	189	342	364	389	403	436	484
Refund of VAT & excise tax for export	..	..	-563	-733	-1 052	-1 136	-1 287	-1 215	-1 387	-1 591
5112 Sales tax	..	..	0	0	0	0	0	0	0	0
5113 Other	..	..	658	1 116	1 723	1 778	1 931	1 150	0	0
Business tax	..	..	658	1 116	1 723	1 778	1 931	1 150	..	..
5120 Taxes on specific goods and services	..	..	483	1 039	1 461	1 586	1 707	1 658	1 797	1 867
5121 Excises	..	..	313	794	1 098	1 193	1 348	1 302	1 362	1 420
Domestic excise tax	..	..	221	607	823	891	1 054	1 022	1 023	1 063
Motor vehicles purchase tax	..	..	88	179	260	289	279	267	328	345
Leaf tobacco tax	..	..	5	8	15	14	14	13	12	11
5122 Profits of fiscal monopolies	..	..	0	0	0	0	0	0	0	0
5123 Customs and import duties	..	..	143	203	263	284	256	260	300	285
5124 Taxes on exports	..	..	0	0	0	0	0	0	0	0
5125 Taxes on investment goods	..	..	0	0	0	0	0	0	0	0
5126 Taxes on specific services	..	..	0	0	0	0	0	0	0	0
5127 Other taxes on internat. trade and transactions	..	..	0	0	0	0	0	0	0	0

	1997	2000	2007	2010	2013	2014	2015	2016	2017	2018
5128 Other taxes	..	..	26	42	101	108	103	95	135	163
Resources tax	..	..	26	42	101	108	103	95	135	163
5130 Unallocable between 5110 and 5120	..	..	0	0	0	0	0	0	0	0
5200 Taxes on use of goods and to perform activities	..	..	27	116	233	265	276	276	248	235
5210 Recurrent taxes	..	..	7	24	47	54	61	68	77	83
Vehicle and vessel tax	..	..	7	24	47	54	61	68	77	83
5211 Paid by households: motor vehicles	..	..	..	..	..	..	..	..	..	..
5212 Paid by others: motor vehicles	..	..	..	..	..	..	..	..	..	..
5213 Paid in respect of other goods	..	..	..	..	..	..	..	..	..	..
5220 Non-recurrent taxes	..	..	20	92	185	210	214	208	170	152
Cultivated land use tax	..	..	19	89	181	206	210	203	165	132
Vessel tonnage tax	..	..	2	3	4	5	5	5	5	5
Environmental protection tax	..	..	0	0	0	0	0	0	0	15
5300 Unallocable between 5100 and 5200	..	..	0	0	0	0	0	0	0	0
6000 Other taxes	..	..	0	0	0	0	0	0	0	0
6100 Paid solely by business	..	..	..	..	..	..	..	..	..	..
6200 Other	..	..	..	..	..	..	..	..	..	..

Note: Year ending 31st December.

The data are on a cash basis.

Heading 2000: Detailed data on revenues from social security contributions were not available.

Heading 5111: Revenues from import VAT and import excises, urban maintenance and construction tax and refunds on export VAT and export excises are taxes levied on both VAT and excises, however it is not possible to distinguish revenues between the two sources. Therefore all revenues have been allocated to heading 5111 as VAT represents the majority of these revenues.

Source: Ministry of Finance of China.

StatLink ᵐˢᴾ https://stat.link/cuy8ix

Table 4.4. Cook Islands
Details of tax revenue
Thousand NZD

	1997	2000	2007	2010	2013	2014	2015	2016	2017	2018
Total tax revenue	..	..	78 330	91 161	92 464	90 572	117 445	126 010	142 539	163 423
1000 Taxes on income, profits and capital gains	..	..	30 685	35 916	29 860	23 213	41 090	42 210	52 127	63 029
1100 Of individuals	..	..	22 163	26 277	20 848	14 189	27 696	26 055	30 039	38 432
1110 On income and profits	..	..	22 163	26 277	20 848	14 189	27 696	26 055	30 039	38 432
Net Income Tax	..	..	22 163	26 361	20 032	11 963	24 768	24 298	28 197	36 929
Withholding Tax	..	..	0	-84	816	2 226	2 928	1 757	1 842	1 504
1120 On capital gains	..	..	0	0	0	0	0	0	0	0
1200 Corporate	..	..	8 523	9 638	9 012	9 024	13 394	16 155	22 089	24 596
1210 On profits	..	..	8 523	9 638	9 012	9 024	13 394	16 155	22 089	24 596
1220 On capital gains of corporates	..	..	0	0	0	0	0	0	0	0
1300 Unallocable between 1100 and 1200	..	..	0	0	0	0	0	0	0	0
2000 Social security contributions	..	..	0	0	0	0	0	0	0	0
2100 Employees	..	..	..	..	..	..	..	..	..	..
2110 On a payroll basis	..	..	..	..	..	..	..	..	..	..
2120 On an income tax basis	..	..	..	..	..	..	..	..	..	..
2200 Employers	..	..	..	..	..	..	..	..	..	..
2210 On a payroll basis	..	..	..	..	..	..	..	..	..	..
2220 On an income tax basis	..	..	..	..	..	..	..	..	..	..
2300 Self-employed or non-employed	..	..	..	..	..	..	..	..	..	..
2310 On a payroll basis	..	..	..	..	..	..	..	..	..	..
2320 On an income tax basis	..	..	..	..	..	..	..	..	..	..
2400 Unallocable between 2100, 2200 and 2300	..	..	..	..	..	..	..	..	..	..
2410 On a payroll basis	..	..	..	..	..	..	..	..	..	..
2420 On an income tax basis	..	..	..	..	..	..	..	..	..	..
3000 Taxes on payroll and workforce	..	..	0	0	0	0	0	0	0	0
4000 Taxes on property	..	..	0	0	0	0	0	0	0	0
4100 Recurrent taxes on immovable property	..	..	..	..	..	..	..	..	..	..
4110 Households	..	..	..	..	..	..	..	..	..	..
4120 Others	..	..	..	..	..	..	..	..	..	..
4200 Recurrent taxes on net wealth	..	..	..	..	..	..	..	..	..	..
4210 Individual	..	..	..	..	..	..	..	..	..	..
4220 Corporate	..	..	..	..	..	..	..	..	..	..
4300 Estate, inheritance and gift taxes	..	..	..	..	..	..	..	..	..	..
4310 Estate and inheritance taxes	..	..	..	..	..	..	..	..	..	..
4320 Gift taxes	..	..	..	..	..	..	..	..	..	..
4400 Taxes on financial and capital transactions	..	..	..	..	..	..	..	..	..	..
4500 Other non-reccurrent taxes on property	..	..	..	..	..	..	..	..	..	..
4510 On net wealth	..	..	..	..	..	..	..	..	..	..
4520 Other non-recurrent taxes	..	..	..	..	..	..	..	..	..	..
4600 Other recurrent taxes on property	..	..	..	..	..	..	..	..	..	..
5000 Taxes on goods and services	..	..	47 645	55 246	62 604	67 359	76 355	83 800	90 411	100 394
5100 Taxes on production, sale, transfer, etc	..	..	46 772	54 398	61 589	66 142	75 495	82 703	89 199	99 252
5110 General taxes on goods and services	..	..	33 973	37 444	41 682	47 459	54 708	58 140	63 330	72 958
5111 Value added taxes	..	..	33 955	37 381	41 681	47 453	54 659	58 124	63 330	72 958
VAT revenues (gross)	..	..	41 689	45 454	52 902	62 549	67 855	70 574	82 054	86 189
VAT refunds	..	..	-5 043	-4 365	-7 521	-7 507	-7 433	-7 796	-9 965	-3 697
VAT on Crown Appropriations	..	..	-2 692	-3 707	-3 700	-7 589	-5 763	-4 653	-8 759	-9 535
5112 Sales tax	..	..	0	0	0	0	0	0	0	0
5113 Other	..	..	18	63	2	6	49	16	0	0
5120 Taxes on specific goods and services	..	..	12 799	16 955	19 907	18 682	20 787	24 564	25 869	26 294
5121 Excises	..	..	0	0	0	0	0	0	0	0
5122 Profits of fiscal monopolies	..	..	0	0	0	0	0	0	0	0
5123 Customs and import duties	..	..	9 810	11 052	11 899	10 536	12 320	14 330	15 098	14 566
5124 Taxes on exports	..	..	0	0	0	0	0	0	0	0
5125 Taxes on investment goods	..	..	0	0	0	0	0	0	0	0
5126 Taxes on specific services	..	..	2 989	5 903	8 008	8 146	8 468	10 234	10 771	11 729
5127 Other taxes on internat. trade and transactions	..	..	0	0	0	0	0	0	0	0
5128 Other taxes	..	..	0	0	0	0	0	0	0	0
5130 Unallocable between 5110 and 5120	..	..	0	0	0	0	0	0	0	0
5200 Taxes on use of goods and to perform activities	..	..	873	847	1 015	1 217	860	1 097	1 212	1 142
5210 Recurrent taxes	..	..	218	207	189	186	229	209	291	271
5211 Paid by households: motor vehicles	..	..	0	0	0	0	0	0	0	0
5212 Paid by others: motor vehicles	..	..	0	0	0	0	0	0	0	0
5213 Paid in respect of other goods	..	..	218	207	189	186	229	209	291	271
5220 Non-recurrent taxes	..	..	655	640	827	1 032	631	888	922	871
5300 Unallocable between 5100 and 5200	..	..	0	0	0	0	0	0	0	0
6000 Other taxes	..	..	0	0	0	0	0	0	0	0

	1997	2000	2007	2010	2013	2014	2015	2016	2017	2018
6100 Paid solely by business	..	..	..	..	..	..	..	..	..	..
6200 Other	..	..	..	..	..	..	..	..	..	..

Note: Data are reported on a fiscal year basis beginning 1st July. For example, the data for 2018 represent the period from July 2018 to June 2019.
The data are on a cash basis.

Figures exclude tax revenues collected by sub-national governments as the data are not available.

Source: Ministry of Finance and Economic Management of the Cook Islands.

StatLink ⊞⊡ https://stat.link/261sci

Table 4.5. Fiji
Details of tax revenue
Million FJD

	1997	2000	2007	2010	2013	2014	2015	2016	2017	2018
Total tax revenue	..	..	..	1 304	1 830	2 080	2 318	2 387	2 679	2 739
1000 Taxes on income, profits and capital gains	..	..	..	426	439	514	598	730	845	769
1100 Of individuals	..	..	..	184	162	209	211	222	231	224
1110 On income and profits	..	..	..	184	145	166	187	198	200	177
PAYE	..	..	..	184	118	140	159	167	167	146
Social responsibility tax	..	..	..	0	9	8	8	11	10	8
Fringe benefit tax	..	..	..	0	18	19	20	21	24	22
1120 On capital gains	..	..	..	0	17	43	24	23	31	47
1200 Corporate	..	..	..	242	277	305	386	508	614	545
1210 On profits	..	..	..	242	277	305	386	508	614	545
Company Tax	..	..	..	161	203	208	291	348	445	385
Dividend and Withholding	..	..	..	73	72	85	85	105	121	120
Provisional tax	..	..	..	11	11	11	10	49	59	61
Other income taxes	..	..	..	30	30	30	45	44	49	57
Income tax refunds	..	..	..	-34	-40	-28	-45	-38	-60	-78
1220 On capital gains of corporates	..	..	..	0	0	0	0	0	0	0
1300 Unallocable between 1100 and 1200	..	..	..	0	0	0	0	0	0	0
2000 Social security contributions	..	..	..	0	0	0	0	0	0	0
2100 Employees	..	..	..	..	..	..	..	..	..	..
2110 On a payroll basis	..	..	..	..	..	..	..	..	..	..
2120 On an income tax basis	..	..	..	..	..	..	..	..	..	..
2200 Employers	..	..	..	..	..	..	..	..	..	..
2210 On a payroll basis	..	..	..	..	..	..	..	..	..	..
2220 On an income tax basis	..	..	..	..	..	..	..	..	..	..
2300 Self-employed or non-employed	..	..	..	..	..	..	..	..	..	..
2310 On a payroll basis	..	..	..	..	..	..	..	..	..	..
2320 On an income tax basis	..	..	..	..	..	..	..	..	..	..
2400 Unallocable between 2100, 2200 and 2300	..	..	..	..	..	..	..	..	..	..
2410 On a payroll basis	..	..	..	..	..	..	..	..	..	..
2420 On an income tax basis	..	..	..	..	..	..	..	..	..	..
3000 Taxes on payroll and workforce	..	..	..	0	0	0	0	0	0	0
4000 Taxes on property	..	..	..	0	44	68	71	78	78	92
4100 Recurrent taxes on immovable property	..	..	..	..	0	0	0	0	0	0
4110 Households	..	..	..	..	..	..	..	..	..	..
4120 Others	..	..	..	..	..	..	..	..	..	..
4200 Recurrent taxes on net wealth	..	..	..	..	0	0	0	0	0	0
4210 Individual	..	..	..	..	..	..	..	..	..	..
4220 Corporate	..	..	..	..	..	..	..	..	..	..
4300 Estate, inheritance and gift taxes	..	..	..	..	0	0	0	0	0	0
4310 Estate and inheritance taxes	..	..	..	..	..	..	..	..	..	..
4320 Gift taxes	..	..	..	..	..	..	..	..	..	..
4400 Taxes on financial and capital transactions	..	..	..	..	44	68	71	78	78	92
4500 Other non-reccurrent taxes on property	..	..	..	..	0	0	0	0	0	0
4510 On net wealth	..	..	..	..	..	..	..	..	..	..
4520 Other non-recurrent taxes	..	..	..	..	..	..	..	..	..	..
4600 Other recurrent taxes on property	..	..	..	..	0	0	0	0	0	0
5000 Taxes on goods and services	..	..	..	878	1 347	1 498	1 650	1 580	1 757	1 879
5100 Taxes on production, sale, transfer, etc	..	..	..	877	1 345	1 496	1 648	1 578	1 755	1 877
5110 General taxes on goods and services	..	..	..	526	803	852	958	774	864	882
5111 Value added taxes	..	..	..	496	751	794	893	653	744	789
VAT revenues (gross)	..	..	..	646	1 020	1 102	1 204	943	987	1 049
VAT refunds	..	..	..	-150	-269	-308	-311	-290	-243	-259
5112 Sales tax	..	..	..	0	0	0	0	0	0	0
5113 Other	..	..	..	31	52	58	65	121	121	93
5120 Taxes on specific goods and services	..	..	..	350	543	644	690	804	890	995
5121 Excises	..	..	..	88	127	139	145	246	313	394
Environmental levy	..	..	..	0	0	0	0	67	108	161
Import excises	..	..	..	20	38	43	43	47	54	61
Domestic excises	..	..	..	81	92	98	106	134	154	174
Other excises	..	..	..	5	2	2	2	2	2	2
Rebates	..	..	..	-17	-5	-6	-6	-5	-5	-4
5122 Profits of fiscal monopolies	..	..	..	0	0	0	0	0	0	0
5123 Customs and import duties	..	..	..	252	311	365	392	398	419	441
5124 Taxes on exports	..	..	..	9	4	10	10	10	10	9
5125 Taxes on investment goods	..	..	..	0	0	0	0	0	0	0
5126 Taxes on specific services	..	..	..	0	101	130	143	150	148	150
5127 Other taxes on internat. trade and transactions	..	..	..	0	0	0	0	0	0	0

	1997	2000	2007	2010	2013	2014	2015	2016	2017	2018
5128 Other taxes	..	..	..	0	0	0	0	0	0	0
5130 Unallocable between 5110 and 5120	..	..	..	0	0	0	0	0	0	0
5200 Taxes on use of goods and to perform activities	..	..	..	2	2	2	2	2	2	2
5210 Recurrent taxes	..	..	..	2	2	2	1	1	2	2
5211 Paid by households: motor vehicles	..	..	..	0	0	0	0	0	0	0
5212 Paid by others: motor vehicles	..	..	..	0	0	0	0	0	0	0
5213 Paid in respect of other goods	..	..	..	2	2	2	1	1	2	2
5220 Non-recurrent taxes	..	..	..	0	0	0	0	0	0	0
5300 Unallocable between 5100 and 5200	..	..	..	0	0	0	0	0	0	0
6000 Other taxes	..	..	..	**0**	**0**	**0**	**0**	**0**	**0**	**0**
6100 Paid solely by business	..	..	..	..	..	..	..	..	..	..
6200 Other	..	..	..	..	..	..	..	..	..	..

Note: Year ending 31st December.

The data are on a cash basis.

Figures exclude tax revenues collected by sub-national governments as the data are not available.

The resource tax and the tourist VAT refund registration fee (about 0.7% of GDP in 2018) are not included in tax revenues. These revenues are considered as non-tax revenue in accordance with the OECD classification, as set out in the Interpretative Guide in Annex A.

Source: Revenue and Customs Service of Fiji.

StatLink 🔗 https://stat.link/69oe0c

Table 4.6. Indonesia
Details of tax revenue
Billion IDR

	1997	2000	2007	2010	2013	2014	2015	2016	2017	2018
Total tax revenue	57 340	119 697	525 969	779 484	1 191 766	1 285 634	1 395 963	1 489 358	1 566 729	1 765 590
1000 Taxes on income, profits and capital gains	27 062	57 073	238 431	357 036	506 442	546 181	602 308	666 213	646 800	749 977
1100 Of individuals	..	..	77 250	59 373	187 262	206 288	180 502	164 225	182 835	156 428
1110 On income and profits	..	..	0	59 369	187 255	206 283	180 489	164 217	182 833	156 419
1120 On capital gains	..	..	0	4	7	5	13	8	1	10
1200 Corporate	..	..	161 181	297 662	319 180	339 893	421 806	501 987	463 965	593 549
1210 On profits	..	..	0	288 014	300 456	321 457	382 892	456 391	450 657	578 121
1220 On capital gains	..	..	0	9 648	18 725	18 436	38 915	45 596	13 308	15 428
1300 Unallocable between 1100 and 1200	0	0	0	0	0	0	0	0	0	0
2000 Social security contributions	..	..	..	..	..	..	7 715	47 220	54 401	61 993
2100 Employees	..	..	..	..	..	..	1 590	1 829	2 121	2 496
2110 On a payroll basis	..	..	..	..	..	..	..	..	..	..
2120 On an income tax basis	..	..	..	..	..	..	..	..	..	..
2200 Employers	..	..	..	..	..	..	3 505	4 108	4 650	5 323
2210 On a payroll basis	..	..	..	..	..	..	..	..	..	..
2220 On an income tax basis	..	..	..	..	..	..	..	..	..	..
2300 Self-employed or non-employed	..	..	..	..	..	..	..	..	..	..
2310 On a payroll basis	..	..	..	..	..	..	..	..	..	..
2320 On an income tax basis	..	..	..	..	..	..	..	..	..	..
2400 Unallocable between 2100, 2200 and 2300	..	..	..	..	..	..	2 620	41 283	47 630	54 174
2410 On a payroll basis	..	..	..	..	..	..	..	..	..	..
2420 On an income tax basis	..	..	..	..	..	..	..	..	..	..
3000 Taxes on payroll and workforce	0	0	0	0	0	0	0	0	0	0
4000 Taxes on property	2 413	4 456	29 677	40 546	29 570	28 409	33 836	23 885	21 854	24 901
4100 Recurrent taxes on immovable property	2 413	3 525	23 724	28 581	25 305	23 476	29 250	19 443	16 770	19 445
4110 Households	..	..	..	..	..	..	..	..	..	..
4120 Others	..	..	..	..	..	..	..	..	..	..
4200 Recurrent taxes on net wealth	0	0	0	0	0	0	0	0	0	0
4210 Individual	..	..	..	..	..	..	..	..	..	..
4220 Corporate	..	..	..	..	..	..	..	..	..	..
4300 Estate, inheritance and gift taxes	0	0	0	0	0	0	0	0	0	0
4310 Estate and inheritance taxes	..	..	..	..	..	..	..	..	..	..
4320 Gift taxes	..	..	..	..	..	..	..	..	..	..
4400 Taxes on financial and capital transactions	0	931	5 953	11 966	4 265	4 932	4 586	4 441	5 084	5 456
Tax on acquisition of land and buildings	..	931	5 953	0	..	..	..	0	0	0
4500 Non-recurrent taxes	0	0	0	0	0	0	0	0	0	0
4510 On net wealth	..	..	..	..	..	..	..	..	..	..
4520 Other non-recurrent taxes	..	..	..	..	..	..	..	..	..	..
4600 Other recurrent taxes on property	0	0	0	0	0	0	0	0	0	0
5000 Taxes on goods and services	27 274	53 547	220 143	325 685	540 967	571 303	603 869	592 291	674 209	743 395
5100 Taxes on production, sale, transfer, etc	27 274	53 547	220 143	325 685	540 967	571 303	603 869	592 291	674 209	743 395
5110 General taxes	20 351	35 232	154 527	230 605	385 058	409 570	424 288	413 295	481 707	537 924
5111 Value added taxes	20 351	35 232	154 527	218 133	365 859	393 463	410 391	395 616	464 477	520 390
5112 Sales tax	0	0	0	12 472	19 199	16 107	13 897	17 680	17 230	17 534
5113 Other	0	0	0	0	0	0	0	0	0	0
5120 Taxes on specific goods and services	6 923	18 315	65 616	95 080	155 909	161 734	179 581	178 996	192 502	205 470
5121 Excises	4 263	11 287	44 679	66 166	108 452	118 086	144 641	143 525	153 288	159 589
5122 Profits of fiscal monopolies	0	0	0	0	0	0	0	0	0	0
5123 Customs and import duties	2 579	6 697	16 699	20 017	31 621	32 319	31 213	32 472	35 066	39 117
5124 Taxes on exports	81	331	4 237	8 898	15 835	11 329	3 727	2 999	4 147	6 765
5125 Taxes on investment goods	0	0	0	0	0	0	0	0	0	0
5126 Taxes on specific services	0	0	0	0	0	0	0	0	0	0
5127 Other taxes on internat. trade and transactions	0	0	0	0	0	0	0	0	0	0
5128 Other taxes	0	0	0	0	0	0	0	0	0	0
5130 Unallocable between 5110 and 5120	0	0	0	0	0	0	0	0	0	0
5200 Taxes on use of goods and to perform activities	0	0	0	0	0	0	0	0	0	0
5210 Recurrent taxes	..	..	..	..	..	..	..	..	..	..
5211 Paid by households: motor vehicles	..	..	..	..	..	..	..	..	..	..
5212 Paid by others: motor vehicles	..	..	..	..	..	..	..	..	..	..
5213 Paid in respect of other goods	..	..	..	..	..	..	..	..	..	..
5220 Non-recurrent taxes	..	..	..	..	..	..	..	..	..	..
5300 Unallocable between 5100 and 5200	0	0	0	0	0	0	0	0	0	0
6000 Other taxes	591	4 621	37 718	56 216	114 787	139 741	148 234	159 749	169 465	185 325
6100 Paid solely by business	0	0	0	0	0	0	0	0	0	0
6200 Other	591	4 621	37 718	56 216	114 787	139 741	148 234	159 749	169 465	185 325
Other local level	0	3 784	34 981	56 177	114 460	138 769	147 829	157 167	168 798	184 807
Other non local level	591	837	2 738	39	328	973	406	2 582	667	517

Note: Year ending 31st December.

The data are on a cash basis.

Revenue data in 2016 and 2017 include revenues from the "Tax Amnesty" policy which will not be repeated in the following year.

Heading 2100: Includes Death Benefit (JK), a life insurance with payment for participants upon the death of their wives/husbands/children or for families upon the death of participants.

Heading 2200: Includes Work Accident Insurance (JKK) which provides protection against the risks of work-related accidents.

Heading 2400: Includes Pension Insurance (JP), and mandatory contributions from BPJS Health for formal workers. Data in 2015 only include Pension Insurance (JP). Contributions from the BPJS Health for 2018 have been estimated.

Source: Fiscal Policy Agency, Ministry of Finance of Indonesia.

StatLink https://stat.link/70hvwp

Table 4.7. Japan
Details of tax revenue

Billion JPY

	1997	2000	2007	2010	2013	2014	2015	2016	2017	2018
Total tax revenue	**139 617**	**136 236**	**146 248**	**132 484**	**146 405**	**156 886**	**163 533**	**164 963**	**171 751**	**104 457**
1000 Taxes on income, profits and capital gains	**51 673**	**47 398**	**53 174**	**40 034**	**47 534**	**49 939**	**50 969**	**50 448**	**52 658**	**55 682**
1100 Of individuals	29 809	28 677	28 600	24 663	28 150	29 655	30 847	30 670	32 325	32 993
1110 On income and profits	29 809	28 677	28 600	24 663	28 150	29 655	30 847	30 670	32 325	32 993
Income tax	19 183	18 789	16 080	12 984	15 865	17 139	18 178	17 978	19 276	19 885
Prefectural inhabitants tax	3 183	3 621	5 008	4 699	5 090	5 215	5 252	5 128	5 376	4 903
Municipal inhabitants tax	7 172	6 044	7 294	6 795	7 015	7 114	7 224	7 365	7 471	8 000
Enterprise tax	271	223	218	184	181	186	194	198	203	206
1120 On capital gains	0	0	0	0	0	0	0	0	0	0
1200 Corporate	21 864	18 721	24 573	15 372	19 384	20 284	20 122	19 778	20 333	22 689
1210 On profits	21 864	18 721	24 573	15 372	19 384	20 284	20 122	19 778	20 333	22 689
Corporation tax	13 477	11 747	14 744	8 968	11 698	11 464	10 832	10 332	11 995	12 296
Prefectural inhabitants tax	1 026	879	1 206	777	854	963	859	763	762	829
Municipal inhabitants tax	2 532	2 176	3 015	1 954	2 157	2 445	2 324	2 392	2 224	2 392
Enterprise tax	4 830	3 918	5 608	2 253	2 674	3 017	3 510	4 395	3 991	4 395
Local special corporate tax	0	0	0	1 420	2 001	2 395	2 081	1 782	1 858	2 114
Local corporate tax	0	0	0	0	0	1	516	629	654	664
1220 On capital gains	0	0	0	0	0	0	0	0	0	0
1300 Unallocable between 1100 and 1200	0	0	0	0	0	0	0	0	0	0
2000 Social security contributions	**47 861**	**47 968**	**53 325**	**54 461**	**59 803**	**62 252**	**64 465**	**66 614**	**68 562**	**..**
2100 Employees	19 682	19 830	21 975	23 593	25 984	27 168	28 224	29 311	30 340	..
2110 On a payroll basis	19 682	19 830	21 975	23 593	25 984	27 168	28 224	29 311	30 340	..
2120 On an income tax basis	0	0	0	0	0	0	0	0	0	..
2200 Employers	22 826	22 456	24 243	24 674	27 143	28 374	29 479	30 560	31 637	..
2210 On a payroll basis	22 826	22 456	24 243	24 674	27 143	28 374	29 479	30 560	31 637	..
2220 On an income tax basis	0	0	0	0	0	0	0	0	0	..
2300 Self-employed or non-employed	5 352	5 683	7 108	6 194	6 676	6 710	6 763	6 742	6 585	..
2310 On a payroll basis	5 352	5 683	7 108	6 194	6 676	6 710	6 763	6 742	6 585	..
2320 On an income tax basis	0	0	0	0	0	0	0	0	0	..
2400 Unallocable between 2100, 2200 and 2300	0	0	0	0	0	0	0	0	0	..
2410 On a payroll basis	..	..	..	..	..	..	..	..	..	..
2420 On an income tax basis	..	..	..	..	..	..	..	..	..	..
3000 Taxes on payroll and workforce	**0**	**0**	**0**	**0**	**0**	**0**	**0**	**0**	**0**	**0**
4000 Taxes on property	**15 679**	**14 294**	**13 138**	**12 878**	**12 940**	**13 306**	**13 400**	**13 772**	**14 073**	**14 085**
4100 Recurrent taxes on immovable property	10 410	10 414	9 949	10 225	9 882	10 016	10 005	10 165	10 323	10 377
Prefectural property tax	8	11	14	5	2	2	2	3	4	11
Municipal property tax	8 822	9 041	8 729	8 961	8 653	8 769	8 755	9 077	9 025	9 077
City planning tax	1 326	1 318	1 202	1 256	1 227	1 244	1 244	1 262	1 277	1 289
Special landholding tax	94	43	4	3	1	2	3	7	1	0
Water and land utilization tax	0	0	0	0	0	0	0	0	0	0
Land value tax	160	1	0	0	0	0	0	0	0	0
4110 Households	..	..	..	..	..	..	..	..	..	..
4120 Others	..	..	..	..	..	..	..	..	..	..
4200 Recurrent taxes on net wealth	0	0	0	0	0	0	0	0	0	0
4210 Individual	..	..	..	..	..	..	..	..	..	..
4220 Corporate	..	..	..	..	..	..	..	..	..	..
4300 Estate, inheritance and gift taxes	2 413	1 782	1 503	1 250	1 574	1 883	1 968	2 131	2 292	2 240
4310 Estate and inheritance taxes	..	..	..	..	..	..	..	..	..	..
Inheritance tax	..	..	..	..	..	..	..	..	..	..
4320 Gift taxes	..	..	..	..	..	..	..	..	..	..
Tax on gifts	..	..	..	..	..	..	..	..	..	..
4400 Taxes on financial and capital transactions	2 856	2 099	1 686	1 403	1 483	1 407	1 426	1 476	1 458	1 467
Bourse tax	40	0	0	0	0	0	0	0	0	0
Securities transaction	404	0	0	0	0	0	0	0	0	0
Bank of Japan note issue tax	0	0	0	0	0	0	0	0	0	0
Stamp revenues	1 681	1 532	1 202	1 024	1 126	1 035	1 050	1 079	1 052	1 054
Real property acquisition tax	731	567	485	379	357	372	377	397	407	413
4500 Non-recurrent taxes	0	0	0	0	0	0	0	0	0	0
4510 On net wealth	..	..	..	..	..	..	..	..	..	..
4520 Other non-recurrent taxes	..	..	..	..	..	..	..	..	..	..
4600 Other recurrent taxes on property	0	0	0	0	0	0	0	0	0	0
5000 Taxes on goods and services	**24 058**	**26 227**	**26 256**	**24 730**	**25 744**	**30 991**	**34 286**	**33 711**	**36 031**	**34 254**
5100 Taxes on production, sale, transfer, etc.	21 132	23 180	23 241	22 160	23 313	28 587	31 871	31 254	33 582	31 762
5110 General taxes	10 112	12 350	12 841	12 675	13 479	19 135	22 400	21 931	22 249	22 531
5111 Value added taxes	10 112	12 350	12 841	12 675	13 479	19 135	22 400	21 931	22 249	22 531
5112 Sales tax	0	0	0	0	0	0	0	0	0	..
5113 Other	0	0	0	0	0	0	0	0	0	..

	1997	2000	2007	2010	2013	2014	2015	2016	2017	2018
5120 Taxes on specific goods and services	11 021	10 830	10 400	9 485	9 834	9 452	9 470	9 323	11 333	9 231
5121 Excise duties	9 764	9 837	9 374	8 622	8 728	8 308	8 351	8 316	10 241	8 144
Liquor tax	1 962	1 816	1 524	1 389	1 371	1 328	1 338	1 320	1 304	1 311
Sugar excises	0	0	0	0	0	0	0	0	0	0
Local gasoline tax	276	296	302	294	275	266	264	261	256	249
Gasoline tax	2 583	2 769	2 820	2 750	2 574	2 486	2 465	2 434	2 396	2 330
Liquefied petroleum gas tax	29	28	27	24	21	19	18	17	17	16
Aviation fuel tax	104	104	104	89	67	67	66	66	67	67
Commodity tax	0	0	0	0	0	0	0	0	0	0
Playing-card tax	0	0	0	0	0	0	0	0	0	0
Prefectural tobacco tax	248	282	278	256	173	155	153	149	141	139
Municipal tobacco tax	799	865	853	788	983	950	936	911	862	851
Timber delivery tax	0	0	0	0	0	0	0	0	0	0
Mineral product tax	2	2	2	2	2	2	2	2	2	2
Electricity and gas tax	0	0	0	0	0	0	0	0	0	0
Diesel oil tax	1 331	1 208	1 034	918	943	936	925	933	949	954
Vehicle acquisition tax	562	464	425	192	193	86	137	146	190	191
Promotion of power resources development tax	354	375	352	349	328	321	316	320	326	323
Petroleum and coal tax	497	489	513	502	600	631	630	702	691	709
Tobacco tax	1 018	876	925	908	1 038	919	954	914	864	874
Special tobacco tax	0	264	214	163	161	142	148	141	134	129
5122 Profits of fiscal monopolies	0	0	0	0	0	0	0	0	0	0
Monopoly profits	..	..	..	..	..	..	..	..	..	..
5123 Customs and import duties	1 012	877	941	786	1 034	1 073	1 049	939	1 024	1 022
Customs duty	1 012	877	941	786	1 034	1 073	1 049	939	1 024	1 022
5124 Taxes on exports	0	0	0	0	0	0	0	0	0	0
5125 Taxes on investment goods	0	0	0	0	0	0	0	0	0	0
5126 Taxes on specific services	245	116	85	77	71	70	70	68	67	65
Travel tax	0	0	0	0	0	0	0	0	0	0
Admission tax	0	0	0	0	0	0	0	0	0	0
Local entertainment tax	0	0	0	0	0	0	0	0	0	0
Golf course utilization tax	98	81	60	55	49	48	48	46	45	43
Meal and lodging tax	0	0	0	0	0	0	0	0	0	0
Special local consumption tax	125	12	0	0	0	0	0	0	0	0
Bathing tax	22	23	25	22	22	22	23	22	23	22
5127 Other taxes on internat. trade and transactions	0	0	0	0	0	0	0	0	0	0
5128 Other taxes	0	0	0	0	0	0	0	0	0	0
5130 Unallocable between 5110 and 5120	0	0	0	0	0	0	0	0	0	0
5200 Taxes on use of goods and perform activities	2 926	3 047	3 015	2 570	2 431	2 404	2 416	2 457	2 450	2 492
5210 Recurrent taxes	2 905	3 027	2 993	2 548	2 409	2 382	2 393	2 435	2 427	2 470
Automobile tax	1 705	1 765	1 717	1 616	1 574	1 556	1 543	1 535	1 541	1 545
Light vehicle tax	113	125	164	178	189	195	200	238	249	257
Motor vehicle tonnage tax	1 084	1 134	1 110	753	643	629	649	660	637	666
Hunter licence tax	2	2	0	0	0	0	0	0	0	0
Hunting tax	1	1	2	2	2	2	1	1	1	1
Mine lot tax	1	1	0	0	0	0	0	0	0	0
5211 Paid by households: motor vehicles	..	..	..	..	..	..	..	..	0	0
5212 Paid by others: motor vehicles	..	..	..	..	..	..	..	..	0	0
5213 Paid in respect of other goods	..	..	..	..	..	..	..	..	0	0
5220 Non-recurrent taxes	21	20	22	21	22	23	22	22	22	23
5300 Unallocable between 5100 and 5200	0	0	0	0	0	0	0	0	0	0
6000 Other taxes	**346**	**348**	**356**	**381**	**384**	**399**	**413**	**418**	**427**	**436**
6100 Paid solely by business	325	324	313	330	348	356	361	366	371	374
Business office tax	325	324	313	330	348	356	361	366	371	374
6200 Other	22	24	43	52	36	43	52	52	56	62
Taxes not in local tax law	21	24	43	52	36	43	52	52	56	62
Other	0	0	0	0	0	0	0	0	0	0

Note: Data are on a fiscal year basis beginning 1st April. From 1990, data are on accrual basis. The figures for different groups of taxes are reported on different reporting bases, namely: Social security contributions (heading 2000) : in principle accrual basis, Central government taxes : accrual basis (revenues accrued during the fiscal year plus cash receipts collected before the end of April until 1977), Local government taxes : accrual basis (due to be paid during the fiscal year and cash receipts collected before the end of May). The Japanese authorities take the view that the Enterprise tax (classified in 1100 and 1200) and the Mineral product tax (classified in 5121) should be classified in heading 6000 since under articles 72 and 519 of the Local Tax Law these taxes are regarded as levies on the business or mining activity itself.
Heading 2000 includes some unidentifiable voluntary contributions.
Heading 2300: Includes contributions to the National pension, National Health Insurance and the Farmer's pension fund. Contributions to the Farmer's pension fund are not available for the years before 1999.
Heading 4100: Municipal property tax, includes Prefectural property tax from 1990 to 1994 because data is not available to provide a breakdown.
Heading 5121: Municipal tobacco tax, includes Prefectural tobacco tax from 1990 to 1994 because data is not available to provide a breakdown.
Heading 5121: In sub-item Petroleum and coal tax, the data before 2003 refer to petroleum tax.
Source: Tax Bureau, Ministry of Finance.

StatLink ᵃᵢₛₗ https://stat.link/xoaykq

Table 4.8. Kazakhstan
Details of tax revenue
Million KZT

	1997	2000	2007	2010	2013	2014	2015	2016	2017	2018
Total tax revenue	..	517 777	3 349 317	5 182 379	8 130 631	8 365 069	6 352 963	7 006 053	8 690 678	10 383 770
1000 Taxes on income, profits and capital gains	..	214 545	1 797 785	2 072 357	2 928 127	3 113 992	2 467 977	2 610 413	3 128 907	3 972 562
1100 Of individuals		51 016	221 025	312 332	492 991	552 280	598 807	691 778	750 212	838 394
1110 On income and profits		51 016	221 025	312 332	492 991	552 280	598 807	691 778	750 212	838 394
From non-foreign citizens		51 016	221 025	276 089	442 561	492 913	566 974	688 023	744 662	831 567
From foreign citizens		0	0	36 243	50 430	59 367	31 832	3 755	5 550	6 828
1120 On capital gains		..	..	..	..	..	..	..	..	..
1200 Corporate		163 529	1 576 760	1 760 025	2 435 136	2 561 712	1 869 170	1 918 635	2 378 695	3 134 167
1210 On profits		163 529	1 576 760	1 760 025	2 435 136	2 561 712	1 869 170	1 918 635	2 378 695	3 134 167
From non-oil companies		163 529	766 979	847 057	1 039 044	1 172 635	1 236 561	1 445 066	1 545 293	1 703 353
From oil companies		0	0	0	0	0	0	0	0	0
From oil companies to National Fund		0	809 782	912 968	1 396 092	1 389 077	632 609	473 569	833 402	1 430 814
1220 On capital gains		..	..	..	..	..	..	..	..	..
1300 Unallocable between 1100 and 1200		0	0	0	0	0	0	0	0	0
2000 Social security contributions	..	0	49 904	131 041	203 361	225 948	240 590	264 710	280 537	230 206
2100 Employees	..	..	..	..	..	..	..	..	..	..
2110 On a payroll basis	..	..	..	..	..	..	..	..	..	..
2120 On an income tax basis	..	..	..	..	..	..	..	..	..	..
2200 Employers	..	..	..	..	..	..	..	..	..	..
2210 On a payroll basis	..	..	..	..	..	..	..	..	..	..
2220 On an income tax basis	..	..	..	..	..	..	..	..	..	..
2300 Self-employed or non-employed	..	..	..	..	..	..	..	..	..	..
2310 On a payroll basis	..	..	..	..	..	..	..	..	..	..
2320 On an income tax basis	..	..	..	..	..	..	..	..	..	..
2400 Unallocable between 2100, 2200 and 2300	..	..	49 904	131 041	203 361	225 948	240 590	264 710	280 537	230 206
2410 On a payroll basis	..	..	..	..	..	..	..	..	..	..
2420 On an income tax basis	..	..	..	..	..	..	..	..	..	..
3000 Taxes on payroll and workforce	..	99 082	295 733	253 830	380 477	427 985	464 674	530 440	576 607	618 505
The social tax		99 082	295 733	253 830	380 477	427 985	464 674	530 440	576 607	618 505
4000 Taxes on property	..	21 013	73 822	124 632	160 845	192 063	226 853	227 862	257 012	298 617
4100 Recurrent taxes on immovable property	..	20 504	71 592	122 146	157 424	188 331	224 752	226 815	255 868	298 455
4110 Households	..	3 230	2 936	4 402	6 153	9 385	10 164	11 906	3 922	22 374
4120 Others	..	17 274	68 655	117 744	151 271	178 946	214 588	214 909	251 946	276 082
Uniform land tax		235	428	762	830	876	833	944	1 004	1 036
Property tax		13 699	59 140	104 745	138 015	165 795	200 710	200 685	236 542	269 534
Land tax		3 340	9 086	12 238	12 426	12 275	13 045	13 281	14 401	5 512
4200 Recurrent taxes on net wealth	..	0	0	0	0	0	0	0	0	0
4210 Individual	..	..	..	..	..	..	..	..	..	..
4220 Corporate	..	..	..	..	..	..	..	..	..	..
4300 Estate, inheritance and gift taxes	..	0	0	0	0	0	0	0	0	0
4310 Estate and inheritance taxes	..	..	..	..	..	..	..	..	..	..
4320 Gift taxes	..	..	..	..	..	..	..	..	..	..
4400 Taxes on financial and capital transactions	..	509	2 231	2 486	3 421	3 732	2 101	1 047	1 143	161
4500 Non-recurrent taxes	..	0	0	0	0	0	0	0	0	0
4510 On net wealth	..	..	..	..	..	..	..	..	..	..
4520 Other non-recurrent taxes	..	..	..	..	..	..	..	..	..	..
4600 Other recurrent taxes on property	..	0	0	0	0	0	0	0	0	0
5000 Taxes on goods and services	..	179 452	1 131 164	2 600 514	4 457 717	4 405 005	2 952 727	3 372 218	4 437 419	5 259 064
5100 Taxes on production, sale, transfer, etc	..	168 678	1 032 930	2 497 709	4 300 462	4 237 236	2 816 629	3 238 137	4 285 158	5 080 971
5110 General taxes		115 159	629 279	677 229	1 327 433	1 197 258	943 051	1 495 682	1 664 699	2 034 314
5111 Value added taxes		115 159	629 279	677 229	1 327 433	1 197 258	943 051	1 495 682	1 664 699	2 034 314
Domestic VAT		75 625	137 290	197 358	445 876	333 943	203 247	525 318	532 864	800 800
VAT on imported goods		39 534	464 361	435 869	819 129	789 302	667 404	860 801	1 017 876	1 124 959
Other VAT		0	27 628	44 002	62 428	74 013	72 399	109 563	113 959	108 554
5112 Sales tax	..	0	0	0	0	0	0	0	0	0
5113 Other	..	0	0	0	0	0	0	0	0	0
5120 Taxes on specific goods and services		53 519	403 651	1 820 480	2 973 029	3 039 978	1 873 579	1 742 455	2 620 458	3 046 657
5121 Excises		19 285	58 753	61 423	103 651	147 057	161 168	205 231	255 994	311 856
Alcohol		12 939	18 189	15 691	29 659	38 788	36 345	40 712	58 793	79 874
Tobacco		5 182	10 953	22 903	45 644	78 695	98 346	121 403	137 791	163 140
Petroleum product	..	1 164	20 970	20 966	24 139	25 221	26 216	42 042	58 146	67 504
Automobiles	..	0	8 641	1 864	4 208	4 352	931	0	0	0
Others	..	0	0	0	2	0	-770	1 075	1 265	1 338
5122 Profits of fiscal monopolies	..	0	0	0	0	0	0	0	0	0
5123 Customs and import duties	..	18 471	150 355	354 487	297 959	279 313	189 522	266 484	296 905	331 629

	1997	2000	2007	2010	2013	2014	2015	2016	2017	2018
5124 Taxes on exports	..	0	611	492 870	1 466 254	1 513 573	920 175	807 011	1 154 883	1 586 728
Taxes on exports	..	..	0	22 060	585 857	778 853	692 855	688 122	904 476	1 099 662
Taxes on exports to National Fund	..	..	611	470 810	880 397	734 720	227 320	118 889	250 408	487 066
5125 Taxes on investment goods	..	0	0	0	0	0	0	0	0	0
5126 Taxes on specific services	..	0	6 184	14 566	18 862	21 036	24 798	25 856	27 144	43 076
Telecommunication	..	..	3 624	5 535	5 476	6 167	8 151	8 124	8 286	8 596
Placement of outdoor advertisements	..	..	2 560	3 723	5 652	5 981	6 076	5 855	5 510	5 615
Gambling business	..	..	0	3 693	6 385	7 598	9 231	10 518	11 746	26 846
Others	..	..	0	1 614	1 350	1 291	1 340	1 359	1 602	2 018
5127 Other taxes on internat. trade and transactions	..	0	0	0	0	0	0	0	0	0
5128 Other taxes	..	15 763	187 748	897 133	1 086 303	1 078 999	578 015	437 873	885 532	773 369
Production of useful minerals of non-oil sector companies	..	15 763	16 510	122 128	168 186	122 909	118 073	159 276	259 183	308 717
Production of useful minerals of oil sector companies	..	0	0	0	0	0	0	0	0	0
Production of useful minerals of oil sector co. to National Fund	..	0	171 238	775 005	918 117	956 090	459 942	278 597	626 350	464 652
5130 Unallocable between 5110 and 5120	..	0	0	0	0	0	0	0	0	0
5200 Taxes on use of goods and perform activities	..	10 774	98 234	102 806	157 255	167 769	136 098	134 081	152 261	178 093
5210 Recurrent taxes	..	5 901	11 382	26 327	36 116	38 930	42 319	46 879	59 981	67 191
5211 Paid by households: motor vehicles	..	3 930	8 099	21 565	29 629	31 656	34 466	38 572	51 271	57 814
5212 Paid by others: motor vehicles	..	1 971	3 241	4 697	6 401	7 188	7 812	8 307	8 710	9 377
5213 Paid in respect of other goods	..	0	42	65	86	86	41	0	0	0
5220 Non-recurrent taxes	..	4 873	86 852	76 478	121 140	128 840	93 779	87 202	92 280	110 902
Emissions into the environment	..	0	70 958	57 982	93 179	97 712	63 379	67 216	72 529	87 126
Others	..	4 873	15 894	18 497	27 960	31 128	30 399	19 985	19 752	23 776
5300 Unallocable between 5100 and 5200	..	0	0	0	0	0	0	0	0	0
6000 Other taxes	..	**3 684**	**909**	**6**	**103**	**75**	**141**	**410**	**10 198**	**4 816**
6100 Paid solely by business	..	0	0	0	0	0	0	0	0	0
6200 Other	..	3 684	909	6	103	75	141	410	10 198	4 816

Note: Year ending 31st December.

Data are on a cash basis.

The share of the Republic of Kazakhstan under production sharing contracts of oil companies, the bonuses of oil and non-oil sector companies, the levy for the use of the radio-frequency spectrum, the payment to compensate for historic costs as well as certain other items are classified as non-tax revenues according to the OECD Interpretative Guide, but are considered as tax revenues in Kazakhstan.

Headings 1210, 5124 and 5128: These categories includes revenues that are paid to the National Fund of the Republic of Kazakhstan. This fund was created in 2000 as a stabilisation fund and includes revenues levied from oil and gas companies.

Heading 2000: Social security contribution revenues are not considered as tax revenues in Kazakhstan, but are considered as tax revenues under the OECD Interpretative Guide, subject to certain criteria.

Heading 4120: The uniform land tax is a presumptive tax for farmers and peasants' households. Such payers are not obliged to pay personal income tax, land tax, environmental fees, transport tax, property tax and other mandatory payments to the budget. The uniform land tax is levied on the value of land in use.

Source: Ministry of Finance of the Republic of Kazakhstan.

StatLink ᵐˢ⁰ https://stat.link/hfvkpw

Table 4.9. Korea

Details of tax revenue
Billion KRW

	1997	2000	2007	2010	2013	2014	2015	2016	2017	2018
Total tax revenue	**102 916**	**136 295**	**258 571**	**295 968**	**347 332**	**365 428**	**393 559**	**430 752**	**465 470**	**506 548**
1000 Taxes on income, profits and capital gains	**26 916**	**39 254**	**82 239**	**82 905**	**101 792**	**106 353**	**119 151**	**134 503**	**149 420**	**172 976**
1100 Of individuals	16 543	19 950	43 276	42 098	53 311	59 457	67 600	75 711	83 121	93 274
1110 On income and profits	14 586	18 569	31 984	33 935	46 654	51 410	55 744	62 028	67 987	75 251
Income tax	0	0	0	0	0	0	0	0	0	0
Dividends and interest income tax	0	0	4 682	4 425	4 889	4 628	4 561	4 125	4 517	4 982
Wages and salaries income tax	0	0	14 124	15 517	21 931	25 359	27 055	30 994	34 034	38 000
Other income tax	0	0	2 607	2 986	3 432	3 805	4 467	5 346	5 333	5 975
Global income tax	12 911	16 128	6 151	6 369	10 901	11 486	12 784	14 348	16 049	17 483
Defence tax on income tax	0	0	0	0	0	0	0	0	0	0
Education tax on income tax	0	0	0	0	0	0	0	0	0	0
Rural dev. tax on interest, bus. Inc. & cap. gains relief	149	156	160	179	124	115	105	109	104	111
Inhabitant tax on income tax (local)	1 526	2 285	4 260	4 459	5 377	6 017	6 772	7 106	7 950	8 700
1120 On capital gains	1 957	1 381	11 292	8 163	6 657	8 047	11 856	13 683	15 134	18 023
Capital gains tax	1 957	1 381	11 292	8 163	6 657	8 047	11 856	13 683	15 134	18 023
1200 Corporate	10 158	19 271	38 963	40 807	48 481	46 896	51 551	58 792	66 299	79 702
1210 On profits	10 158	19 271	38 963	40 807	48 481	46 896	51 551	58 792	66 299	79 702
Corporation tax - withholding	5 501	8 577	8 360	9 095	12 176	12 172	12 317	11 986	11 990	13 174
Corporation tax - final returns	3 924	9 302	27 057	28 173	31 679	30 478	32 713	40 130	47 187	57 763
Defence tax on corporation tax	0	0	0	0	0	0	0	0	0	0
Inhabitant tax on corporation tax (local)	733	1 142	3 152	3 094	4 118	3 882	6 217	6 270	6 785	8 307
Rural development tax corporate income	0	251	394	445	508	364	304	406	337	458
Excess profit tax	0	0	0	0	0	0	0	0	0	0
1220 On capital gains	0	0	0	0	0	0	0	0	0	0
Capital gains tax	..	..	..	..	..	..	..	..	..	..
1300 Unallocable between 1100 and 1200	215	33	0	0	0	0	0	0	0	0
Business income tax	0	0	..	..	..	..	..	..	..	..
Real estate income tax	0	0	..	..	..	..	..	..	..	..
Defence tax on real estate & business income	0	0	..	..	..	..	..	..	..	..
Rural dev. tax on bus. inc. & cap. gains relief	211	30	..	..	..	..	..	..	..	..
Inhabitant tax before 1990 (local)	1	0	..	..	..	..	..	..	..	..
Farm land tax (local)	3	3	..	..	..	..	..	..	..	..
Inhabitant tax on farm land tax (local)	0	0	..	..	..	..	..	..	..	..
2000 Social security contributions	**14 583**	**22 759**	**53 588**	**69 090**	**91 596**	**98 184**	**104 693**	**112 658**	**119 676**	**128 660**
2100 Employees	6 376	8 578	21 773	28 213	38 396	41 355	44 281	48 077	51 125	55 257
Veterans' relief fund	0	0	0	0	0	0	0	0	0	0
Soldiers' annuity fund	0	0	0	0	0	0	0	0	0	0
Unemployment assurance	264	598	1 164	1 358	2 418	2 866	3 076	3 251	3 418	3 666
National welfare pension fund	3 597	4 325	9 338	11 004	13 890	14 823	15 821	16 862	17 864	19 090
Social benefit fund	0	0	0	0	0	0	0	0	0	0
Health Insurance	1 149	2 066	8 180	11 783	17 128	18 492	19 868	21 470	22 814	24 920
Teachers' pensions	219	279	581	868	1 077	1 081	1 125	1 410	1 507	1 595
Government employees pensions	1 013	1 144	2 202	2 878	3 435	3 593	3 876	4 533	4 934	5 371
Military personal pensions	134	166	308	322	448	500	515	551	588	615
2110 On a payroll basis	..	8 578	21 773	28 213	38 396	41 355	44 281	48 077	51 125	55 257
2120 On an income tax basis	..	0	0	0	0	0	0	0	0	0
2200 Employers	5 901	9 409	23 557	30 856	41 518	44 806	47 846	51 190	54 063	58 712
Ind. works' insurance fund	1 819	1 876	4 431	4 632	5 436	5 797	6 062	6 283	6 429	7 346
Soldiers' annuity fund	0	0	0	0	0	0	0	0	0	0
Pneumoconiosis fund	0	0	0	0	0	0	0	0	0	0
Unemployment insurance	653	1 449	2 474	2 860	4 545	5 150	5 499	5 790	6 082	6 517
Veterans' relief fund	0	0	0	0	0	0	0	0	0	0
National welfare pension fund	1 814	4 340	9 383	11 052	13 958	14 909	15 895	16 928	17 922	19 155
Social benefit fund	0	0	0	0	0	0	0	0	0	0
Health Insurance	1 459	1 547	6 844	11 718	16 826	18 133	19 493	21 074	22 397	24 346
Teachers' pensions	156	197	425	594	753	817	897	1 115	1 233	1 348
Government employees pensions	0	0	0	0	0	0	0	0	0	0
2210 On a payroll basis	..	9 409	23 557	30 856	41 518	44 806	47 846	51 190	54 063	58 712
2220 On an income tax basis	..	0	0	0	0	0	0	0	0	..
2300 Self-employed or non-employed	2 306	4 772	8 258	10 021	11 682	12 023	12 566	13 391	14 488	14 691
2310 On a payroll basis	0	0	0	0	0	0	0	0	0	0
2320 On an income tax basis	2 306	4 772	8 258	10 021	11 682	12 023	12 566	13 391	14 488	14 691
2400 Unallocable between 2100, 2200 and 2300	0	0	0	0	0	0	0	0	0	0
2410 On a payroll basis	..	..	..	..	..	..	..	..	..	..
2420 On an income tax basis	..	..	..	..	..	..	..	..	..	..

	1997	2000	2007	2010	2013	2014	2015	2016	2017	2018
3000 Taxes on payroll and workforce	**309**	**258**	**619**	**714**	**981**	**1 042**	**1 122**	**1 293**	**1 376**	**1 492**
Workshop tax on workforce (local)	309	258	619	714	981	1 042	1 122	1 293	1 376	1 492
Vocational training promotion fund	0	0	0	0	0	0	0	0	0	0
4000 Taxes on property	**13 088**	**16 846**	**33 109**	**33 516**	**35 847**	**40 305**	**48 625**	**49 820**	**54 406**	**58 811**
4100 Recurrent taxes on immovable property	2 986	3 385	9 196	9 270	10 809	11 654	12 486	13 095	14 319	15 589
Property tax (local)	577	728	3 755	4 817	8 267	8 780	9 294	9 930	10 662	11 532
City planning tax on urban real estate (local)	731	815	1 883	2 465	0	0	0	0	0	0
Community facilities tax (local)	268	341	543	650	912	1 138	1 351	1 450	1 513	1 626
Tax on excessive land holdings (local)	0	0	0	0	0	0	0	0	0	0
Tax on aggregate land holdings (local)	1 279	1 282	5	0	0	0	0	0	0	0
Rural dev. tax on local agg. land holdings tax	63	81	1	0	0	0	0	0	0	0
Tax on excessively increased land value	-1	0	0	0	0	0	0	0	0	0
Comprehensive real estate tax	0	0	2 414	1 029	1 224	1 307	1 399	1 294	1 652	1 873
Rural dev. tax on comprehensive real estate tax	0	0	483	208	250	265	267	240	302	356
4110 Households	0	0	0	0	0	0	0	0	0	..
4120 Others	68	138	112	101	156	164	175	181	190	202
Workshop tax on property (local)	68	138	112	101	156	164	175	181	190	202
4200 Recurrent taxes on net wealth	0	0	0	0	0	0	0	0	0	0
4210 Individual	..	..	..	..	..	..	..	..	..	..
4220 Corporate	..	..	..	..	..	..	..	..	..	..
4300 Estate, inheritance and gift taxes	1 161	989	2 842	3 076	4 290	4 625	5 044	5 350	6 785	7 359
4310 Estate and inheritance taxes	605	449	1 059	1 203	1 587	1 696	1 944	1 995	2 342	2 832
Inheritance tax	605	449	1 059	1 203	1 587	1 696	1 944	1 995	2 342	2 832
Defence tax on inheritance tax	0	0	0	0	0	0	0	0	0	0
4320 Gift taxes	556	540	1 783	1 873	2 703	2 929	3 100	3 355	4 443	4 527
Gift tax	556	540	1 783	1 873	2 703	2 929	3 100	3 355	4 443	4 527
Defence tax on gift tax	0	0	0	0	0	0	0	0	0	0
4400 Taxes on financial and capital transactions	8 774	11 935	21 071	21 170	20 748	24 026	31 095	31 375	33 302	35 863
Registration tax (local)	4 257	4 528	7 254	7 370	1 312	1 485	1 831	1 708	1 608	1 718
Registration tax	0	0	0	0	0	0	0	0	0	0
Defence tax on registration tax	0	0	0	0	0	0	0	0	0	0
Rural dev. tax on local acquisition tax	164	246	627	632	874	843	969	954	1 028	993
Rural dev. tax on local registration tax	211	66	143	144	1	1	1	0	0	0
Securities transactions tax	262	2 736	3 469	3 667	3 077	3 121	4 670	4 468	4 508	6 241
Rural dev. tax on securities transaction tax	170	823	1 729	2 010	1 529	1 459	1 861	1 637	1 775	2 217
Acquisition tax (local)	3 319	3 148	7 261	6 825	13 318	16 391	20 810	21 702	23 487	23 813
Stamp tax	390	388	588	522	637	726	953	906	896	881
4500 Non-recurrent taxes	167	537	0	0	0	0	0	0	0	0
Asset revaluation tax	167	537	..	..	..	..	..	..	..	..
4510 On net wealth	..	..	..	..	..	..	..	..	..	..
4520 Other non-recurrent taxes	..	..	..	..	..	..	..	..	..	..
4600 Other recurrent taxes on property	0	0	0	0	0	0	0	0	0	..
5000 Taxes on goods and services	**43 978**	**52 271**	**80 861**	**99 769**	**106 717**	**109 451**	**110 326**	**121 197**	**129 065**	**133 095**
5100 Taxes on production, sale, transfer, etc.	41 699	50 023	78 414	96 573	99 970	102 531	103 254	113 644	121 293	125 207
5110 General taxes	19 488	23 212	40 942	51 800	59 105	62 975	60 162	68 229	74 361	77 471
5111 Value added taxes	19 488	23 212	40 942	51 800	59 105	62 975	60 162	68 229	74 361	77 471
Value added tax	19 488	23 212	40 942	51 800	59 105	62 975	60 162	68 229	74 361	77 471
5112 Sales tax	0	0	0	0	0	0	0	0	0	0
Business tax	..	..	..	..	..	..	..	..	..	..
5113 Other	0	0	0	0	0	0	0	0	0	..
5120 Taxes on specific goods and services	22 211	26 811	37 472	44 773	40 865	39 556	43 092	45 415	46 932	47 736
5121 Excise duties	14 616	18 155	27 880	31 340	27 661	28 226	31 857	34 762	35 779	36 218
Commodity tax	0	0	0	0	0	0	0	0	0	0
Defence tax on commodity tax	0	0	0	0	0	0	0	0	0	0
Liquor tax	1 790	1 963	2 268	2 878	2 947	2 852	3 228	3 209	3 035	3 261
Defence tax on liquor tax	0	0	0	0	0	0	0	0	0	0
Education tax on liquor tax	418	516	580	724	764	728	808	813	745	788
Textile tax	0	0	0	0	0	0	0	0	0	0
Petroleum tax	0	0	0	0	0	0	0	0	0	0
Transport tax on petrol products	5 547	8 404	11 464	13 970	13 248	13 440	14 055	15 303	15 553	15 335
Education tax on transport tax	758	1 247	1 715	2 133	1 895	2 074	2 154	2 289	2 320	2 304
Electricity and gas tax	0	0	0	0	0	0	0	0	0	0
Special excise tax	3 036	2 985	5 161	5 066	5 484	5 624	8 001	8 881	9 861	10 451
Defence tax on special excise tax	0	0	0	0	0	0	0	0	0	0
Education tax on special excise tax	804	498	607	501	485	495	515	463	602	545
Rural development on special excise tax	26	37	54	24	56	60	61	60	60	56
Tobacco sales tax (local)	0	0	0	0	0	0	0	0	0	0
Tobacco consumption tax (local)	2 236	2 251	2 761	2 875	2 782	2 953	3 035	3 744	3 603	3 478
Motor fuel tax (local)	0	254	3 270	3 169	0	0	0	0	0	0
5122 Profits of fiscal monopolies	0	0	0	0	0	0	0	0	0	0
Monopoly profit	..	..	..	..	..	..	..	..	..	..

	1997	2000	2007	2010	2013	2014	2015	2016	2017	2018
5123 Customs and import duties	5 941	5 936	7 690	11 046	11 012	9 132	8 907	8 434	8 938	9 213
Customs duties	5 798	5 800	7 411	10 666	10 562	8 721	8 495	8 045	8 529	8 815
Defence tax on customs duties	0	0	0	0	0	0	0	0	0	0
Special customs duties	0	0	0	0	0	0	0	0	0	0
Tonnage tax	0	0	0	0	0	0	0	0	0	0
Education tax on imports	116	99	234	336	429	390	390	366	382	370
Rural dev. tax on customs exemptions	27	37	45	44	21	21	22	23	27	28
Previous year receipts	0	0	0	0	0	0	0	0	0	0
5124 Taxes on exports	0	0	0	0	0	0	0	0	0	..
5125 Taxes on investment goods	0	0	0	0	0	0	0	0	0	..
5126 Taxes on specific services	1 654	2 720	1 902	2 387	2 192	2 198	2 328	2 219	2 215	2 305
Telephone tax	789	1 457	0	0	0	0	0	0	0	0
Defence tax on telephone tax	0	0	0	0	0	0	0	0	0	0
Entertainment tax	0	0	0	0	0	0	0	0	0	0
Defence tax on entertainment tax	0	0	0	0	0	0	0	0	0	0
Entertainment tax (local)	0	0	0	0	0	0	0	0	0	0
Travel tax	0	0	0	0	0	0	0	0	0	0
Admission tax	0	0	0	0	0	0	0	0	0	0
Defence tax on admission tax	0	0	0	0	0	0	0	0	0	0
Education tax on banking & insurance	369	473	721	951	938	920	1 004	951	959	1 092
Horse race tax (local)	361	566	864	1 068	1 042	1 073	1 089	1 060	1 051	1 016
Rural dev. tax on horse race tax	18	84	165	215	212	205	235	208	205	197
Butchery tax (local)	47	51	52	58	0	0	0	0	0	0
Regional development tax (local)	71	89	100	95	0	0	0	0	0	0
5127 Other taxes on internat. trade and transactions	0	0	0	0	0	0	0	0	0	..
5128 Other taxes	0	0	0	0	0	0	0	0	0	..
5130 Unallocable between 5110 and 5120	0	0	0	0	0	0	0	0	0	..
5200 Taxes on use of goods and perform activities	2 279	2 248	2 447	3 196	6 747	6 920	7 072	7 553	7 772	7 888
5210 Recurrent taxes	2 279	2 248	2 447	3 196	6 747	6 920	7 072	7 553	7 772	7 888
License tax (local)	225	241	77	76	0	0	0	0	0	0
Automobile tax (local)	2 054	2 007	2 370	3 120	6 747	6 920	7 072	7 553	7 772	7 888
5211 Paid by households: motor vehicles	..	..	..	..	..	..	..	..	..	..
5212 Paid by others: motor vehicles	..	..	..	..	..	..	..	..	..	..
5213 Paid in respect of other goods	..	..	..	..	..	..	..	..	..	..
5220 Non-recurrent taxes	0	0	0	0	0	0	0	0	0	..
5300 Unallocable between 5100 and 5200	0	0	0	0	0	0	0	0	0	..
6000 Other taxes	**4 041**	**4 907**	**8 155**	**9 974**	**10 399**	**10 093**	**9 642**	**11 281**	**11 527**	**11 514**
6100 Paid solely by business	0	0	0	0	0	0	0	0	0	..
6200 Other	4 041	4 907	8 155	9 974	10 399	10 093	9 642	11 281	11 527	11 514
Unallocable tax revenue	0	0	0	0	0	0	0	0	0	0
Previous year tax	779	1 474	2 965	4 449	4 774	4 049	3 435	4 147	4 389	4 430
Previous year tax (local)	340	474	672	654	601	589	392	868	715	540
Unallocable defence tax	-8	-3	0	0	0	0	0	0	0	0
Education tax on local taxes	2 931	2 962	4 518	4 871	5 024	5 455	5 815	6 266	6 423	6 544

Note: Year ending 31st December.

Data are on cash basis.

Heading 2000: From 1997 the contributions to the three funds (civil servant pension fund, private school teachers pension fund and medical insurance fund) are classified as security social contributions. The reasons for the change are that the contributions either became mandatory or the fund started to be managed by public authorities in that year, thereby meeting the OECD definition of social security contributions.

Heading 2200: From 2007, this includes long-term care insurance.

Source: Ministry of Finance and Economy, Ministry of Home Affairs.

StatLink ᵃᵗˢᴸ https://stat.link/finhmr

Table 4.10. Malaysia

Details of tax revenue

Million MYR

	1997	2000	2007	2010	2013	2014	2015	2016	2017	2018
Total tax revenue	55 493	50 083	98 569	113 573	160 920	169 513	170 971	175 325	183 537	180 707
1000 Taxes on income, profits and capital gains	27 648	27 339	65 671	75 058	114 113	120 284	105 751	103 967	110 260	123 953
1100 Of individuals	6 429	7 015	11 661	17 805	23 055	24 423	26 321	27 566	28 945	32 605
1110 On income and profits	6 429	7 015	11 661	17 805	23 055	24 423	26 321	27 566	28 945	32 605
1120 On capital gains	..	..	..	..	..	..	..	..	..	0
1200 Corporate	20 552	19 923	52 615	55 156	87 949	92 223	75 275	72 127	76 226	86 556
1210 On profits	20 552	19 923	52 615	55 156	87 949	92 223	75 275	72 127	76 226	86 556
Company income tax	16 688	13 905	32 149	36 266	58 175	65 240	63 679	63 625	64 465	66 474
Petroleum income tax	3 861	6 010	20 453	18 713	29 753	26 956	11 559	8 422	11 761	20 082
Offshore business activity tax	3	8	13	15	20	27	37	81	0	0
Levy on Electricity	0	0	0	162	1	0	0	0	0	0
1220 On capital gains of corporates	..	..	..	..	..	..	..	..	..	0
1300 Unallocable between 1100 and 1200	666	402	1 395	2 097	3 109	3 639	4 155	4 274	5 089	4 792
Cooperatives income tax	143	87	189	378	286	169	80	90	74	171
Withholding income tax	0	0	1 190	1 268	2 008	2 184	2 316	2 562	3 266	3 117
Other income tax	0	0	17	21	23	24	30	43	51	37
Real property gains tax	523	247	0	303	785	1 210	1 729	1 492	1 697	1 467
Exit levy	0	41	0	0	0	0	0	0	0	0
Windfall levy on crude palm oil	0	0	0	0	0	0	0	0	0	0
Windfall levy on crude palm kernel oil	0	26	0	0	0	0	0	0	0	0
Levy on fresh fruit bunch	0	0	0	127	7	51	1	87	0	0
2000 Social security contributions	0	990	1 690	2 008	2 518	2 689	2 847	3 216	3 561	3 944
2100 Employees	..	218	371	439	552	588				
2110 On a payroll basis	..	218	371	439	552	588				
2120 On an income tax basis	..	0	0	0	0	0	..	..	..	..
2200 Employers	..	772	1 319	1 569	1 966	2 101	..	..	..	..
2210 On a payroll basis	..	772	1 319	1 569	1 966	2 101	..	..	..	..
2220 On an income tax basis	..	0	0	0	0	0	..	..	..	..
2300 Self-employed or non-employed	..	0	0	0	0	0	..	..	..	..
2310 On a payroll basis	..	..	..	..	..	..	..	..	..	..
2320 On an income tax basis	..	..	..	..	..	..	..	..	..	..
2400 Unallocable between 2100, 2200 and 2300	..	0	0	0	0	0	2 847	3 216	3 561	3 944
2410 On a payroll basis	..	..	..	..	..	..	..	..	..	0
2420 On an income tax basis	..	..	..	..	..	..	..	..	..	0
3000 Taxes on payroll and workforce	0	0	0	0	0	0	0	0	0	0
4000 Taxes on property	19	2	..	..	1	2	1	3	0	0
4100 Recurrent taxes on immovable property	0	0	..	..	0	0	0	0	0	0
4110 Households	..	..	..	..	..	..	..	..	..	..
4120 Others	..	..	..	..	..	..	..	..	..	..
4200 Recurrent taxes on net wealth	0	0	..	..	0	0	0	0	0	0
4210 Individual	..	..	..	..	..	..	..	..	..	..
4220 Corporate	..	..	..	..	..	..	..	..	..	..
4300 Estate, inheritance and gift taxes	19	2	..	..	1	2	1	3	0	0
4310 Estate and inheritance taxes	19	2	..	..	1	2	1	3	0	0
Estate Duty	19	2	..	..	1	2	1	3	0	0
4320 Gift taxes	0	0	..	..	0	0	0	0	0	0
4400 Taxes on financial and capital transactions	0	0	..	..	0	0	0	0	0	0
4500 Other non-reccurrent taxes on property	0	0	..	..	0	0	0	0	0	0
4510 On net wealth	..	..	..	..	..	..	..	..	..	..
4520 Other non-recurrent taxes	..	..	..	..	..	..	..	..	..	..
4600 Other recurrent taxes on property	..	..	..	..	0	..	..	..	..	..
5000 Taxes on goods and services	25 061	19 910	27 483	32 268	37 871	40 030	56 353	62 415	63 952	46 729
5100 Taxes on production, sale, transfer, etc	23 195	17 990	25 772	30 218	35 421	37 411	53 669	59 649	61 148	43 810
5110 General taxes on goods and services	6 167	5 968	6 642	8 171	10 068	10 939	32 235	41 309	44 337	24 207
5111 Value added taxes	0	0	0	0	0	0	27 012	41 206	44 290	20 236
5112 Sales tax	6 167	5 968	6 642	8 171	10 068	10 939	5 223	103	47	3 971
Sales tax on local goods	4 160	3 894	4 178	4 886	5 626	6 130	3 207			1 095
Sales tax on imported goods	2 008	2 074	2 464	3 285	4 442	4 809	2 016			2 876
5113 Other	0	0	0	0	0	0	0	0	0	0
5120 Taxes on specific goods and services	15 266	10 245	16 897	19 624	22 756	23 930	18 862	15 854	14 266	16 986
5121 Excises	6 053	3 803	8 990	11 770	12 193	12 925	11 890	11 705	10 112	10 779
Excise duties on domestic goods	6 053	3 803	7 910	9 350	8 395	8 456	7 999	7 721	5 519	4 918
Malt beer (domestic)	..	..	..	..	..	..	..	..	..	1 696
Cigarettes (domestic)	..	..	..	..	..	..	..	..	..	234
Passenger vehicles (domestic)	..	..	..	..	..	..	..	..	..	2 483
Other products (domestic)	..	..	..	..	..	..	..	..	..	505
Excise duties on imported goods	0	0	1 081	2 420	3 798	4 468	3 891	3 984	4 593	5 861

	1997	2000	2007	2010	2013	2014	2015	2016	2017	2018
Cigarettes (imported)	..	..	..	..	..	..	..	..	..	2 681
Motor vehicles (imported)	..	..	..	..	..	..	..	..	..	2 803
Other products (imported)	..	..	..	..	..	..	..	..	..	378
5122 Profits of fiscal monopolies	0	0	0	0	0	0	0	0	0	0
5123 Customs and import duties	6 524	3 599	2 424	1 966	2 524	2 670	2 732	2 905	2 784	2 897
Import duty on vehicles	..	..	..	..	..	..	..	..	..	562
Import duty on motors, machines and spare parts	..	..	..	..	..	..	..	..	..	681
Import duty on alcoholic beverages	..	..	..	..	..	..	..	..	..	100
Import duty on steel and metal products	..	..	..	..	..	..	..	..	..	305
Import duty on other products	..	..	..	..	..	..	..	..	..	1 248
5124 Taxes on exports	1 053	1 032	2 322	1 810	1 930	1 893	1 039	980	1 355	1 725
Export duty on petroleom	..	..	..	..	..	..	..	..	..	1 513
Export duty on other products	..	..	..	..	..	..	..	..	..	212
5125 Taxes on investment goods	0	0	0	0	0	0	0	0	0	0
5126 Taxes on specific services	1 475	1 701	3 013	3 926	5 944	6 278	3 038	103	15	1 473
Pool betting duties and sweepstakes	0	0	0	0	0	0	0	0	0	0
Service tax	1 475	1 701	3 013	3 926	5 944	6 278	3 038	103	15	1 473
5127 Other taxes on internat. trade and transactions	160	110	147	151	165	165	163	160	0	113
5128 Other taxes	0	0	0	0	0	0	0	0	0	0
5130 Unallocable between 5110 and 5120	1 761	1 777	2 233	2 423	2 597	2 542	2 572	2 486	2 545	2 617
5200 Taxes on use of goods and to perform activities	1 866	1 920	1 711	2 050	2 450	2 619	2 684	2 766	2 805	2 919
5210 Recurrent taxes	1 863	1 918	1 709	2 047	2 447	2 617	2 681	2 763	2 805	2 919
5211 Paid by households: motor vehicles	1 852	1 909	1 688	1 992	2 407	2 532	2 630	2 714	2 805	2 919
Motor vehicle licences	1 852	1 909	1 688	1 992	2 407	2 532	2 630	2 714	2 805	2 919
5212 Paid by others: motor vehicles	11	9	20	18	3	3	3	3	0	0
Commercial vehicle licences	11	9	19	17	3	3	3	3	0	0
Tour vehicle licences	0	0	1	1	0	0	0	0	0	0
5213 Paid in respect of other goods	0	0	0	38	37	81	48	46	0	0
Petroleum Permits	0	0	0	1	0	4	2	2	0	0
Bank Licences Fees	0	0	0	37	37	78	46	44	0	0
5220 Non-recurrent taxes	3	2	3	2	2	2	3	3	0	0
Environment Pollution Licences	2	2	3	2	2	2	3	3	0	0
Film rental tax	1	0	0	0	0	0	0	0	0	0
5300 Unallocable between 5100 and 5200	0	0	0	0	0	0	0	0	0	0
6000 Other taxes	**2 764**	**1 841**	**3 725**	**4 240**	**6 417**	**6 508**	**6 018**	**5 724**	**5 764**	**6 081**
6100 Paid solely by business	0	0	0	0	0	0	0	0	0	0
6200 Other	2 764	1 841	3 725	4 240	6 417	6 508	6 018	5 724	5 764	6 081
Share transfer tax	0	0	0	0	0	0	0	0	0	0
Stamp duties	2 714	1 799	3 404	4 192	6 364	6 458	5 974	5 688	5 665	5 924
Other direct taxes	50	42	321	48	53	51	45	37	99	157

Note: Year ending 31st December.

The data are on a cash basis.

More granular data have been presented in this edition based on additional information from the government.

Heading 2000: Starting from 2015, Social Security Contribution data is given as a lump sum. Data for 2018 has been estimated using growth rate of 2016-2017.

Source: Ministry of Finance of Malaysia; Social Security Organisation of Malaysia (PERKESO).

StatLink 🔗 https://stat.link/o82135

Table 4.11. Mongolia
Details of tax revenue
Billion MNT

	1997	2000	2007	2010	2013	2014	2015	2016	2017	2018
Total tax revenue	..	..	1 406	2 470	4 503	4 481	4 421	4 567	6 005	7 788
1000 Taxes on income, profits and capital gains	..	..	649	975	1 109	1 101	1 171	1 043	1 613	2 091
1100 Of individuals	..	..	75	161	449	480	482	523	651	814
1110 On income and profits	..	..	75	161	449	480	482	523	651	814
1120 On capital gains	..	..	0	0	0	0	0	0	0	0
1200 Corporate	..	..	574	814	660	621	689	520	962	1 277
1210 On profits	..	..	574	814	660	621	689	520	962	1 277
Corporate tax income revenue	..	..	220	391	660	621	689	520	962	1 277
Windfall profit tax	..	..	354	423	0	0	0	0	0	0
1220 On capital gains of corporates	..	..	0	0	0	0	0	0	0	0
1300 Unallocable between 1100 and 1200	..	..	0	0	0	0	0	0	0	0
2000 Social security contributions	..	..	161	323	819	871	972	1 058	1 259	1 569
2100 Employees	..	..	8	170	364	423	438	465	535	541
2110 On a payroll basis	..	..	..	..	..	..	..	..	..	..
2120 On an income tax basis	..	..	..	..	..	..	..	..	..	..
2200 Employers	..	..	147	129	399	440	447	494	578	640
2210 On a payroll basis	..	..	..	..	..	..	..	..	..	..
2220 On an income tax basis	..	..	..	..	..	..	..	..	..	..
2300 Self-employed or non-employed	..	..	0	0	0	0	0	0	0	0
2310 On a payroll basis	..	..	..	..	..	..	..	..	..	..
2320 On an income tax basis	..	..	..	..	..	..	..	..	..	..
2400 Unallocable between 2100, 2200 and 2300	..	..	6	24	56	8	87	99	146	388
2410 On a payroll basis	..	..	..	..	..	..	..	..	..	..
2420 On an income tax basis	..	..	..	..	..	..	..	..	..	..
3000 Taxes on payroll and workforce	..	..	0	0	0	0	0	0	0	0
4000 Taxes on property	..	..	28	47	111	115	117	125	157	169
4100 Recurrent taxes on immovable property	..	..	20	33	67	66	60	54	62	67
4110 Households	..	..	..	..	..	..	..	..	..	..
4120 Others	..	..	..	..	..	..	..	..	..	..
4200 Recurrent taxes on net wealth	..	..	8	14	44	50	58	72	94	102
4210 Individual	..	..	0	0	0	0	0	0	0	0
4220 Corporate	..	..	8	14	44	50	58	72	94	102
4300 Estate, inheritance and gift taxes	..	..	0	0	0	0	0	0	0	0
4310 Estate and inheritance taxes	..	..	..	..	..	..	..	..	..	..
4320 Gift taxes	..	..	..	..	..	..	..	..	..	..
4400 Taxes on financial and capital transactions	..	..	0	0	0	0	0	0	0	0
4500 Other non-reccurrent taxes on property	..	..	0	0	0	0	0	0	0	0
4510 On net wealth	..	..	..	..	..	..	..	..	..	..
4520 Other non-recurrent taxes	..	..	..	..	..	..	..	..	..	..
4600 Other recurrent taxes on property	..	..	0	0	0	0	0	0	0	0
5000 Taxes on goods and services	..	..	568	1 125	2 465	2 393	2 161	2 341	2 976	3 960
5100 Taxes on production, sale, transfer, etc	..	..	508	1 048	2 288	2 206	1 990	2 129	2 686	3 671
5110 General taxes on goods and services	..	..	265	579	1 435	1 372	1 050	1 141	1 619	2 196
5111 Value added taxes	..	..	265	579	1 435	1 372	1 050	1 141	1 619	2 196
Domestic VAT	..	..	108	208	574	551	485	558	734	898
Import VAT	..	..	199	423	938	917	672	684	1 032	1 412
VAT refunds	..	..	-42	-51	-76	-95	-107	-102	-148	-114
5112 Sales tax	..	..	0	0	0	0	0	0	0	0
5113 Other	..	..	0	0	0	0	0	0	0	0
5120 Taxes on specific goods and services	..	..	243	469	853	835	941	989	1 067	1 475
5121 Excises	..	..	140	276	460	466	604	641	532	768
Alcoholic drinks (excluding beer)	..	..	48	93	228	261	210	222	247	269
Beer	..	..	7	17	32	36	28	27	27	29
Tobacco	..	..	10	11	40	46	32	33	33	29
Vehicles	..	..	39	55	104	90	44	27	89	214
Fuel and gasoline	..	..	36	100	56	34	291	332	137	227
5122 Profits of fiscal monopolies	..	..	0	0	0	0	0	0	0	0
5123 Customs and import duties	..	..	96	193	381	355	321	328	512	682
5124 Taxes on exports	..	..	6	0	0	0	0	0	0	0
5125 Taxes on investment goods	..	..	0	0	0	0	0	0	0	0
5126 Taxes on specific services	..	..	0	0	11	13	16	19	23	25
5127 Other taxes on internat. trade and transactions	..	..	0	0	0	0	0	0	0	0
5128 Other taxes	..	..	0	0	0	0	0	0	0	0
5130 Unallocable between 5110 and 5120	..	..	0	0	0	0	0	0	0	0
5200 Taxes on use of goods and to perform activities	..	..	60	77	177	187	171	212	290	289
5210 Recurrent taxes	..	..	60	74	112	109	157	192	253	247
5211 Paid by households: motor vehicles	..	..	6	10	26	28	29	32	36	38

	1997	2000	2007	2010	2013	2014	2015	2016	2017	2018
5212 Paid by others: motor vehicles	..	..	0	0	0	0	0	0	0	0
5213 Paid in respect of other goods	..	..	54	63	87	80	128	160	218	208
5220 Non-recurrent taxes	..	..	0	3	65	78	14	20	37	42
5300 Unallocable between 5100 and 5200	..	..	0	0	0	0	0	0	0	0
6000 Other taxes	..	..	**0**	**0**	**0**	**0**	**0**	**0**	**0**	**0**
6100 Paid solely by business	..	..	..	..	..	..	..	..	..	..
6200 Other	..	..	..	..	..	..	..	..	..	..

Note: Year ending December 31st.
    The data are on a cash basis.
Source: Ministry of Finance of Mongolia.

StatLink https://stat.link/nez1hq

Table 4.12. Nauru
Details of tax revenue
Thousand AUD

	1997	2000	2007	2010	2013	2014	2015	2016	2017	2018
Total tax revenue	..	..	..	..	..	9 552	24 106	21 459	42 087	56 565
1000 Taxes on income, profits and capital gains	..	..	..	..	..	0	12 593	12 590	27 320	39 731
1100 Of individuals	..	..	..	..	..	0	0	0	0	0
1110 On income and profits	..	..	..	..	..	0	0	0	0	0
1120 On capital gains	..	..	..	..	..	0	0	0	0	0
1200 Corporate	..	..	..	..	..	0	0	0	0	0
1210 On profits	..	..	..	..	..	..	..	..	..	..
1220 On capital gains of corporates	..	..	..	..	..	..	..	..	..	..
1300 Unallocable between 1100 and 1200	..	..	..	..	..	0	12 593	12 590	27 320	39 731
Employment Services Tax	..	..	..	..	..	0	12 593	10 131	8 657	17 531
Business Tax	..	..	..	..	..	0	0	2 459	18 663	22 200
2000 Social security contributions	..	..	..	..	..	0	0	0	0	0
2100 Employees	..	..	..	..	..	..	..	..	..	..
2110 On a payroll basis	..	..	..	..	..	..	..	..	..	..
2120 On an income tax basis	..	..	..	..	..	..	..	..	..	..
2200 Employers	..	..	..	..	..	..	..	..	..	..
2210 On a payroll basis	..	..	..	..	..	..	..	..	..	..
2220 On an income tax basis	..	..	..	..	..	..	..	..	..	..
2300 Self-employed or non-employed	..	..	..	..	..	..	..	..	..	..
2310 On a payroll basis	..	..	..	..	..	..	..	..	..	..
2320 On an income tax basis	..	..	..	..	..	..	..	..	..	..
2400 Unallocable between 2100, 2200 and 2300	..	..	..	..	..	..	..	..	..	..
2410 On a payroll basis	..	..	..	..	..	..	..	..	..	..
2420 On an income tax basis	..	..	..	..	..	..	..	..	..	..
3000 Taxes on payroll and workforce	..	..	..	..	..	0	0	0	0	0
4000 Taxes on property	..	..	..	..	..	0	0	0	0	0
4100 Recurrent taxes on immovable property	..	..	..	..	..	..	..	..	..	..
4110 Households	..	..	..	..	..	..	..	..	..	..
4120 Others	..	..	..	..	..	..	..	..	..	..
4200 Recurrent taxes on net wealth	..	..	..	..	..	..	..	..	..	..
4210 Individual	..	..	..	..	..	..	..	..	..	..
4220 Corporate	..	..	..	..	..	..	..	..	..	..
4300 Estate, inheritance and gift taxes	..	..	..	..	..	..	..	..	..	..
4310 Estate and inheritance taxes	..	..	..	..	..	..	..	..	..	..
4320 Gift taxes	..	..	..	..	..	..	..	..	..	..
4400 Taxes on financial and capital transactions	..	..	..	..	..	..	..	..	..	..
4500 Other non-reccurrent taxes on property	..	..	..	..	..	..	..	..	..	..
4510 On net wealth	..	..	..	..	..	..	..	..	..	..
4520 Other non-recurrent taxes	..	..	..	..	..	..	..	..	..	..
4600 Other recurrent taxes on property	..	..	..	..	..	..	..	..	..	..
5000 Taxes on goods and services	..	..	..	..	..	9 552	11 513	8 869	14 767	16 834
5100 Taxes on production, sale, transfer, etc	..	..	..	..	..	8 747	10 747	8 200	14 011	15 750
5110 General taxes on goods and services	..	..	..	..	..	0	0	0	0	0
5111 Value added taxes	..	..	..	..	..	..	..	..	..	..
5112 Sales tax	..	..	..	..	..	..	..	..	..	..
5113 Other	..	..	..	..	..	..	..	..	..	..
5120 Taxes on specific goods and services	..	..	..	..	..	8 747	10 747	8 200	14 011	15 750
5121 Excises	..	..	..	..	..	0	0	0	0	0
5122 Profits of fiscal monopolies	..	..	..	..	..	0	0	0	0	0
5123 Customs and import duties	..	..	..	..	..	7 581	8 271	5 121	12 055	10 000
5124 Taxes on exports	..	..	..	..	..	0	0	0	0	0
5125 Taxes on investment goods	..	..	..	..	..	0	0	0	0	0
5126 Taxes on specific services	..	..	..	..	..	1 166	2 476	3 079	1 955	5 750
DCA Departure tax	..	..	..	..	..	286	579	615	259	1 747
DCA Pax levy	..	..	..	..	..	278	991	689	289	1 846
Telecom tax	..	..	..	..	..	602	906	1 775	1 407	2 158
5127 Other taxes on internat. trade and transactions	..	..	..	..	..	0	0	0	0	0
5128 Other taxes	..	..	..	..	..	0	0	0	0	0
5130 Unallocable between 5110 and 5120	..	..	..	..	..	0	0	0	0	0
5200 Taxes on use of goods and to perform activities	..	..	..	..	..	805	766	670	757	1 084
5210 Recurrent taxes	..	..	..	..	..	213	228	286	334	455
5211 Paid by households: motor vehicles	..	..	..	..	..	0	0	0	0	0
5212 Paid by others: motor vehicles	..	..	..	..	..	0	0	0	0	32
5213 Paid in respect of other goods	..	..	..	..	..	213	228	286	334	423
5220 Non-recurrent taxes	..	..	..	..	..	592	538	384	423	629
5300 Unallocable between 5100 and 5200	..	..	..	..	..	0	0	0	0	0
6000 Other taxes	..	..	..	..	..	0	0	0	0	0

	1997	2000	2007	2010	2013	2014	2015	2016	2017	2018
6100 Paid solely by business	..	..	..	..	..	..	..	..	..	..
6200 Other	..	..	..	..	..	..	..	..	..	..

Note: Data are on a fiscal year basis beginning 1st July. For example, the data for 2018 represent the period from July 2018 to July 2019.
The data are on a cash basis.
Source: Nauru Revenue Office.

StatLink https://stat.link/dsrit3

Table 4.13. New Zealand

Details of tax revenue

Million NZD

	1997	2000	2007	2010	2013	2014	2015	2016	2017	2018
Total tax revenue	**35 560**	**39 765**	**64 046**	**62 310**	**72 187**	**76 609**	**81 500**	**86 601**	**92 661**	**98 056**
1000 Taxes on income, profits and capital gains	**21 260**	**23 861**	**40 308**	**33 494**	**39 415**	**41 818**	**44 724**	**48 134**	**51 505**	**54 482**
1100 Of individuals	15 669	17 126	26 965	23 519	26 555	28 726	30 298	31 869	35 020	36 154
1110 On income and profits	15 669	17 126	26 965	23 519	26 555	28 726	30 298	31 869	35 020	36 154
1120 On capital gains	0	0	0	0	0	0	0	0	0	0
1200 Corporate	3 926	4 914	9 069	7 609	10 344	10 250	11 407	13 461	13 584	15 317
1210 On profits	3 926	4 914	9 069	7 609	10 344	10 250	11 407	13 461	13 584	15 317
1220 On capital gains	0	0	0	0	0	0	0	0	0	0
1300 Unallocable between 1100 and 1200	1 665	1 821	4 274	2 366	2 516	2 842	3 019	2 804	2 901	3 011
NRWT	662	760	1 506	467	427	470	733	594	619	656
Property speculation	0	0	0	0	0	0	0	0	0	0
Absentee income tax	0	0	0	0	0	0	0	0	0	0
Interest	961	990	2 699	1 704	1 643	1 829	1 660	1 468	1 530	1 613
Dividends	42	71	69	195	446	543	626	742	752	742
Other	0	0	0	0	0	0	0	0	0	0
2000 Social security contributions	**0**	**0**	**0**	**0**	**0**	**0**	**0**	**0**	**0**	**0**
2100 Employees	0	0	0	0	0	0	0	0	0	0
2110 On a payroll basis	..	..	..	..	..	..	..	..	..	..
2120 On an income tax basis	..	..	..	..	..	..	..	..	..	..
2200 Employers	0	0	0	0	0	0	0	0	0	0
2210 On a payroll basis	..	..	..	..	..	..	..	..	..	..
2220 On an income tax basis	..	..	..	..	..	..	..	..	..	..
2300 Self-employed or non-employed	0	0	0	0	0	0	0	0	0	0
2310 On a payroll basis	..	..	..	..	..	..	..	..	..	..
2320 On an income tax basis	..	..	..	..	..	..	..	..	..	..
2400 Unallocable between 2100, 2200 and 2300	0	0	0	0	0	0	0	0	0	0
2410 On a payroll basis	..	..	..	..	..	..	..	..	..	..
2420 On an income tax basis	..	..	..	..	..	..	..	..	..	..
3000 Taxes on payroll and workforce	**0**	**0**	**0**	**0**	**0**	**0**	**0**	**0**	**0**	**0**
4000 Taxes on property	**1 918**	**2 112**	**3 417**	**4 119**	**4 585**	**4 793**	**5 046**	**5 257**	**5 543**	**5 862**
4100 Recurrent taxes on immovable property	1 732	2 049	3 322	4 031	4 492	4 693	4 962	5 178	5 436	5 764
Local govt rates and services	1 732	2 049	3 322	4 031	4 492	4 693	4 962	5 178	5 436	5 764
Land tax	0	0	0	0	0	0	0	0	0	0
4110 Households	..	..	..	..	..	..	..	..	..	..
4120 Others	..	..	..	..	..	..	..	..	..	..
4200 Recurrent taxes on net wealth	0	0	0	0	0	0	0	0	0	0
4210 Individual	..	..	..	..	..	..	..	..	..	..
4220 Corporate	..	..	..	..	..	..	..	..	..	..
4300 Estate, inheritance and gift taxes	0	2	3	2	0	0	0	0	0	0
4310 Estate and inheritance taxes	..	0	0	0	..	..	..	..	..	..
4320 Gift taxes	..	2	3	2	..	..	..	..	..	..
4400 Taxes on financial and capital transactions	186	61	92	86	93	100	84	79	107	98
Instrument duty	173	51	85	82	91	100	84	79	107	98
Cheque duty	13	10	7	4	2	0	0	0	0	0
4500 Non-recurrent taxes	0	0	0	0	0	0	0	0	0	0
4510 On net wealth	..	..	..	..	..	..	..	..	..	..
4520 Other non-recurrent taxes	..	..	..	..	..	..	..	..	..	..
4600 Other recurrent taxes on property	0	0	0	0	0	0	0	0	0	0
5000 Taxes on goods and services	**12 382**	**13 792**	**20 290**	**24 692**	**28 184**	**29 996**	**31 728**	**33 203**	**35 612**	**37 707**
5100 Taxes on production, sale, transfer, etc.	11 603	12 887	18 832	23 107	26 344	28 011	29 584	30 925	33 220	35 024
5110 General taxes	8 696	9 885	15 046	19 143	22 063	23 306	24 587	25 847	27 951	29 475
5111 Value added taxes	8 696	9 885	15 046	19 143	22 063	23 306	24 587	25 847	27 951	29 475
5112 Sales tax	0	0	0	0	0	0	0	0	0	0
Motor vehicles	..	..	..	..	..	..	..	..	..	..
Other sales tax	..	..	..	..	..	..	..	..	..	..
5113 Other	0	0	0	0	0	0	0	0	0	0
5120 Taxes on specific goods and services	2 907	3 002	3 786	3 964	4 281	4 705	4 997	5 078	5 269	5 549

	1997	2000	2007	2010	2013	2014	2015	2016	2017	2018
5121 Excise duties	2 018	2 148	1 627	1 782	1 854	2 050	2 280	2 231	2 214	2 455
On alcoholic beverages	439	436	573	622	650	651	672	684	699	725
Beer	218	201	290	207	250	253	262	265	265	275
Wine	106	100	163	181	204	216	216	218	227	235
Spirits	115	135	120	234	196	182	194	201	207	215
Tobacco	681	764	159	220	273	310	362	352	399	477
Motor vehicles	0	0	0	0	0	0	0	0	0	0
Refined sugar	0	0	0	0	0	0	0	0	0	0
CA petroleum fuels	786	810	819	872	865	1 018	1 185	1 137	1 057	1 184
NRF fuel excise	0	0	0	0	0	0	0	0	0	0
Local petroleum fuels	25	27	30	32	31	35	33	34	33	42
CA mileage tax	0	0	0	0	0	0	0	0	0	0
NRF mileage tax	0	0	0	0	0	0	0	0	0	0
Road user charges	0	0	0	0	0	0	0	0	0	0
Energy resources levy	87	111	46	36	35	36	28	24	26	27
5122 Profits of fiscal monopolies	0	0	0	0	0	0	0	0	0	0
5123 Customs and import duties	750	648	1 857	1 916	2 160	2 391	2 442	2 550	2 738	2 792
5124 Taxes on exports	0	0	0	0	0	0	0	0	0	0
5125 Taxes on investment goods	0	0	0	0	0	0	0	0	0	0
5126 Taxes on specific services	139	206	302	266	267	264	275	297	317	302
Lottery (national)	103	167	290	253	254	249	260	281	301	287
Lottery (overseas)	0	0	0	0	0	0	0	0	0	0
Racing	36	39	12	13	13	15	15	16	16	15
Film hire tax	0	0	0	0	0	0	0	0	0	0
Domestic air travel tax	0	0	0	0	0	0	0	0	0	0
5127 Other taxes on internat. trade and transactions	0	0	0	0	0	0	0	0	0	0
Foreign fishing vessels tax	..	..	..	..	..	..	..	..	..	..
Foreign travel tax	..	..	..	..	..	..	..	..	..	..
International departure tax	..	..	..	..	..	..	..	..	..	..
5128 Other taxes	0	0	0	0	0	0	0	0	0	0
5130 Unallocable between 5110 and 5120	0	0	0	0	0	0	0	0	0	0
5200 Taxes on use of goods and perform activities	779	905	1 458	1 585	1 840	1 985	2 144	2 278	2 392	2 683
5210 Recurrent taxes	779	905	1 458	1 585	1 840	1 985	2 144	2 278	2 392	2 683
Motor vehicle registration	158	181	226	172	187	181	214	223	227	236
Heavy traffic fees	466	532	851	1 016	1 205	1 283	1 381	1 469	1 551	1 655
Accident compensation levies	0	0	0	0	0	0	0	0	0	0
5211 Paid by households: motor vehicles	0	0	0	0	0	0	0	0	0	0
5212 Paid by others: motor vehicles	0	0	0	0	0	0	0	0	0	0
5213 Paid in respect of other goods	155	192	381	397	448	521	549	586	614	792
Local authority fees and charges	155	192	381	397	448	521	549	586	614	792
5220 Non-recurrent taxes	0	0	0	0	0	0	0	0	0	0
5300 Unallocable between 5100 and 5200	0	0	0	0	0	0	0	0	0	0
6000 Other taxes	**0**	**0**	**31**	**5**	**3**	**2**	**2**	**7**	**1**	**5**
6100 Paid solely by business	..	..	0	0	0	0	0	0	0	0
6200 Other	..	..	31	5	3	2	2	7	1	5

Note: For the years before 1989 data are on a fiscal year basis ending 31st March. The figures provided for 1989 and onwards relate to the financial year ending 30th June of the following year.

From 1993, data are on accrual basis.

Heading 1000: Tax credits to exporters under the export incentives schemes are non-wastable, but that part of the excess of tax liability paid out to taxpayers is not identifiable.

Heading 1100: The figures up to 1969 include revenues collected by a social security income tax. The base of this tax was the same as the ordinary income tax base and the two have now been incorporated into a single income tax.

Heading 5121: From October 1986 incorporates that portion of the selective impost on wine, spirits, tobacco and motor vehicles which was formerly collected and reported as sales tax. The revenue collected on those imported goods which are subject to the equivalent of the domestic excise has been classified as excise duty. In this respect, there is a discontinuity between the excises recorded before and after October 1986.

Heading 5210: The other local authority licence fees include some small items which could be regarded as non-tax revenues.

Heading for non-wastable tax credits 1110 comprises four Family assistance tax credits. The total in item 1100 is net of the tax expenditure component but not net of the transfer component.

Source: Local Authorities Statistics, Department of Statistics, Wellington.

StatLink ⫘ᴉ𝖘▸ https://stat.link/2zpkxm

Table 4.14. Papua New Guinea
Details of tax revenue
Million PGK

	1997	2000	2007	2010	2013	2014	2015	2016	2017	2018
Total tax revenue	..	..	5 875	6 573	8 773	10 373	9 142	8 606	8 986	9 983
1000 Taxes on income, profits and capital gains	..	936	4 287	4 562	5 878	6 983	5 956	5 286	5 474	6 119
1100 Of individuals	..	552	1 001	1 553	2 827	3 200	3 037	2 844	3 094	3 102
1110 On income and profits	..	552	1 001	1 553	2 827	3 200	3 037	2 844	3 094	3 102
1120 On capital gains	..	0	0	0	0	0	0	0	0	0
1200 Corporate	..	384	3 285	3 009	3 051	3 783	2 919	2 441	2 380	3 017
1210 On profits	..	384	3 285	3 009	3 051	3 783	2 919	2 441	2 380	3 017
Corporate Income Tax	..	262	724	1 201	2 067	2 629	2 375	2 094	1 950	1 933
Mining and Petroleum Tax	..	0	2 334	1 476	667	888	169	92	114	775
Royalty Tax and Management fee	..	4	5	10	28	37	18	44	43	44
Dividend witholding tax	..	54	204	279	245	186	195	133	182	155
Interest witholding tax	..	64	19	42	45	43	162	79	91	111
1220 On capital gains of corporates	..	..	..	..	..	..	..	..	..	..
1300 Unallocable between 1100 and 1200	..	0	0	0	0	0	0	0	0	0
2000 Social security contributions	..	0	0	0	0	0	0	0	0	0
2100 Employees	..	..	..	..	..	..	..	..	..	..
2110 On a payroll basis	..	..	..	..	..	..	..	..	..	..
2120 On an income tax basis	..	..	..	..	..	..	..	..	..	..
2200 Employers	..	..	..	..	..	..	..	..	..	..
2210 On a payroll basis	..	..	..	..	..	..	..	..	..	..
2220 On an income tax basis	..	..	..	..	..	..	..	..	..	..
2300 Self-employed or non-employed	..	..	..	..	..	..	..	..	..	..
2310 On a payroll basis	..	..	..	..	..	..	..	..	..	..
2320 On an income tax basis	..	..	..	..	..	..	..	..	..	..
2400 Unallocable between 2100, 2200 and 2300	..	..	..	..	..	..	..	..	..	..
2410 On a payroll basis	..	..	..	..	..	..	..	..	..	..
2420 On an income tax basis	..	..	..	..	..	..	..	..	..	..
3000 Taxes on payroll and workforce	..	1	2	2	6	16	0	14	11	9
4000 Taxes on property	..	44	85	65	67	137	51	79	42	100
4100 Recurrent taxes on immovable property	..	0	0	0	0	0	0	0	0	0
4110 Households	..	..	..	..	..	..	..	..	..	..
4120 Others	..	..	..	..	..	..	..	..	..	..
4200 Recurrent taxes on net wealth	..	0	0	0	0	0	0	0	0	0
4210 Individual	..	..	..	..	..	..	..	..	..	..
4220 Corporate	..	..	..	..	..	..	..	..	..	..
4300 Estate, inheritance and gift taxes	..	0	0	0	0	0	0	0	0	0
4310 Estate and inheritance taxes	..	..	..	..	..	..	..	..	..	..
4320 Gift taxes	..	..	..	..	..	..	..	..	..	..
4400 Taxes on financial and capital transactions	..	44	85	65	67	137	51	79	42	100
4500 Other non-reccurrent taxes on property	..	0	0	0	0	0	0	0	0	0
4510 On net wealth	..	..	..	..	..	..	..	..	..	..
4520 Other non-recurrent taxes	..	..	..	..	..	..	..	..	..	..
4600 Other recurrent taxes on property	..	0	0	0	0	0	0	0	0	0
5000 Taxes on goods and services	..	325	1 501	1 944	2 822	3 237	3 134	3 227	3 459	3 755
5100 Taxes on production, sale, transfer, etc	..	325	1 501	1 944	2 822	3 237	3 134	3 227	3 459	3 755
5110 General taxes on goods and services	..	325	654	874	1 388	1 636	1 637	1 646	1 617	1 642
5111 Value added taxes	..	321	648	865	1 379	1 623	1 571	1 638	1 581	1 622
Goods and services tax (inland Collection)	..	177	468	629	1 036	1 180	1 068	1 103	1 131	1 120
GST transfers to provinces	..	144	180	236	343	443	503	535	450	502
5112 Sales tax	..	0	0	0	0	0	0	0	0	0
5113 Other	..	4	6	9	9	13	66	8	36	20
5120 Taxes on specific goods and services	..	..	846	1 070	1 434	1 601	1 497	1 581	1 842	2 113
5121 Excises	..	..	455	611	814	889	802	876	1 105	1 168
5122 Profits of fiscal monopolies	..	0	0	0	0	0	0	0	0	0
5123 Customs and import duties	..	..	136	189	257	273	243	243	246	325
5124 Taxes on exports	..	..	155	174	212	275	316	294	297	392
5125 Taxes on investment goods	..	0	0	0	0	0	0	0	0	0
5126 Taxes on specific services	..	61	100	97	151	164	136	168	193	228
Gaming taxes	..	58	97	93	145	158	126	164	179	205
Departure tax	..	3	3	4	6	6	9	4	14	23
5127 Other taxes on internat. trade and transactions	..	0	0	0	0	0	0	0	0	0
5128 Other taxes	..	0	0	0	0	0	0	0	0	0
5130 Unallocable between 5110 and 5120	..	0	0	0	0	0	0	0	0	0
5200 Taxes on use of goods and to perform activities	..	0	0	0	0	0	0	0	0	0
5210 Recurrent taxes	..	..	..	..	..	..	..	..	..	..
5211 Paid by households: motor vehicles	..	..	..	..	..	..	..	..	..	..
5212 Paid by others: motor vehicles	..	..	..	..	..	..	..	..	..	..

	1997	2000	2007	2010	2013	2014	2015	2016	2017	2018
5213 Paid in respect of other goods	..	..	..	..	..	..	..	..	..	..
5220 Non-recurrent taxes	..	..	..	..	..	..	..	..	..	..
5300 Unallocable between 5100 and 5200	..	0	0	0	0	0	0	0	0	0
6000 Other taxes	..	**0**	**0**	**0**	**0**	**0**	**0**	**0**	**0**	**0**
6100 Paid solely by business	..	..	..	..	..	..	..	..	..	..
6200 Other	..	..	..	..	..	..	..	..	..	..

Note: Year ending 31st December.

The data are on a cash basis.

Figures exclude tax revenues collected by sub-national governments as the data are not available.

Total tax revenues are not available for 2000 and 2001 as the data are incomplete, and do not include customs revenues for these two years.

Source: Ministry of Treasury and Finance of Papua New Guinea.

StatLink ᐟᎮᏂᏚᏞ https://stat.link/ib1g3e

Table 4.15. Philippines
Details of tax revenue
Million PHP

	1997	2000	2007	2010	2013	2014	2015	2016	2017	2018
Total tax revenue	447 976	564 343	1 121 594	1 330 768	1 868 601	2 111 568	2 265 139	2 460 823	2 779 895	3 173 684
1000 Taxes on income, profits and capital gains	164 170	217 798	453 338	521 707	767 819	840 680	912 229	994 543	1 106 711	1 124 589
1100 Of individuals	59 749	83 006	141 673	167 605	246 894	283 873	309 439	344 081	391 049	386 748
1110 On income and profits	53 370	78 229	135 504	158 325	232 725	267 703	292 548	325 446	367 166	359 901
1120 On capital gains	6 379	4 777	6 170	9 280	14 169	16 170	16 891	18 635	23 883	26 847
1200 Corporate	95 449	116 980	282 504	326 967	486 898	523 183	569 485	619 067	683 929	700 990
1210 On profits	94 427	114 871	280 090	323 116	476 311	513 978	561 465	609 301	676 868	690 641
1220 On capital gains of corporates	1 022	2 110	2 414	3 851	10 587	9 205	8 020	9 766	7 061	10 348
1300 Unallocable between 1100 and 1200	8 973	17 812	29 160	27 135	34 027	33 624	33 305	31 395	31 732	36 851
2000 Social security contributions	36 500	74 200	131 830	168 430	236 575	284 360	319 106	343 545	372 420	433 580
2100 Employees	0	0	0	0	0	0	0	0	0	0
2110 On a payroll basis	..	..	..	..	..	..	..	..	..	..
2120 On an income tax basis	..	..	..	..	..	..	..	..	..	..
2200 Employers	2 800	19 900	26 520	34 300	54 662	80 130	97 598	101 003	111 496	128 526
2210 On a payroll basis	..	..	..	..	..	..	..	..	..	..
2220 On an income tax basis	..	..	..	..	..	..	..	..	..	..
2300 Self-employed or non-employed	0	0	0	0	0	0	0	0	0	0
2310 On a payroll basis	0	..	..	..	..	..	..	..	..	..
2320 On an income tax basis	0	..	..	..	..	..	..	..	..	..
2400 Unallocable between 2100, 2200 and 2300	33 700	54 300	105 310	134 130	181 913	204 230	221 508	242 542	260 925	305 054
2410 On a payroll basis	..	..	..	..	..	..	..	..	..	..
2420 On an income tax basis	..	..	..	..	..	..	..	..	..	..
3000 Taxes on payroll and workforce	..	..	..	..	..	..	..	..	..	..
4000 Taxes on property	4 178	17 401	32 354	39 070	56 269	60 026	63 982	66 265	78 269	81 373
4100 Recurrent taxes on immovable property	0	14 947	27 387	31 876	41 191	45 458	48 991	50 829	61 891	64 474
Real property tax (local government)	0	14 947	27 387	31 876	41 191	45 458	48 991	50 829	61 891	64 474
4110 Households	0	0	0	0	0	0	0	0	0	0
4120 Others	0	0	0	0	0	0	0	0	0	0
4200 Recurrent taxes on net wealth	0	0	0	0	0	0	0	0	0	0
4210 Individual	0	0	0	0	0	0	0	0	0	0
4220 Corporate	0	0	0	0	0	0	0	0	0	0
4300 Estate, inheritance and gift taxes	881	480	962	1 981	3 275	5 450	5 636	6 638	7 467	7 155
4310 Estate and inheritance taxes	677	302	650	1 451	1 650	3 489	3 341	4 723	5 001	3 654
4320 Gift taxes	204	178	312	531	1 625	1 960	2 294	1 915	2 466	3 501
4400 Taxes on financial and capital transactions	3 297	1 974	4 005	5 213	11 803	9 118	9 356	8 798	8 910	9 744
Stock transactions (RA 7717)	3 297	1 974	4 005	5 213	11 803	9 118	9 356	8 798	8 910	9 744
4500 Other non-reccurrent taxes on property	0	0	0	0	0	0	0	0	0	0
4510 On net wealth	0	0	0	0	0	0	0	0	0	0
4520 Other non-recurrent taxes	0	0	0	0	0	0	0	0	0	0
4600 Other recurrent taxes on property	0	0	0	0	0	0	0	0	0	0
5000 Taxes on goods and services	225 025	237 243	456 497	549 890	735 896	844 442	884 132	962 763	1 118 976	1 364 987
5100 Taxes on production, sale, transfer, etc	222 627	234 202	448 164	540 595	724 888	832 656	872 832	949 396	1 103 612	1 349 375
5110 General taxes on goods and services	47 273	53 879	145 013	173 284	250 149	278 794	295 502	331 414	365 235	358 169
5111 Value added taxes	47 273	53 879	145 013	173 284	250 149	278 794	295 502	331 414	365 235	358 169
5112 Sales tax	0	0	0	0	0	0	0	0	0	0
5113 Other	0	0	0	0	0	0	0	0	0	0
5120 Taxes on specific goods and services	175 354	180 323	303 151	367 312	474 739	553 862	577 330	617 982	738 376	991 206
5121 Excises	63 048	61 677	54 998	67 203	118 856	135 315	158 319	163 505	209 493	290 612
Alcohol products	13 412	12 997	18 786	21 781	33 535	37 525	42 214	50 272	61 050	68 809
Tobacco products	16 027	17 427	23 206	31 730	71 608	82 725	99 505	95 055	125 910	136 005
Petroleum products	29 272	28 297	10 036	9 832	8 503	9 419	11 888	13 111	15 512	39 002
Automobiles	0	0	0	0	2 542	2 636	2 452	3 128	4 308	5 814
Mineral products	77	243	942	1 306	2 494	2 814	2 079	1 758	2 251	4 918
Others	4 259	2 712	2 028	2 555	174	196	182	181	462	36 064
5122 Profits of fiscal monopolies	0	0	0	0	0	0	0	0	0	0
5123 Customs and import duties	94 800	95 006	209 439	259 241	304 925	369 277	367 534	396 365	458 184	593 111
5124 Taxes on exports	0	0	0	0	0	0	0	0	0	0
5125 Taxes on investment goods	0	0	0	0	0	0	0	0	0	0
5126 Taxes on specific services	17 506	23 639	38 714	40 868	50 958	49 270	51 477	58 111	70 700	107 483
Banks and financial institutions	9 696	9 538	19 434	22 857	30 199	26 677	26 915	29 602	33 471	33 087
Travel tax (CHED/NCAA)	386	1 043	1 581	1 512	1 885	1 827	1 770	1 694	2 894	3 084
Immigration tax (BID)	18	47	42	59	69	72	72	87	115	105
Other	7 406	13 011	17 657	16 440	18 805	20 694	22 720	26 728	34 220	71 207
5127 Other taxes on internat. trade and transactions	0	0	0	0	0	0	0	0	0	0
5128 Other taxes	0	0	0	0	0	0	0	0	0	0
5130 Unallocable between 5110 and 5120	0	0	0	0	0	0	0	0	0	0
5200 Taxes on use of goods and to perform activities	2 398	3 041	8 333	9 295	11 008	11 786	11 300	13 367	15 364	15 612

	1997	2000	2007	2010	2013	2014	2015	2016	2017	2018
5210 Recurrent taxes	2 398	3 041	8 333	9 295	11 008	11 786	11 300	13 367	15 364	15 612
LTO-Motor Vehicle Users' Tax	2 398	3 041	8 333	9 295	11 008	11 786	11 300	13 367	15 364	15 612
5211 Paid by households: motor vehicles	0	0	0	0	0	0	0	0	0	0
5212 Paid by others: motor vehicles	0	0	0	0	0	0	0	0	0	0
5213 Paid in respect of other goods	0	0	0	0	0	0	0	0	0	0
5220 Non-recurrent taxes	0	0	0	0	0	0	0	0	0	0
5300 Unallocable between 5100 and 5200	0	0	0	0	0	0	0	0	0	0
6000 Other taxes	**18 103**	**17 702**	**47 575**	**51 671**	**72 042**	**82 060**	**85 690**	**93 706**	**103 520**	**169 155**
6100 Paid solely by business	0	0	0	0	0	0	0	0	0	0
6200 Other	18 103	17 702	47 575	51 671	72 042	82 060	85 690	93 706	103 520	169 155
Documentary Stamp Tax	16 477	16 170	35 147	42 629	60 356	69 036	72 073	80 151	85 916	139 168
DENR-Forest charges	116	175	164	239	132	133	128	136	164	192
Miscellaneous taxes	1 510	1 356	8 944	4 391	5 874	6 051	6 219	5 888	9 086	19 708
Other taxes (local government)	0	0	3 319	4 412	5 679	6 840	7 270	7 531	8 354	10 086

Note: Year ending 31st December.

The data are on a cash basis.

Heading 5123: This category includes VAT on imports as well as excises levied on imports.

Source: Department of Finance of the Philippines.

StatLink ⧉ https://stat.link/a07run

Table 4.16. Samoa
Details of tax revenue
Million WST

	1997	2000	2007	2010	2013	2014	2015	2016	2017	2018
Total tax revenue	..	..	330	341	427	440	495	514	523	572
1000 Taxes on income, profits and capital gains	..	..	78	84	103	107	114	117	116	132
1100 Of individuals	..	..	42	46	58	59	64	69	68	68
1110 On income and profits	..	..	42	46	58	59	64	69	68	68
1120 On capital gains	..	..	0	0	0	0	0	0	0	0
1200 Corporate	..	..	36	38	45	48	51	48	48	64
1210 On profits	..	..	36	38	45	48	51	48	48	64
1220 On capital gains of corporates	..	..	0	0	0	0	0	0	0	0
1300 Unallocable between 1100 and 1200	..	..	0	0	0	0	0	0	0	0
2000 Social security contributions	..	..	0	0	0	0	0	0	0	0
2100 Employees	..	..	..	..	..	..	..	..	..	..
2110 On a payroll basis	..	..	..	..	..	..	..	..	..	..
2120 On an income tax basis	..	..	..	..	..	..	..	..	..	..
2200 Employers	..	..	..	..	..	..	..	..	..	..
2210 On a payroll basis	..	..	..	..	..	..	..	..	..	..
2220 On an income tax basis	..	..	..	..	..	..	..	..	..	..
2300 Self-employed or non-employed	..	..	..	..	..	..	..	..	..	..
2310 On a payroll basis	..	..	..	..	..	..	..	..	..	..
2320 On an income tax basis	..	..	..	..	..	..	..	..	..	..
2400 Unallocable between 2100, 2200 and 2300	..	..	..	..	..	..	..	..	..	..
2410 On a payroll basis	..	..	..	..	..	..	..	..	..	..
2420 On an income tax basis	..	..	..	..	..	..	..	..	..	..
3000 Taxes on payroll and workforce	..	..	0	0	0	0	0	0	0	0
4000 Taxes on property	..	..	2	0	0	0	0	0	0	0
4100 Recurrent taxes on immovable property	..	..	0	0	0	0	0	0	..	..
4110 Households	..	..	..	..	..	..	..	..	..	..
4120 Others	..	..	..	..	..	..	..	..	..	..
4200 Recurrent taxes on net wealth	..	..	0	0	0	0	0	0	0	0
4210 Individual	..	..	..	..	..	..	..	..	..	..
4220 Corporate	..	..	..	..	..	..	..	..	..	..
4300 Estate, inheritance and gift taxes	..	..	0	0	0	0	0	0	0	0
4310 Estate and inheritance taxes	..	..	..	..	..	..	..	..	..	..
4320 Gift taxes	..	..	..	..	..	..	..	..	..	..
4400 Taxes on financial and capital transactions	..	..	2	0	0	0	0	0	0	0
4500 Other non-reccurrent taxes on property	..	..	0	0	0	0	0	0	0	0
4510 On net wealth	..	..	..	..	..	..	..	..	..	..
4520 Other non-recurrent taxes	..	..	..	..	..	..	..	..	..	..
4600 Other recurrent taxes on property	..	..	0	0	0	0	0	0	..	..
5000 Taxes on goods and services	..	..	251	257	324	332	380	397	408	440
5100 Taxes on production, sale, transfer, etc	..	..	251	257	324	332	380	397	408	440
5110 General taxes on goods and services	..	..	126	119	170	177	200	198	209	229
5111 Value added taxes	..	..	126	119	170	177	200	198	209	229
VAGST on Imports	..	..	100	0	0	0	0	0	..	..
VAGST on sales of goods and services	..	..	26	0	0	0	0	0	..	..
5112 Sales tax	..	..	0	0	0	0	0	0	0	0
5113 Other	..	..	0	0	0	0	0	0	0	0
5120 Taxes on specific goods and services	..	..	125	137	154	155	181	199	199	211
5121 Excises	..	..	78	95	96	99	120	134	127	133
Petroleum Levy	..	..	3	..	..	..	..	..	..	..
Import Excise	..	..	29	..	..	..	..	..	..	..
Domestic Excise	..	..	47	..	..	..	..	..	..	..
5122 Profits of fiscal monopolies	..	..	0	0	0	0	0	0	0	0
5123 Customs and import duties	..	..	43	38	53	50	54	55	59	63
5124 Taxes on exports	..	..	0	0	0	0	0	0	0	0
5125 Taxes on investment goods	..	..	0	0	0	0	0	0	0	0
5126 Taxes on specific services	..	..	4	4	5	6	6	10	13	15
5127 Other taxes on internat. trade and transactions	..	..	0	0	0	0	0	0	0	0
5128 Other taxes	..	..	0	0	0	0	0	0	0	0
5130 Unallocable between 5110 and 5120	..	..	0	0	0	0	0	0	0	0
5200 Taxes on use of goods and to perform activities	..	..	0	0	0	0	0	0	0	0
5210 Recurrent taxes	..	..	..	..	..	..	..	..	..	..
5211 Paid by households: motor vehicles	..	..	..	..	..	..	..	..	..	..
5212 Paid by others: motor vehicles	..	..	..	..	..	..	..	..	..	..
5213 Paid in respect of other goods	..	..	..	..	..	..	..	..	..	..
5220 Non-recurrent taxes	..	..	..	..	..	..	..	..	..	..
5300 Unallocable between 5100 and 5200	..	..	0	0	0	0	0	0	0	0
6000 Other taxes	..	..	0	0	0	0	0	0	0	0

	1997	2000	2007	2010	2013	2014	2015	2016	2017	2018
6100 Paid solely by business	..	..	..	..	..	..	..	..	..	..
6200 Other	..	..	..	..	..	..	..	..	..	..

Note: Data are reported on a fiscal year basis beginning 1st July. For example, the data for 2018 represent the period from July 2018 to June 2019.

The data are on a cash basis.

Figures exclude tax revenues collected by sub-national governments as the data are not available.

The data from 2009 were provided on the basis of the IMF's GFSM 2014 classification. Prior to this year, data were provided on a different basis. The differences between the two sets of data are indicated below for the relevant tax revenue categories.

Heading 1000: Income tax revenues from 2009 onwards are net of income tax refunds. Prior to 2009, the income tax revenue figures are gross of refunds

Heading 5111: VAGST revenues from 2009 onwards net of aid, loan payments by Treasury and VAGST paid by Government departments.

Heading 5123: Import duty from 2009 onwards is net of aid and loan payments by Treasury.

Heading 5126: Data from 2009 include revenues from fisheries' licences. Fisheries' licences revenues are usually classified as non-tax revenues according to the OECD classification set out in Annex A of the Interpretative Guide, but could not be distinguished from other revenues from taxes on specific services.

Source: Bureau of Statistics of Samoa.

StatLink https://stat.link/wtq6k5

Table 4.17. Singapore

Details of tax revenue

Million SGD

	1997	2000	2007	2010	2013	2014	2015	2016	2017	2018
Total tax revenue	..	25 627	36 630	41 848	51 146	54 110	55 647	58 699	66 363	66 203
1000 Taxes on income, profits and capital gains	..	13 538	16 621	18 687	22 050	23 940	24 890	26 378	32 065	30 818
1100 Of individuals	..	3 543	4 537	6 470	7 688	8 927	9 235	10 526	10 724	11 706
1110 On income and profits	..	3 543	4 537	6 470	7 688	8 927	9 235	10 526	10 724	11 706
1120 On capital gains	..	0	0	0	0	0	0	0	0	0
1200 Corporate	..	9 509	10 934	11 260	13 209	13 887	14 253	14 378	19 810	17 523
1210 On profits	..	9 509	10 934	11 260	13 209	13 887	14 253	14 378	19 810	17 523
From corporate profits	..	8 316	9 250	10 687	12 680	13 372	13 815	13 602	14 944	16 032
Statutory board contributions	..	1 192	1 683	573	530	516	438	776	4 866	1 491
1220 On capital gains	..	0	0	0	0	0	0	0	0	0
1300 Unallocable between 1100 and 1200	..	486	1 150	957	1 152	1 126	1 402	1 474	1 532	1 590
Withholding taxes	..	486	1 150	957	1 152	1 126	1 402	1 474	1 532	1 590
2000 Social security contributions	..	0	0	0	0	0	0	0	0	0
2100 Employees	..	..	..	..	..	..	..	..	..	..
2110 On a payroll basis	..	..	..	..	..	..	..	..	..	..
2120 On an income tax basis	..	..	..	..	..	..	..	..	..	..
2200 Employers	..	..	..	..	..	..	..	..	..	..
2210 On a payroll basis	..	..	..	..	..	..	..	..	..	..
2220 On an income tax basis	..	..	..	..	..	..	..	..	..	..
2300 Self-employed or non-employed	..	..	..	..	..	..	..	..	..	..
2310 On a payroll basis	..	..	..	..	..	..	..	..	..	..
2320 On an income tax basis	..	..	..	..	..	..	..	..	..	..
2400 Unallocable between 2100, 2200 and 2300	..	..	..	..	..	..	..	..	..	..
2410 On a payroll basis	..	..	..	..	..	..	..	..	..	..
2420 On an income tax basis	..	..	..	..	..	..	..	..	..	..
3000 Taxes on payroll and workforce	..	0	0	0	0	0	0	0	0	0
4000 Taxes on property	..	2 863	6 259	6 080	8 112	7 124	7 224	7 638	9 345	9 256
4100 Recurrent taxes on immovable property	..	1 535	2 428	2 798	4 179	4 340	4 456	4 359	4 440	4 649
4110 Households	..	..	..	..	..	..	..	..	..	..
4120 Others	..	..	..	..	..	..	..	..	..	..
4200 Recurrent taxes on net wealth	..	0	0	0	0	0	0	0	0	0
4210 Individual	..	..	..	..	..	..	..	..	..	..
4220 Corporate	..	..	..	..	..	..	..	..	..	..
4300 Estate, inheritance and gift taxes	..	71	154	5	3	1	-1	0	0	0
4310 Estate and inheritance taxes	..	71	154	5	3	1	-1	0	0	0
4320 Gift taxes	..	0	0	0	0	0	0	0	0	0
4400 Taxes on financial and capital transactions	..	1 257	3 677	3 277	3 930	2 784	2 769	3 278	4 905	4 607
4500 Non-recurrent taxes	..	0	0	0	0	0	0	0	0	0
4510 On net wealth	..	..	..	..	..	..	..	..	..	..
4520 Other non-recurrent taxes	..	..	..	..	..	..	..	..	..	..
4600 Other recurrent taxes on property	..	0	0	0	0	0	0	0	0	0
5000 Taxes on goods and services	..	7 967	12 053	14 376	15 736	16 949	17 657	18 638	18 933	19 499
5100 Taxes on production, sale, transfer, etc	..	5 462	9 864	12 525	14 081	15 346	15 897	16 490	16 781	16 876
5110 General taxes	..	2 121	6 165	8 198	9 513	10 215	10 345	11 078	10 960	11 137
5111 Value added taxes	..	2 121	6 165	8 198	9 513	10 215	10 345	11 078	10 960	11 137
5112 Sales tax	..	0	0	0	0	0	0	0	0	0
5113 Other	..	0	0	0	0	0	0	0	0	0
5120 Taxes on specific goods and services	..	3 341	3 699	4 327	4 568	5 131	5 552	5 412	5 821	5 739
5121 Excises	..	1 847	1 985	2 048	2 189	2 540	2 833	2 730	3 133	3 075
Liquors	..	..	414	470	518	634	638	640	663	678
Tobacco	..	..	700	889	1 043	1 228	1 205	986	1 174	1 122
Petroleum Products	..	..	386	419	414	419	584	596	827	784
Motor Vehicles	..	..	483	267	206	251	399	502	463	486
Compressed Natural Gas Unit Duty	..	..	0	0	3	3	2	1	1	0
Others	..	..	3	5	5	6	5	5	5	6
5122 Profits of fiscal monopolies	..	0	0	0	0	0	0	0	0	0
5123 Customs and import duties	..	..	..	..	..	..	..	..	..	..
5124 Taxes on exports	..	0	0	0	0	0	0	0	0	0
5125 Taxes on investment goods	..	0	0	0	0	0	0	0	0	0
5126 Taxes on specific services	..	1 494	1 714	2 279	2 379	2 591	2 719	2 682	2 688	2 664
Betting duty	..	1 494	1 714	2 279	2 379	2 591	2 719	2 682	2 688	2 664
5127 Other taxes on internat. trade and transactions	..	0	0	0	0	0	0	0	0	0
5128 Other taxes	..	0	0	0	0	0	0	0	0	0
5130 Unallocable between 5110 and 5120	..	0	0	0	0	0	0	0	0	0
5200 Taxes on use of goods and perform activities	..	2 506	2 189	1 851	1 655	1 603	1 760	2 148	2 153	2 623
5210 Recurrent taxes	..	..	..	..	..	..	..	..	..	..
5211 Paid by households: motor vehicles	..	..	..	..	..	..	..	..	..	..

	1997	2000	2007	2010	2013	2014	2015	2016	2017	2018
5212 Paid by others: motor vehicles	..	..	..	..	..	..	..	..	..	..
5213 Paid in respect of other goods	..	..	..	..	..	..	..	..	..	..
5220 Non-recurrent taxes	..	..	..	..	..	..	..	..	..	..
5300 Unallocable between 5100 and 5200	..	0	0	0	0	0	0	0	0	0
6000 Other taxes	..	**1 259**	**1 698**	**2 706**	**5 248**	**6 097**	**5 876**	**6 045**	**6 019**	**6 629**
6100 Paid solely by business	..	0	0	0	0	0	0	0	0	0
6200 Other	..	1 259	1 698	2 706	5 248	6 097	5 876	6 045	6 019	6 629

Note: Data are on a fiscal year basis ending 31st March. For example, the data for 2018 represent 1 April 2018 to 31 March 2019.

The data are on a cash basis.

Heading 2000: there are no social security contributions in Singapore.

Heading 4100: recurrent taxes on immovable property includes tax levied on all private properties, as well as properties owned by statutory boards.

Heading 5121: comprises excises, customs and import duties.

Source: Ministry of Finance of Singapore.

StatLink https://stat.link/0mcq26

Table 4.18. Solomon Islands
Details of tax revenue
Million SBD

	1997	2000	2007	2010	2013	2014	2015	2016	2017	2018
Total tax revenue	..	..	819	1 376	2 189	2 269	2 392	2 367	2 632	3 000
1000 Taxes on income, profits and capital gains	..	..	189	418	642	622	719	690	780	788
1100 Of individuals	..	..	141	280	403	404	437	411	491	501
1110 On income and profits	..	..	141	280	403	404	437	411	491	501
1120 On capital gains	..	..	0	0	0	0	0	0	0	0
1200 Corporate	..	..	48	137	239	218	283	278	289	288
1210 On profits	..	..	48	137	239	218	283	278	289	288
Dividend Withholding Tax (WHT)	..	..	14	41	87	74	118	106	114	86
Non-resident WHT	..	..	16	43	75	63	71	68	66	59
Resident WHT	..	..	19	53	78	81	94	105	110	143
1220 On capital gains of corporates	..	..	..	..	..	..	..	..	..	..
1300 Unallocable between 1100 and 1200	..	..	0	0	0	0	0	0	0	0
2000 Social security contributions	..	..	0	0	0	0	0	0	0	0
2100 Employees	..	..	..	..	..	..	..	..	..	..
2110 On a payroll basis	..	..	..	..	..	..	..	..	..	..
2120 On an income tax basis	..	..	..	..	..	..	..	..	..	..
2200 Employers	..	..	..	..	..	..	..	..	..	..
2210 On a payroll basis	..	..	..	..	..	..	..	..	..	..
2220 On an income tax basis	..	..	..	..	..	..	..	..	..	..
2300 Self-employed or non-employed	..	..	..	..	..	..	..	..	..	..
2310 On a payroll basis	..	..	..	..	..	..	..	..	..	..
2320 On an income tax basis	..	..	..	..	..	..	..	..	..	..
2400 Unallocable between 2100, 2200 and 2300	..	..	..	..	..	..	..	..	..	..
2410 On a payroll basis	..	..	..	..	..	..	..	..	..	..
2420 On an income tax basis	..	..	..	..	..	..	..	..	..	..
3000 Taxes on payroll and workforce	..	..	0	0	0	0	0	0	0	0
4000 Taxes on property	..	..	9	8	11	14	19	17	14	16
4100 Recurrent taxes on immovable property	..	..	0	0	0	0	0	0	0	0
4110 Households	..	..	..	..	..	..	..	..	..	..
4120 Others	..	..	..	..	..	..	..	..	..	..
4200 Recurrent taxes on net wealth	..	..	0	0	0	0	0	0	0	0
4210 Individual	..	..	..	..	..	..	..	..	..	..
4220 Corporate	..	..	..	..	..	..	..	..	..	..
4300 Estate, inheritance and gift taxes	..	..	0	0	0	0	0	0	0	0
4310 Estate and inheritance taxes	..	..	..	..	..	..	..	..	..	..
4320 Gift taxes	..	..	..	..	..	..	..	..	..	..
4400 Taxes on financial and capital transactions	..	..	9	8	11	14	19	17	14	16
4500 Other non-reccurrent taxes on property	..	..	0	0	0	0	0	0	0	0
4510 On net wealth	..	..	..	..	..	..	..	..	..	..
4520 Other non-recurrent taxes	..	..	..	..	..	..	..	..	..	..
4600 Other recurrent taxes on property	..	..	0	0	0	0	0	0	0	0
5000 Taxes on goods and services	..	..	621	951	1 536	1 633	1 654	1 660	1 838	2 196
5100 Taxes on production, sale, transfer, etc	..	..	616	944	1 527	1 619	1 638	1 643	1 821	2 180
5110 General taxes on goods and services	..	..	621	458	734	747	721	682	773	859
5111 Value added taxes	..	..	0	0	0	0	0	0	0	0
5112 Sales tax	..	..	283	458	734	747	721	682	773	859
5113 Other	..	..	0	0	0	0	0	0	0	0
5120 Taxes on specific goods and services	..	..	333	486	793	872	917	961	1 047	1 321
5121 Excises	..	..	53	106	138	158	144	163	173	233
Tobacco	..	..	29	59	79	96	89	95	109	139
Beer	..	..	23	34	55	59	49	61	63	93
Spirits	..	..	0	12	3	4	6	7	2	0
Other	..	..	0	0	0	0	0	0	0	0
5122 Profits of fiscal monopolies	..	..	0	0	0	0	0	0	0	0
5123 Customs and import duties	..	..	99	136	229	217	214	215	243	295
5124 Taxes on exports	..	..	182	245	426	496	560	582	631	794
Export duty on minerals	..	..	0	2	11	6	1	2	1	1
Export duty on shells	..	..	0	1	1	1	1	0	0	1
Export duty on fish	..	..	7	2	1	1	1	1	2	1
Export duty on timber/log	..	..	174	240	409	487	469	579	627	790
Export duty on other products	..	..	0	0	4	2	88	1	1	1
5125 Taxes on investment goods	..	..	0	0	0	0	0	0	0	0
5126 Taxes on specific services	..	..	0	0	0	0	0	0	0	0
5127 Other taxes on internat. trade and transactions	..	..	0	0	0	0	0	0	0	0
5128 Other taxes	..	..	0	0	0	0	0	0	0	0
5130 Unallocable between 5110 and 5120	..	..	0	0	0	0	0	0	0	0
5200 Taxes on use of goods and to perform activities	..	..	5	7	9	14	16	17	17	16

	1997	2000	2007	2010	2013	2014	2015	2016	2017	2018
5210 Recurrent taxes	..	..	5	7	9	14	16	17	17	16
5211 Paid by households: motor vehicles	..	..	0	0	0	0	0	0	0	0
5212 Paid by others: motor vehicles	..	..	0	0	0	0	0	0	0	0
5213 Paid in respect of other goods	..	..	5	7	9	14	16	17	17	16
5220 Non-recurrent taxes	..	..	0	0	0	0	0	0	0	0
5300 Unallocable between 5100 and 5200	..	..	0	0	0	0	0	0	0	0
6000 Other taxes	..	..	**0**	**0**	**0**	**0**	**0**	**0**	**0**	**0**
6100 Paid solely by business	..	..	..	..	..	..	..	..	..	..
6200 Other	..	..	..	..	..	..	..	..	..	..

Note: Year ending 31st December.

The data are on a cash basis.

Figures exclude tax revenues collected by sub-national governments as the data are not available.

Some revenues (e.g. customs fees, penalties) amounting to about 2.5 million in 2018 are considered as non-tax revenues according to the OECD classification, described in the interpretative guide in Annex A. The national classification of Solomon Islands classifies these revenues as tax revenues.

Source: Solomon Islands Ministry of Finance and Treasury.

StatLink ᠁ https://stat.link/lxi3bp

Table 4.19. Thailand

Details of tax revenue

Million THB

	1997	2000	2007	2010	2013	2014	2015	2016	2017	2018
Total tax revenue	..	**740 147**	**1 553 133**	**1 870 452**	**2 484 572**	**2 410 488**	**2 568 138**	**2 595 796**	**2 673 414**	**2 857 840**
1000 Taxes on income, profits and capital gains	..	**235 421**	**614 883**	**682 860**	**943 208**	**881 591**	**895 205**	**894 058**	**893 754**	**975 030**
1100 Of individuals	..	87 420	177 205	187 687	267 979	237 147	268 290	283 003	275 928	281 123
1110 On income and profits	..	0	0	0	0	0	0	0	0	0
1120 On capital gains	..	0	0	0	0	0	0	0	0	0
1200 Corporate	..	148 001	437 678	495 173	675 229	644 444	626 915	611 055	617 826	693 907
1210 On profits	..	0	0	0	0	0	0	0	0	0
1220 On capital gains of corporates	..	0	0	0	0	0	0	0	0	0
1300 Unallocable between 1100 and 1200	..	0	0	0	0	0	0	0	0	0
2000 Social security contributions	..	**27 073**	**79 809**	**132 394**	**103 112**	**128 174**	**144 803**	**145 693**	**153 488**	**162 127**
2100 Employees	..	12 704	37 717	0	46 633	58 031	66 027	68 574	70 993	75 249
2110 On a payroll basis	..	0	0	0	0	0	0	0	0	0
2120 On an income tax basis	..	0	0	0	0	0	0	0	0	0
2200 Employers	..	14 369	40 567	127 844	51 761	63 615	70 103	72 714	74 681	78 656
2210 On a payroll basis	..	0	0	0	0	0	0	0	0	0
2220 On an income tax basis	..	0	0	0	0	0	0	0	0	0
2300 Self-employed or non-employed	..	0	1 525	4 549	4 718	6 528	8 674	4 405	7 814	8 222
2310 On a payroll basis	..	0	0	0	0	0	0	0	0	0
2320 On an income tax basis	..	0	0	0	0	0	0	0	0	0
2400 Unallocable between 2100, 2200 and 2300	..	0	0	0	0	0	0	0	0	0
2410 On a payroll basis	..	0	0	0	0	0	0	0	0	0
2420 On an income tax basis	..	0	0	0	0	0	0	0	0	0
3000 Taxes on payroll and workforce	..	**0**	**0**	**0**	**0**	**0**	**0**	**0**	**0**	**0**
4000 Taxes on property	..	**16 283**	**18 317**	**24 666**	**57 579**	**62 627**	**68 157**	**60 364**	**73 946**	**78 533**
4100 Recurrent taxes on immovable property	..	9 094	18 317	24 592	23 749	32 396	33 530	33 751	37 955	38 166
4110 Households	..	0	0	0	0	0	0	0	0	0
4120 Others	..	0	0	0	0	0	0	0	0	0
4200 Recurrent taxes on net wealth	..	0	0	74	0	0	0	0	0	0
4210 Individual	..	0	0	0	0	0	0	0	0	0
4220 Corporate	..	0	0	0	0	0	0	0	0	0
4300 Estate, inheritance and gift taxes	..	0	0	0	0	0	0	0	65	218
4310 Estate and inheritance taxes	..	0	0	0	0	0	0	0	0	0
4320 Gift taxes	..	0	0	0	0	0	0	0	0	0
4400 Taxes on financial and capital transactions	..	7 189	0	0	33 830	30 231	34 627	26 613	35 927	40 149
4500 Other non-recurrent taxes on property	..	0	0	0	0	0	0	0	0	0
4510 On net wealth	..	0	0	0	0	0	0	0	0	0
4520 Other non-recurrent taxes	..	0	0	0	0	0	0	0	0	0
4600 Other recurrent taxes on property	..	0	0	0	0	0	0	0	0	0
5000 Taxes on goods and services	..	**457 826**	**829 490**	**1 016 829**	**1 364 677**	**1 322 691**	**1 442 296**	**1 477 287**	**1 533 483**	**1 621 189**
5100 Taxes on production, sale, transfer, etc	..	444 986	808 624	990 052	1 231 684	1 182 176	1 262 437	1 312 202	1 386 480	1 456 652
5110 General taxes on goods and services	..	171 113	319 655	388 856	509 847	527 902	535 121	558 192	584 342	633 623
5111 Value added taxes	..	169 425	319 655	388 856	509 847	527 902	535 121	558 192	584 342	633 623
5112 Sales tax	..	1 688	0	0	0	0	0	0	0	0
5113 Other	..	0	0	0	0	0	0	0	0	0
5120 Taxes on specific goods and services	..	273 873	488 969	601 197	721 838	654 274	727 316	754 010	802 138	823 029
5121 Excises	..	180 884	351 498	478 257	554 529	480 479	559 388	589 363	642 966	662 141
5122 Profits of fiscal monopolies	..	5 310	8 210	4 879	3 458	9 869	8 106	5 148	7 116	174
5123 Customs and import duties	..	84 902	87 440	92 675	109 798	105 270	100 156	97 400	90 485	93 665
5124 Taxes on exports	..	2 329	4 164	168	252	267	202	103	81	143
5125 Taxes on investment goods	..	0	0	0	0	0	0	0	0	0
5126 Taxes on specific services	..	448	37 657	25 218	53 801	58 388	59 463	61 996	61 490	66 905
5127 Other taxes on internat. trade and transactions	..	0	0	0	0	0	0	0	0	0
5128 Other taxes	..	0	0	0	0	0	0	0	0	0
5130 Unallocable between 5110 and 5120	..	0	0	0	0	0	0	0	0	0
5200 Taxes on use of goods and to perform activities	..	12 840	20 866	26 777	132 992	140 515	179 860	165 084	147 003	164 537
5210 Recurrent taxes	..	0	0	0	0	0	0	0	0	0
5211 Paid by households: motor vehicles	..	0	0	0	0	0	0	0	0	0
5212 Paid by others: motor vehicles	..	0	0	0	0	0	0	0	0	0
5213 Paid in respect of other goods	..	0	0	0	0	0	0	0	0	0
5220 Non-recurrent taxes	..	0	0	0	0	0	0	0	0	0
5300 Unallocable between 5100 and 5200	..	0	0	0	0	0	0	0	0	0
6000 Other taxes	..	**3 544**	**10 634**	**13 703**	**15 996**	**15 405**	**17 677**	**18 394**	**18 743**	**20 962**
6100 Paid solely by business	..	0	0	0	0	0	0	0	0	0
6200 Other	..	0	0	0	0	0	0	0	0	0

Note: Data are on a fiscal year basis ending 30th September. For example, the data for 2018 represents 1 October 2017 to 30 September 2018.

The data are on a cash basis. Tax revenues submitted by the Ministry of Finance for 2000 - 2012 are based on data gathered by the IMF.

Source: Ministry of Finance in Thailand.

StatLink https://stat.link/nimsyc

Table 4.20. Tokelau

Details of tax revenue
Thousand NZD

	1997	2000	2007	2010	2013	2014	2015	2016	2017	2018
Total tax revenue	..	..	**1 198**	**1 694**	**1 865**	**2 107**	**2 151**	**2 176**	**2 518**	**2 843**
1000 Taxes on income, profits and capital gains	..	..	**573**	**866**	**1 076**	**1 014**	**1 100**	**1 188**	**1 404**	**1 346**
1100 Of individuals	..	..	573	866	1 076	1 014	1 100	1 188	1 404	1 346
1110 On income and profits	..	..	..	..	..	..	..	..	..	..
1120 On capital gains	..	..	..	..	..	..	..	..	..	..
1200 Corporate	..	..	0	0	0	0	0	0	0	0
1210 On profits	..	..	..	..	..	..	..	..	..	..
1220 On capital gains of corporates	..	..	..	..	..	..	..	..	..	..
1300 Unallocable between 1100 and 1200	..	..	0	0	0	0	0	0	0	0
2000 Social security contributions	..	..	**0**	**0**	**0**	**0**	**0**	**0**	**0**	**0**
2100 Employees	..	..	..	..	..	..	..	..	..	..
2110 On a payroll basis	..	..	..	..	..	..	..	..	..	..
2120 On an income tax basis	..	..	..	..	..	..	..	..	..	..
2200 Employers	..	..	..	..	..	..	..	..	..	..
2210 On a payroll basis	..	..	..	..	..	..	..	..	..	..
2220 On an income tax basis	..	..	..	..	..	..	..	..	..	..
2300 Self-employed or non-employed	..	..	..	..	..	..	..	..	..	..
2310 On a payroll basis	..	..	..	..	..	..	..	..	..	..
2320 On an income tax basis	..	..	..	..	..	..	..	..	..	..
2400 Unallocable between 2100, 2200 and 2300	..	..	..	..	..	..	..	..	..	..
2410 On a payroll basis	..	..	..	..	..	..	..	..	..	..
2420 On an income tax basis	..	..	..	..	..	..	..	..	..	..
3000 Taxes on payroll and workforce	..	..	**0**	**0**	**0**	**0**	**0**	**0**	**0**	**0**
4000 Taxes on property	..	..	**0**	**0**	**0**	**0**	**0**	**0**	**0**	**0**
4100 Recurrent taxes on immovable property	..	..	..	..	..	..	..	..	..	..
4110 Households	..	..	..	..	..	..	..	..	..	..
4120 Others	..	..	..	..	..	..	..	..	..	..
4200 Recurrent taxes on net wealth	..	..	..	..	..	..	..	..	..	..
4210 Individual	..	..	..	..	..	..	..	..	..	..
4220 Corporate	..	..	..	..	..	..	..	..	..	..
4300 Estate, inheritance and gift taxes	..	..	..	..	..	..	..	..	..	..
4310 Estate and inheritance taxes	..	..	..	..	..	..	..	..	..	..
4320 Gift taxes	..	..	..	..	..	..	..	..	..	..
4400 Taxes on financial and capital transactions	..	..	..	..	..	..	..	..	..	..
4500 Other non-reccurrent taxes on property	..	..	..	..	..	..	..	..	..	..
4510 On net wealth	..	..	..	..	..	..	..	..	..	..
4520 Other non-recurrent taxes	..	..	..	..	..	..	..	..	..	..
4600 Other recurrent taxes on property	..	..	..	..	..	..	..	..	..	..
5000 Taxes on goods and services	..	..	**625**	**828**	**789**	**1 093**	**1 051**	**988**	**1 114**	**1 497**
5100 Taxes on production, sale, transfer, etc	..	..	625	828	789	1 093	1 051	988	1 114	1 497
5110 General taxes on goods and services	..	..	0	0	0	0	0	0	0	0
5111 Value added taxes	..	..	..	..	..	..	..	..	..	..
5112 Sales tax	..	..	..	..	..	..	..	..	..	..
5113 Other	..	..	..	..	..	..	..	..	..	..
5120 Taxes on specific goods and services	..	..	625	828	789	1 093	1 051	988	1 114	1 497
5121 Excises	..	..	624	827	767	1 091	1 050	984	1 104	1 489
Duty On Tobacco	..	..	258	379	395	600	558	539	702	966
Duty On Liqour	..	..	178	222	212	288	288	251	200	266
Duty On General Goods : resale	..	..	188	226	160	203	204	194	202	257
5122 Profits of fiscal monopolies	..	..	0	0	0	0	0	0	0	0
5123 Customs and import duties	..	..	0	0	0	0	0	0	0	0
5124 Taxes on exports	..	..	0	0	0	0	0	0	0	0
5125 Taxes on investment goods	..	..	0	0	0	0	0	0	0	0
5126 Taxes on specific services	..	..	1	1	22	2	1	4	10	8
5127 Other taxes on internat. trade and transactions	..	..	0	0	0	0	0	0	0	0
5128 Other taxes	..	..	0	0	0	0	0	0	0	0
5130 Unallocable between 5110 and 5120	..	..	0	0	0	0	0	0	0	0
5200 Taxes on use of goods and to perform activities	..	..	0	0	0	0	0	0	0	0
5210 Recurrent taxes	..	..	..	..	..	..	..	..	..	..
5211 Paid by households: motor vehicles	..	..	..	..	..	..	..	..	..	..
5212 Paid by others: motor vehicles	..	..	..	..	..	..	..	..	..	..
5213 Paid in respect of other goods	..	..	..	..	..	..	..	..	..	..
5220 Non-recurrent taxes	..	..	..	..	..	..	..	..	..	..
5300 Unallocable between 5100 and 5200	..	..	0	0	0	0	0	0	0	0
6000 Other taxes	..	..	**0**	**0**	**0**	**0**	**0**	**0**	**0**	**0**
6100 Paid solely by business	..	..	..	..	..	..	..	..	..	..
6200 Other	..	..	..	..	..	..	..	..	..	..

Note: Data are reported on a fiscal year basis beginning 1st July. For example, the data for 2018 represent the period from July 2018 to June 2019.
The data are on a cash basis.
Source: National Statistics Office of Tokelau.

StatLink https://stat.link/0k4nm3

Table 4.21. Vanuatu

Details of tax revenue

Million VUV

	1997	2000	2007	2010	2013	2014	2015	2016	2017	2018
Total tax revenue	..	6 098	10 267	11 089	13 049	13 737	13 477	13 324	16 249	17 976
1000 Taxes on income, profits and capital gains	..	0	0	0	0	0	0	0	0	0
1100 Of individuals	..	..	..	..	..	..	..	..	..	..
1110 On income and profits	..	..	..	..	..	..	..	..	..	..
1120 On capital gains	..	..	..	..	..	..	..	..	..	..
1200 Corporate	..	..	..	..	..	..	..	..	..	..
1210 On profits	..	..	..	..	..	..	..	..	..	..
1220 On capital gains of corporates	..	..	..	..	..	..	..	..	..	..
1300 Unallocable between 1100 and 1200	..	..	..	..	..	..	..	..	..	..
2000 Social security contributions	..	0	0	0	0	0	0	0	0	0
2100 Employees	..	..	..	..	..	..	..	..	..	..
2110 On a payroll basis	..	..	..	..	..	..	..	..	..	..
2120 On an income tax basis	..	..	..	..	..	..	..	..	..	..
2200 Employers	..	..	..	..	..	..	..	..	..	..
2210 On a payroll basis	..	..	..	..	..	..	..	..	..	..
2220 On an income tax basis	..	..	..	..	..	..	..	..	..	..
2300 Self-employed or non-employed	..	..	..	..	..	..	..	..	..	..
2310 On a payroll basis	..	..	..	..	..	..	..	..	..	..
2320 On an income tax basis	..	..	..	..	..	..	..	..	..	..
2400 Unallocable between 2100, 2200 and 2300	..	..	..	..	..	..	..	..	..	..
2410 On a payroll basis	..	..	..	..	..	..	..	..	..	..
2420 On an income tax basis	..	..	..	..	..	..	..	..	..	..
3000 Taxes on payroll and workforce	..	0	0	0	0	0	0	0	0	0
4000 Taxes on property	..	196	449	485	360	430	402	383	488	566
4100 Recurrent taxes on immovable property	..	..	..	..	..	..	..	..	..	..
4110 Households	..	..	..	..	..	..	..	..	..	..
4120 Others	..	..	..	..	..	..	..	..	..	..
4200 Recurrent taxes on net wealth	..	..	..	..	..	..	..	..	..	..
4210 Individual	..	..	..	..	..	..	..	..	..	..
4220 Corporate	..	..	..	..	..	..	..	..	..	..
4300 Estate, inheritance and gift taxes	..	..	..	..	..	..	..	..	..	..
4310 Estate and inheritance taxes	..	..	..	..	..	..	..	..	..	..
4320 Gift taxes	..	..	..	..	..	..	..	..	..	..
4400 Taxes on financial and capital transactions	..	..	..	..	..	..	..	..	..	..
4500 Other non-reccurrent taxes on property	..	..	..	..	..	..	..	..	..	..
4510 On net wealth	..	..	..	..	..	..	..	..	..	..
4520 Other non-recurrent taxes	..	..	..	..	..	..	..	..	..	..
4600 Other recurrent taxes on property	..	..	..	..	..	..	..	..	..	..
5000 Taxes on goods and services	..	5 902	9 818	10 603	12 688	13 307	13 075	12 941	15 761	17 411
5100 Taxes on production, sale, transfer, etc	..	5 902	9 818	8 829	9 985	10 427	10 898	10 708	13 024	14 714
5110 General taxes on goods and services	..	3 441	5 858	4 301	5 449	5 794	5 769	5 549	6 912	8 236
5111 Value added taxes	..	3 441	5 858	4 301	5 449	5 794	5 769	5 549	6 912	8 236
5112 Sales tax										
5113 Other	..									
5120 Taxes on specific goods and services	..	2 461	3 960	4 528	4 536	4 633	5 130	5 159	6 112	6 478
5121 Excises	..	76	554	1 882	1 898	1 976	2 180	2 219	2 578	2 784
5122 Profits of fiscal monopolies	..	..	..	..	..	..	..	..	..	..
5123 Customs and import duties	..	2 385	3 406	2 646	2 638	2 657	2 950	2 940	3 534	3 694
5124 Taxes on exports	..	..	..	..	..	..	..	..	..	..
5125 Taxes on investment goods	..	..	..	..	..	..	..	..	..	..
5126 Taxes on specific services	..	..	..	..	..	..	..	..	..	..
5127 Other taxes on internat. trade and transactions	..	..	..	..	..	..	..	..	..	..
5128 Other taxes	..	..	..	..	..	..	..	..	..	..
5130 Unallocable between 5110 and 5120	..	..	..	..	..	..	..	..	..	..
5200 Taxes on use of goods and to perform activities	..	0	0	0	0	0	0	0	0	0
5210 Recurrent taxes	..	..	..	..	..	..	..	..	..	..
5211 Paid by households: motor vehicles	..	..	..	..	..	..	..	..	..	..
5212 Paid by others: motor vehicles	..	..	..	..	..	..	..	..	..	..
5213 Paid in respect of other goods	..	..	..	..	..	..	..	..	..	..
5220 Non-recurrent taxes	..	..	..	..	..	..	..	..	..	..
5300 Unallocable between 5100 and 5200	..	0	0	1 774	2 703	2 880	2 177	2 233	2 737	2 697
6000 Other taxes	..	0	0	0	0	0	0	0	0	0
6100 Paid solely by business	..	..	..	..	..	..	..	..	..	..
6200 Other	..	..	..	..	..	..	..	..	..	..

Note: Year ending December 31st.The data are on a cash basis.
Source: Department of Finance and Treasury of Vanuatu.

StatLink ᵐᵉᵈ https://stat.link/6jse3l

5 Comparative and country tables, non-tax revenues, 2007-2018

Non-tax revenue tables, 2007-2017

In all of the following tables a ("..") indicates not available. The main series in this volume cover the years 2007 to 2018.

Complete series for the comparative tables are available on line at OECD (2020), "Revenue Statistics - Asian and Pacific Economies: Comparative tables", OECD Tax statistics (database). Full time series for the country tables can be accessed at https://stats.oecd.org/ within the theme Public Sector, Taxation and Market Regulation/Taxation/Revenue Statistics Asian and Pacific Economies.

Table 5.1. Total non-tax revenue as percentage of GDP in selected economies, 2008-18

	2008	2009	2010	2011	2012	2013	2014	2015	2016	2017	2018
Bhutan	25.5	26.5	21.9	21.5	16.6	20.6	14.8	17.7	15.0	16.4	12.9
Cook Islands	5.2	9.2	13.5	8.2	8.4	14.3	16.2	13.9	16.4	14.3	12.9
Fiji	0.0	0.0	2.6	3.3	2.8	2.7	2.9	2.9	3.2	3.5	3.6
Kazakhstan	1.6	1.2	1.2	1.6	2.2	1.3	0.7	0.5	1.4	1.2	1.7
Mongolia	6.4	7.9	6.5	7.4	6.9	7.2	7.8	6.3	5.1	4.3	4.6
Nauru	..	..	..	..	..	..	28.6	65.2	63.7	70.8	92.7
Papua New Guinea	4.1	3.5	4.7	3.3	3.1	2.4	3.1	3.2	3.2	3.2	3.6
Philippines	..	..	..	..	..	..	1.9	2.2	1.9	1.8	1.9
Samoa[1]	9.7	3.4	9.0	6.0	4.8	7.0	4.8	4.8	4.7	5.6	6.1
Thailand	2.9	2.9	3.3	2.7	2.8	2.9	3.1	3.5	3.6	3.5	3.7
Tokelau[2]	157.6	165.2	154.6	196.4	192.6	246.6	173.4	252.5	236.5	177.9	236.4
Vanuatu	6.5	7.0	8.3	5.9	5.2	4.2	5.8	14.8	9.6	14.2	18.2

.. Not available

Note: Figures include non-tax revenue data collected by sub-national governments for Kazakhstan, Mongolia and the Philippines. Figures exclude non-tax revenue collected by sub-national governments for the remaining economies as the data are not available.

1. The data prior to 2009 are reported on a different basis (for more information see Table 5.7).

2. Tokelau receives significant revenues from foreign vessels for access to Tokelau fishing waters. In the 2008 SNA, these revenues are recorded as part of GNI, but they do not add to GDP.

StatLink 🔗 https://stat.link/om2fjp

Table 5.2. Non-tax revenue of main headings as percentage of GDP in selected economies, 2018

	Grants	Property income	Sales of goods and services	Fines, penalties and forfeits	Miscellaneous and unidentified revenue
Bhutan	6.0	6.1	0.7	0.1	0.0
Cook Islands	6.0	5.2	0.6	0.4	0.7
Fiji	0.5	1.5	1.5	0.0	0.1
Kazakhstan	0.0	1.4	0.2	0.1	0.0
Mongolia	0.3	2.1	0.5	0.3	1.4
Nauru	0.0	46.1	36.0	0.0	10.6
Papua New Guinea	2.2	1.3	0.0	0.0	0.0
Philippines	0.0	0.8	0.5	0.0	0.6
Samoa	2.1	1.0	3.0	0.0	0.0
Thailand	0.0	1.9	1.3	0.1	0.3
Tokelau[1]	85.8	141.9	8.7	0.0	0.0
Vanuatu	6.1	0.0	0.0	0.0	12.1

Note: Figures include non-tax revenue data collected by sub-national governments for Kazakhstan, Mongolia and the Philippines. Figures exclude non-tax revenue collected by sub-national governments for the remaining economies as the data are not available.

1. Tokelau receives significant revenues from foreign vessels for access to Tokelau fishing waters. In the 2008 SNA, these revenues are recorded as part of GNI, but they do not add to GDP.

StatLink https://stat.link/alr3ib

Table 5.3. Non-tax revenue of main headings as percentage of total non-tax revenues in selected economies, 2018

	Grants	Property income	Sales of goods and services	Fines, penalties and forfeits	Miscellaneous and unidentified revenue
Bhutan	46.2	47.7	5.2	0.9	0.0
Cook Islands	46.7	40.0	4.5	3.3	5.6
Fiji	13.7	42.9	40.8	0.4	2.2
Kazakhstan	0.0	81.5	11.6	7.0	0.0
Mongolia	6.0	44.8	11.5	7.6	30.1
Nauru	0.0	49.7	38.9	0.0	11.4
Papua New Guinea	62.6	36.3	1.1	0.1	0.0
Philippines	0.0	40.5	26.9	0.0	32.6
Samoa	33.8	16.0	50.1	0.1	0.0
Thailand	0.4	51.9	36.4	2.9	8.3
Tokelau	36.3	60.0	3.7	0.0	0.0
Vanuatu	33.6	0.0	0.0	0.0	66.4

Note: Figures include non-tax revenue data collected by sub-national governments for Kazakhstan, Mongolia and the Philippines. They exclude non-tax revenue collected by sub-national governments as the data are not available for the remaining economies.

StatLink ⟪📊⟫ https://stat.link/3ze2na

Table 5.4. Total non-tax revenue in selected economies in millions of US dollars at market exchange rates

	2008	2009	2010	2011	2012	2013	2014	2015	2016	2017	2018
Bhutan	366.7	370.2	364.0	423.3	326.3	411.9	295.5	391.1	344.4	407.1	349.9
Cook Islands	12.3	19.8	33.1	23.2	24.6	43.2	55.0	42.7	53.2	51.3	49.1
Fiji	0.0	0.2	89.8	135.4	118.6	121.0	142.9	134.7	158.0	187.6	199.0
Kazakhstan	2 185.9	1 437.0	1 803.1	3 041.6	4 537.6	3 020.8	1 501.3	909.3	1 855.8	2 073.7	3 108.5
Mongolia	360.4	360.1	470.4	772.7	851.1	902.0	948.6	740.4	566.0	494.6	602.5
Nauru	..	..	..	..	..	..	30.1	56.8	63.8	77.6	114.9
Papua New Guinea	475.8	407.3	671.6	588.5	657.6	513.0	718.5	703.0	658.8	753.3	894.8
Philippines	..	..	..	..	..	..	5 380.0	6 356.5	5 795.3	5 688.2	6 446.1
Samoa	65.8	20.6	61.8	44.1	36.8	54.7	39.8	40.4	38.2	47.1	53.5
Thailand	8 444.1	8 095.9	11 153.4	10 084.7	11 074.1	12 270.1	12 658.7	14 144.7	15 005.6	16 191.8	18 712.0
Tokelau	10.5	9.9	10.7	15.9	16.5	23.3	17.8	25.1	24.5	22.4	25.8
Vanuatu	38.9	42.5	56.4	44.7	40.3	33.7	47.6	114.4	76.3	125.0	167.2

.. Not available

Note: This table is derived by dividing the total non-tax revenue figures for each country (in millions of national currency) by the exchange rate figures shown in Table 3.20.

StatLink https://stat.link/qvmyne

Table 5.5. Bhutan

Details of non-tax revenue
Million BTN

	2008	2009	2010	2011	2012	2013	2014	2015	2016	2017	2018
Total non-tax revenue	**14 802**	**17 689**	**16 981**	**19 188**	**16 404**	**22 598**	**18 163**	**24 270**	**22 838**	**26 865**	**22 740**
Grants	6 575	11 119	10 498	12 502	9 563	14 236	9 955	14 890	12 987	14 847	10 516
Property income	4 944	5 841	5 627	5 949	6 083	7 573	7 288	8 295	8 748	10 763	10 838
Rents and royalties	757	681	711	1 115	1 231	1 382	1 564	1 565	1 938	3 855	4 640
Interest and dividends	4 186	5 160	4 915	4 834	4 852	6 191	5 724	6 729	6 810	6 907	6 198
Druk Holding and Investments (DHI) dividends	0	1 444	1 470	1 500	1 552	1 800	1 812	3 781	4 037	4 020	3 349
DGPC dividends	1 597	1 570	1 519	1 439	1 479	1 969	1 877	0	0	0	0
Other dividends	318	5	8	8	5	10	4	5	5	41	57
Net surplus transfers from the Royal Monetary Authority (RMA)	576	447	187	223	0	0	0	789	874	1 001	1 550
Interest receipt from corporations	1 695	1 694	1 731	1 664	1 816	2 412	2 031	2 155	1 895	1 846	1 242
Other property income	0	0	0	0	0	0	0	0	0	0	0
Sales of goods and services	3 250	698	838	669	674	707	805	993	1 026	1 148	1 186
Fines, penalties and forfeits	0	0	0	0	0	0	0	92	77	108	200
Miscellaneous and unidentified revenue	34	32	19	69	84	81	115	0	0	0	0
Total tax and non-tax revenue	20 462	26 606	27 797	32 675	30 496	37 305	34 881	42 685	42 361	49 269	44 486

Note: Data are reported on a fiscal year basis beginning 1st July. For example, the data for 2018 represent the period from July 2018 to June 2019.
The data are on a cash basis.
Source: Ministry of Finance, Bhutan.

StatLink ᵐᵃᵛˢᵖ https://stat.link/mzqfhg

Table 5.6. Cook Islands
Details of non-tax revenue
Thousand NZD

	2008	2009	2010	2011	2012	2013	2014	2015	2016	2017	2018
Total non-tax revenue	17 270	31 279	45 942	29 270	30 322	52 704	66 251	60 999	76 336	72 214	70 821
Grants	6 003	12 807	22 411	16 808	17 908	32 018	44 449	35 902	47 172	47 449	33 060
Crown Aid Revenue	0	0	0	0	0	0	0	1 000	1 877	0	0
OIDGF Aid Fund	109	348	306	1	0	27 374	22 619	0	7 730	0	0
NZODA Revenue	4 907	10 412	20 123	15 617	15 508	0	8 645	20 889	26 081	25 021	21 876
AusAid Revenue	0	0	0	0	0	0	0	498	84	2 250	66
UNESCO Revenue	47	48	0	0	1	86	87	84	110	1 371	0
UNDP Revenue	607	220	619	301	424	507	1 122	1 559	206	2 302	2 183
EU Revenue	0	78	179	187	91	1 929	955	603	6 826	6 587	945
Other	334	1 702	1 183	701	1 884	2 121	11 021	11 269	4 258	9 918	7 989
Property income	7 219	7 421	9 327	8 542	8 994	10 839	15 613	11 307	21 366	18 680	28 321
Rents and royalties	1 091	2 844	3 528	3 872	4 877	5 503	10 887	7 714	18 057	12 797	20 522
Fishing Licences	1 091	2 844	3 528	3 872	4 196	1 855	8 064	7 714	14 197	7 651	15 164
Fisheries Catch Revenue	0	0	0	0	0	2 877	1 777	0	2 312	255	0
Fisheries - US Treaties	0	0	0	0	681	771	1 046	0	1 548	4 890	5 358
Interest and dividends	6 128	4 577	5 800	4 670	4 117	5 336	4 725	3 593	3 309	5 883	7 799
Dividend Income	2 948	2 328	2 672	2 099	2 060	0	0	0	0	0	0
Interest Income (Crown Accounts)	3 114	2 183	3 100	2 547	2 058	2 145	1 820	1 673	2 140	2 372	2 483
Interest Inc from SOE Advances	66	65	28	24	0	707	976	1 102	787	791	760
Other dividends	0	0	0	0	0	2 484	1 929	818	382	2 720	4 556
Other property income	0	0	0	0	0	0	0	0	0	0	0
Sales of goods and services	2 409	3 015	2 843	2 813	2 477	2 450	3 347	3 497	2 401	3 682	3 176
Immigration Fees	512	509	496	562	534	663	656	715	886	935	1 064
Financial Supervisory Comm	177	732	605	486	279	303	899	917	324	262	279
Numismatic Revenue	517	515	457	439	400	274	501	600	354	511	537
Drivers Licence Fees	677	717	718	715	557	452	125	292	87	214	289
Censorship Fees	29	19	12	10	8	6	5	2	2	3	2
Upper Air Space Fees	361	392	442	463	506	460	985	545	545	545	577
Other fees	136	131	112	138	193	294	175	426	203	1 212	428
Fines, penalties and forfeits	118	131	72	59	39	35	1 249	23	553	248	2 302
Miscellaneous and unidentified revenue	1 521	7 905	11 289	1 048	904	7 362	1 594	10 271	4 844	2 155	3 962
Total tax and non-tax revenue	97 308	121 922	137 104	117 408	129 510	145 168	156 823	178 444	202 346	214 752	234 243

Note: Data are reported on a fiscal year basis beginning 1st July. For example, the data for 2018 represent the period from July 2018 to June 2019.
The data are on a cash basis.
Figures exclude non-tax revenues collected by sub-national governments as the data are not available.
Other grants include revenue from Japan and China
Source: Ministry of Finance and Economic Management of the Cook Islands.

StatLink https://stat.link/9lafb3

Details of non-tax revenue
Million FJD

	2008	2009	2010	2011	2012	2013	2014	2015	2016	2017	2018
Total non-tax revenue	**0**	**0**	**172**	**242**	**212**	**223**	**270**	**282**	**331**	**388**	**415**
Grants	0	0	9	7	13	16	26	18	26	20	57
Property income	0	0	54	89	89	78	102	109	143	174	178
Rents and royalties	0	0	1	40	31	31	36	40	49	63	81
Interest and dividends	0	0	52	50	58	47	66	70	94	111	97
Other property income	0	0	0	0	0	0	0	0	0	0	0
Sales of goods and services	0	0	99	129	101	113	125	136	136	178	169
Fines, penalties and forfeits	0	0	3	2	2	3	4	3	3	3	2
Miscellaneous and unidentified revenue	0	0	8	15	7	13	13	16	22	13	9
Total tax and non-tax revenue	*1 245*	*1 212*	*1 476*	*1 780*	*1 905*	*2 053*	*2 350*	*2 601*	*2 719*	*3 067*	*3 155*

Note: Year ending 31st December.

The data are on a cash basis.

Figures exclude non-tax revenues collected by sub-national governments as the data are not available.

Source: Ministry of Economy, Fiji.

StatLink https://stat.link/syrq15

Table 5.8. Kazakhstan
Details of non-tax revenue
Million KZT

	2008	2009	2010	2011	2012	2013	2014	2015	2016	2017	2018
Total non-tax revenue	262 965	211 952	265 698	445 958	676 607	459 552	269 025	201 621	634 927	676 014	1 071 522
Grants	0	0	0	0	0	0	0	0	0	0	0
Property income	132 167	81 628	121 760	277 974	431 903	234 100	24 467	56 070	305 424	342 509	872 985
Rents and royalties	112 411	61 179	103 118	251 170	257 708	209 807	25	9 908	278 626	309 080	837 280
Interest and dividends	14 499	17 458	16 289	24 946	171 046	17 664	19 319	43 783	24 014	30 784	33 709
Other property income	5 258	2 990	2 352	1 857	3 149	6 629	5 124	2 379	2 785	2 645	1 996
Sales of goods and services	54 193	51 574	65 825	84 555	70 441	73 411	58 905	93 915	183 868	129 057	123 938
Fines, penalties and forfeits	38 245	39 371	39 057	41 713	85 842	75 560	92 421	24 381	69 835	102 234	74 572
Miscellaneous and unidentified revenue	115	9	0	4	2 578	922	810	2 874	5 965	-21	26
Total tax and non-tax revenue	3 895 501	2 959 402	4 476 966	6 530 889	6 782 429	7 130 288	6 972 779	4 790 162	5 661 453	7 162 886	9 068 539

Note: Year ending 31st December.
   Data are on a cash basis.
   The share of the Republic of Kazakhstan under production sharing contracts of oil companies, the bonuses of oil and non-oil sector companies, the levy for
   the use of the radio-frequency spectrum, the payment to compensate for historic costs as well as certain other items are classified as non-tax revenues
   according to the OECD Interpretative Guide, but are considered as tax revenues in Kazakhstan.
Source: Ministry of Finance of the Republic of Kazakhstan.

StatLink ⬛🔢💻 https://stat.link/paxcog

Table 5.9. Mongolia
Details of non-tax revenue
Billion MNT

	2008	2009	2010	2011	2012	2013	2014	2015	2016	2017	2018
Total non-tax revenue	420	518	639	978	1 157	1 375	1 724	1 459	1 214	1 207	1 486
Grants	16	19	39	2	25	0	0	53	77	62	89
Property income	211	282	320	595	753	790	960	824	470	482	670
Rents and royalties	178	174	265	507	598	702	916	813	466	446	593
Interest and dividends	33	109	55	89	155	89	44	12	4	36	77
Other property income	0	0	0	0	0	0	0	0	0	0	0
Sales of goods and services	20	23	33	37	41	59	70	98	118	150	170
Fines, penalties and forfeits	30	36	36	58	79	187	210	178	193	75	113
Miscellaneous and unidentified revenue	143	157	211	286	259	339	484	305	355	438	445
Total tax and non-tax revenue	2 167	1 985	3 109	4 203	4 854	5 878	6 205	5 879	5 781	7 211	9 275

Note: Year ending December 31st.
Source: Ministry of Finance, Mongolia.

StatLink https://stat.link/o8ymae

Table 5.10. Nauru

Details of non-tax revenue
Thousand AUD

	2008	2009	2010	2011	2012	2013	2014	2015	2016	2017	2018
Total non-tax revenue	..	..	..	..	..	..	32 744	67 955	87 608	102 859	148 234
Grants	..	..	..	..	..	..	0	0	0	0	0
Property income	..	..	..	..	..	..	17 998	38 618	48 042	48 170	73 684
Rents and royalties	..	..	..	..	..	..	17 557	38 160	46 910	47 111	72 492
Fishing days, licences and support vessels	..	..	..	..	..	..	16 762	37 477	46 897	46 363	71 374
DCA Air navigation and rental fees	..	..	..	..	..	..	795	683	13	748	1 118
Interest and dividends	..	..	..	..	..	..	441	458	1 132	1 059	1 192
Other property income	..	..	..	..	..	..	0	0	0	0	0
Sales of goods and services	..	..	..	..	..	..	14 746	28 043	33 591	49 802	57 661
Visa Fees RPB	..	..	..	..	..	..	12 804	24 978	27 844	28 357	20 282
DJBC Operations	..	..	..	..	..	..	0	729	3 740	2 657	5 450
Other sales of goods and services	..	..	..	..	..	..	1 942	2 335	2 007	18 788	31 929
Fines, penalties and forfeits	..	..	..	..	..	..	0	0	0	0	0
Miscellaneous and unidentified revenue	..	..	..	..	..	..	0	1 295	5 975	4 887	16 889
Total tax and non-tax revenue	..	..	..	..	..	..	42 296	92 061	109 067	144 946	204 799

.. Not available
Note: Data are on a fiscal year basis beginning 1st July. For example, the data for 2018 represent the period from July 2018 to July 2019.
Source: Nauru Revenue Office.

StatLink ᵐˢᴸ https://stat.link/134ex7

Table 5.11. Papua New Guinea

Details of non-tax revenue

Million PGK

	2008	2009	2010	2011	2012	2013	2014	2015	2016	2017	2018
Total non-tax revenue	1 285	1 122	1 826	1 395	1 370	1 151	1 768	1 946	2 064	2 402	2 934
Grants	1 002	878	1 391	1 045	1 091	878	868	820	1 430	1 440	1 836
Property income	189	145	341	253	172	55	666	911	529	842	1 064
Rents and royalties	0	0	0	0	0	0	0	0	0	0	30
Interest and dividends	189	145	341	253	172	55	666	911	529	842	1 034
Dividends	26	0	40	49	50	55	152	455	228	279	380
Mining and Petroleum Dividends	163	138	299	191	122	0	514	456	301	562	654
SWF Receipts	0	0	0	0	0	0	0	0	0	0	0
Interests and fees from lending	1	7	1	13	0	0	0	0	0	0	0
Other property income	0	0	0	0	0	0	0	0	0	0	0
Sales of goods and services	0	0	0	0	0	0	0	0	0	0	32
Fines, penalties and forfeits	0	0	0	0	0	0	0	0	0	0	3
Miscellaneous and unidentified revenue	93	100	95	98	106	219	235	215	105	121	0
Total tax and non-tax revenue	7 141	6 213	8 399	9 921	9 773	9 925	12 141	11 088	10 670	11 388	12 917

Note: Year ending 31st December.

The data are on a cash basis.

Figures exclude non-tax revenues collected by sub-national governments as the data are not available.

Source: Ministry of Treasury and Finance of Papua New Guinea.

StatLink https://stat.link/ikobzw

Table 5.12. Philippines
Details of non-tax revenue
Million PHP

	2008	2009	2010	2011	2012	2013	2014	2015	2016	2017	2018
Total non-tax revenue	..	..	..	..	..	..	**238 844**	**289 238**	**275 231**	**286 706**	**339 462**
Grants	..	..	..	..	..	..	233	164	78	39	51
Property income	..	..	..	..	..	..	107 253	125 070	118 984	120 400	137 641
Rents and royalties	..	..	..	..	..	..	2 683	1 307	1 086	1 126	1 187
Interest and dividends	..	..	..	..	..	..	873	1 288	1 772	2 202	2 131
Other property income	..	..	..	..	..	..	103 697	122 475	116 126	117 072	134 323
Sales of goods and services	..	..	..	..	..	..	60 232	66 857	72 722	76 860	91 228
Fines, penalties and forfeits	..	..	..	..	..	..	0	0	0	0	0
Miscellaneous and unidentified revenue	..	..	..	..	..	..	71 126	97 147	83 447	89 407	110 542
Total tax and non-tax revenue	1 254 204	1 205 348	1 330 768	1 469 547	1 669 306	1 868 601	2 350 412	2 554 377	2 736 054	3 066 601	3 513 146

.. Not available
Note: Year ending 31st December.
The data are on a cash basis.
Source: Department of Finance of the Philippines.

StatLink ᴍˢᴸ https://stat.link/rg0asq

Table 5.13. Samoa

Details of non-tax revenue

Million WST

	2008	2009	2010	2011	2012	2013	2014	2015	2016	2017	2018
Total non-tax revenue	167	59	157	105	85	125	92	98	100	120	135
Grants	111	14	105	49	48	82	41	45	41	61	46
Property income	31	15	8	18	4	3	11	7	6	7	22
Rents and royalties	31	1	1	1	1	1	1	1	1	2	3
Interest and dividends	0	15	7	18	3	2	11	6	6	6	18
Other property income	0	0	0	0	0	0	0	0	0	0	0
Sales of goods and services	25	17	31	23	19	23	33	37	41	40	67
Administrative fees	..	..	28	19	13	15	23	26	28	24	38
Incidental sales by nonmarket establishments	..	..	2	5	6	8	10	11	13	17	30
Fines, penalties and forfeits	0	2	1	1	2	3	7	8	11	11	0
Miscellaneous and unidentified revenue	0	10	11	13	12	15	0	0	0	0	0
Total tax and non-tax revenue	492	411	498	464	488	552	532	593	614	643	706

.. Not available

Note: Data are reported on a fiscal year basis beginning 1st July. For example, the data for 2018 represent the period from July 2018 to June 2019.

The data are on a cash basis.

Figures exclude non-tax revenues collected by sub-national governments as the data are not available.

The data from 2009 were provided on the basis of the IMF's GFSM 2014 classification. Prior to this year, data were provided on a different basis. The differences between the two sets of data are indicated below for the relevant non-tax revenue categories.

Heading Grants: Data from 2009 includes only cash grants whereas data prior to that year also includes aid-funded projects.

Heading Sales of Goods and services: Data from 2009 exclude fisheries' licences currently included in tax revenue under heading "5126 taxes on specific services" (more information can be found in Table 4.12). Fisheries' licences revenues are usually classified as non-tax revenues according to the OECD classification set out in Annex A of the Interpretative Guide.

Source: Bureau of Statistics of Samoa.

StatLink https://stat.link/ce4o2x

Table 5.14. Thailand
Details of non-tax revenue
Million THB

	2008	2009	2010	2011	2012	2013	2014	2015	2016	2017	2018
Total non-tax revenue	281 300	277 573	353 402	307 501	344 217	377 011	411 153	484 461	529 570	549 443	604 726
Grants	2 100	2 058	2 081	2 737	1 644	2 163	5 369	1 450	5 934	8 905	2 401
Property income	180 800	161 558	191 289	169 637	230 436	245 741	287 830	306 528	281 647	300 896	314 124
Rents and royalties	53 200	51 204	46 429	32 814	67 067	93 718	101 284	88 895	80 580	75 554	81 704
Interest and dividends	127 600	110 353	144 442	136 823	163 369	152 022	186 546	217 633	201 067	225 343	232 420
Other property income	0	0	418	0	0	0	0	0	0	0	0
Sales of goods and services	79 500	99 518	103 797	73 876	99 266	101 057	97 574	127 522	185 322	174 056	220 257
Fines, penalties and forfeits	7 100	8 901	9 197	6 035	8 761	9 165	7 429	13 287	23 063	14 095	17 733
Miscellaneous and unidentified revenue	11 800	5 539	47 037	55 215	4 109	18 885	12 952	35 672	33 603	51 491	50 211
Total tax and non-tax revenue	1 952 900	1 842 168	2 223 854	2 411 738	2 518 776	2 861 583	2 821 641	3 052 599	3 125 365	3 222 857	3 462 566

Note: Data are on a fiscal year basis ending 30th September. For example, the data for 2018 represents 1 October 2017 to 30 September 2018. The data are on a cash basis.
Source: Ministry of Finance in Thailand.

StatLink https://stat.link/b48365

Table 5.15. Tokelau

Details of non-tax revenue
Thousand NZD

	2008	2009	2010	2011	2012	2013	2014	2015	2016	2017	2018
Total non-tax revenue	**14 704**	**15 582**	**14 836**	**20 129**	**20 402**	**28 361**	**21 424**	**35 911**	**35 088**	**31 507**	**37 212**
Grants	12 858	13 899	13 115	14 680	11 700	20 293	12 354	12 000	12 000	11 010	13 500
New Zealand Budgetary Grants	12 858	13 899	13 115	14 680	11 700	20 283	12 305	12 000	12 000	11 010	13 500
External donor funding	0	0	0	0	0	10	49	0	0	0	0
Property income	1 225	1 162	1 051	4 668	7 915	7 244	8 363	23 139	22 340	19 726	22 335
Rents and royalties	1 043	1 081	955	4 578	7 864	7 188	8 067	23 039	21 866	18 909	21 684
Tokelau EEZ Revenues	1 043	1 081	955	4 578	7 864	7 188	8 067	23 039	21 866	18 909	21 684
Interest and dividends	182	81	96	90	51	56	296	100	474	817	651
Other property income	0	0	0	0	0	0	0	0	0	0	0
Sales of goods and services	621	521	670	781	787	824	707	772	748	771	1 377
Handicrafts & Tourism (ENDRE)	0	0	0	0	0	0	0	154	4	7	7
Commemorative coins	0	0	0	64	60	30	71	0	0	0	115
Stamp sales	0	0	0	5	6	7	0	0	0	0	0
Transport - Boatfares	147	115	117	140	112	151	132	123	174	243	295
Transport - Freights Payments	374	318	409	329	350	316	397	386	430	398	618
Transport - Sale of Assets	0	0	1	3	0	8	0	6	10	0	4
Charter fees	12	0	10	0	0	0	0	0	0	0	171
Postage	1	2	3	3	2	2	1	1	0	0	0
Registry Certificates: Birth & Death	2	2	1	1	1	2	2	2	4	5	10
Service Fees	15	18	45	122	121	25	22	20	37	31	73
Miscellaneous Revenues	0	0	1	42	61	97	0	0	0	0	3
Revenue - Debt Recovery (MISC)	0	0	0	0	0	118	0	0	2	0	0
Gains - Sale of Assets (Vehicles)	0	0	0	0	0	0	0	66	19	0	0
House Rental Subsidies	39	52	46	46	43	56	66	1	55	74	62
Tokelau Savings Bank Passbook Fees	0	0	0	0	0	0	1	2	1	0	1
Tokelau Higano: accommodation	31	14	37	26	31	12	15	11	12	13	18
Fines, penalties and forfeits	0	0	0	0	0	0	0	0	0	0	0
Miscellaneous and unidentified revenue	0	0	0	0	0	0	0	0	0	0	0
Total tax and non-tax revenue	16 207	17 043	16 530	21 723	22 022	30 226	23 531	38 062	37 264	34 025	40 055

Note: Data are reported on a fiscal year basis beginning 1st July. For example, the data for 2018 represent the period from July 2018 to June 2019.
The data are on a cash basis.
Source: Tokelau National Statistics Office.

StatLink ᐁᕕᔅ᠊ https://stat.link/1ypk9l

Table 5.16. Vanuatu
Details of non-tax revenue
Million VUV

	2008	2009	2010	2011	2012	2013	2014	2015	2016	2017	2018
Total non-tax revenue	3 996	4 560	5 619	4 174	3 789	3 197	4 615	12 244	8 340	13 470	18 147
Grants	3 961	4 529	4 431	2 954	2 176	1 692	3 072	8 943	4 551	7 032	6 100
Property income	..	..	..	..	..	..	..	..	..	..	..
Rents and royalties	..	..	..	..	..	..	..	..	..	..	..
Interest and dividends	..	..	..	..	..	..	..	..	..	..	..
Other property income	..	..	..	..	..	..	..	..	..	..	..
Sales of goods and services	..	..	..	..	..	..	..	..	..	..	..
Fines, penalties and forfeits	..	..	..	..	..	..	..	..	..	..	..
Miscellaneous and unidentified revenue	35	31	1 187	1 220	1 613	1 505	1 542	3 302	3 789	6 438	12 047
Total tax and non-tax revenue	15 837	16 053	16 708	15 804	15 789	16 246	18 352	25 721	21 664	29 719	36 123

.. Not available
Note: Year ending December 31st.
Source: Department of Finance and Treasury of Vanuatu.

StatLink 🖳 https://stat.link/z2rj56

Annex A.
The OECD Classification of Taxes and Interpretative Guide

Table of Contents

A.1.   The OECD Classification of Taxes

A.2.   Coverage

A.3.   Basis of reporting

A.4.   General classification criteria

A.5.   Commentaries on items of the list

A.6.   Conciliation with National Accounts

A.7.   Memorandum item on the financing of social security benefits

A.8.   Memorandum item on identifiable taxes paid by government

A.9.   Relation of OECD classification of taxes to national accounting systems

A.10. Relation of OECD classification of taxes to the international monetary fund system

A.11. Comparison of the OECD classification of taxes with other international classifications

A.12. Attribution of tax revenues by subsectors of general government

A.13. Provisional classification of revenues from bank levies and payments to deposit insurance and financial stability schemes

A.1 the OECD Classification of Taxes

1. **1000. Taxes on income, profits and capital gains**

    1100. Taxes on income, profits and capital gains of individuals

        1110. On income and profits

        1120. On capital gains

    1200. Corporate taxes on income, profits and capital gains

        1210. On income and profits

        1220. On capital gains

    1300. Unallocable as between 1100 and 1200

2. **2000. Social security contributions**

    2100. Employees

        2110. On a payroll basis

        2120. On an income tax basis

    2200. Employers

        2210. On a payroll basis

        2220. On an income tax basis

    2300. Self-employed or non-employed

        2310. On a payroll basis

        2320. On an income tax basis

    2400 Unallocable as between 2100, 2200 and 2300

        2410. On a payroll basis

        2420. On an income tax basis

3. **3000. Taxes on payroll and workforce**

4. **4000. Taxes on property**

    4100. Recurrent taxes on immovable property

        4110. Households

        4120. Other

    4200 Recurrent taxes on net wealth

        4210. Individual

        4220. Corporate

    4300. Estate, inheritance and gift taxes

        4310. Estate and inheritance taxes

        4320. Gift taxes

4400. Taxes on financial and capital transactions

4500. Other non-recurrent taxes on property

    4510. On net wealth

    4520. Other non-recurrent taxes

4600. Other recurrent taxes on property

5. **5000. Taxes on goods and services**

5100. Taxes on production, sale, transfer, leasing and delivery of goods and rendering of services

    5110. General taxes

        5111. Value added taxes

        5112. Sales taxes

        5113. Turnover and other general taxes on goods and services

    5120. Taxes on specific goods and services

        5121. Excises

        5122. Profits of fiscal monopolies

        5123. Customs and import duties

        5124. Taxes on exports

        5125. Taxes on investment goods

        5126 . Taxes on specific services

        5127. Other taxes on international trade and transactions

        5128. Other taxes on specific goods and services

    5130. Unallocable as between 5110 and 5120

5200. Taxes on use of goods, or on permission to use goods or perform activities

    5210. Recurrent taxes

        5211. Paid by households in respect of motor vehicles

        5212. Paid by others in respect of motor vehicles

        5213. Other recurrent taxes

    5220. Non-recurrent taxes

5300. Unallocable as between 5100 and 5200

6. **6000. Other taxes**

6100. Paid solely by business

6200. Paid by other than business or unidentifiable

A.2 Coverage

General criteria

1.	In the OECD classification the term "taxes" is confined to compulsory unrequited payments to general government. Taxes are unrequited in the sense that benefits provided by government to taxpayers are not normally in proportion to their payments.

2.	The term "tax" does not include fines, penalties and compulsory loans paid to government. Borderline cases between tax and non-tax revenues in relation to certain fees and charges are discussed in §11–14.

3.	General government consists of the central administration, agencies whose operations are under its effective control, state and local governments and their administrations, certain social security schemes and autonomous governmental entities, excluding public enterprises. This definition of government follows that of the 2008 *System of National Accounts* (SNA).[1] In that publication, the general government sector and its sub-sectors are defined in Chapter 4, paragraphs 4.117 to 4.165.

4.	 Extra-budgetary units are part of the general government system. These are general government entities with individual budgets that are not fully covered by the main or general budget. These entities operate under the authority or control of a central, state, or local government. Extra-budgetary entities may have their own revenue sources, which may be supplemented by grants (transfers) from the general budget or from other sources. Even though their budgets may be subject to approval by the legislature, similar to that of budgetary accounts, they have discretion over the volume and composition of their spending. Such entities may be established to carry out specific government functions, such as road construction, or the nonmarket production of health or education services. Budgetary arrangements vary widely across countries, and various terms are used to describe these entities, but they are often referred to as "extra-budgetary funds" or "decentralised agencies."

5.	Compulsory payments to supra-national bodies and their agencies are no longer included as taxes as from 1998, with some exceptions. However, custom duties collected by EU member states on behalf of the European Union are still identified as memorandum items and included in overall tax revenue amounts in the country tables (Chapter 5) of the country in which they are collected. (See §99). In countries where the church forms part of general government church taxes are included, provided they meet the criteria set out in §1 above. As the data refer to receipts of general government, levies paid to non-government bodies, welfare agencies or social insurance schemes outside general government, trade unions or trade associations, even where such levies are compulsory, are excluded. Compulsory payments to general government earmarked for such bodies are, however, included, provided that the government is not simply acting in an agency capacity.[2] Profits from fiscal monopolies are distinguished from those of other public enterprises and are treated as taxes because they reflect the exercise of the taxing power of the state by the use of monopoly powers (see §65–67), as are profits received by the government from the purchase and sale of foreign exchange at different rates (see §74).

6.	Taxes paid by governments (e.g., social security contributions and payroll taxes paid by governments in their capacity as an employer, consumption taxes on their purchases or taxes on their property) are not excluded from the data provided. However, where it is possible to identify the amounts of revenue involved,[3] they are shown in Table 5.38 of this Report.

7.	The relationship between this classification and that of the System of National Accounts (SNA) is set out in Sections A.9 and A.11 below. Because of the differences between the two classifications, the data shown in national accounts are sometimes calculated or classified differently from the practice set out in this guide. These and other differences are mentioned where appropriate (e.g., in §30 below) but it is not possible to refer to all of them. There may also be some differences between this classification and that employed domestically by certain national administrations (e.g., see §12 below), so that OECD and national statistics data may not always be consistent: any such differences, however, are likely to be very slight in terms of amounts of revenues involved.

Social security contributions

8.   Compulsory social security contributions, as defined in §39, and paid to general government, are treated here as tax revenues. Being compulsory payments to general government they clearly resemble taxes. They may, however, differ from other taxes in that the receipt of social security benefits depends, in most countries, upon appropriate contributions having been made, although the size of the benefits is not necessarily related to the amount of the contributions. Better comparability between countries is obtained by treating social security contributions as taxes, but they are listed under a separate heading so that they can be distinguished in any analysis.

9.   The strict dividing line between tax revenues (compulsory unrequited payments to general government) and non-tax compulsory payments (NTCPs) (payments that are either requited or made to other institutions) is clearly defined. However, within the range of different compulsory payments to governments existing across countries, it is not always straightforward in practice to decide whether specific payments are either taxes or NTCPs. For example, compulsory pension savings that are controlled by general government and that accumulate on an individual account earning a market return or a rate that compensates for inflation would at first sight be categorised as NTCPs as opposed to taxes. However, even these payments might still be 'unrequited' and therefore classify as taxes instead of NTCPs (for example if these pension savings are not paid out when the taxpayer dies before reaching the pension age and the funds are then used to provide a minimum pension to all taxpayers that are insured). These issues result in the social security revenue figures reported for most countries being based on the premise that all types of compulsory payments to general government are judged to some extent to have a re-distributional element. It should be noted that this conclusion is based on a typically broad interpretation of the term 'unrequited' in the tax definition.

10.   Social security contributions which are either voluntary or not payable to general government (see §1) are not treated as taxes, though in some countries, as indicated in the country footnotes, there are difficulties in completely eliminating voluntary contributions and certain compulsory payments to the private sector from the revenue figures. Imputed social security contributions are also not treated as taxes.

Fees, user charges and licence fees

11.   Apart from vehicle licence fees, which are universally regarded as taxes, it is not easy to distinguish between those fees and user charges which are to be treated as taxes and those which are not, since, whilst a fee or charge is levied in connection with a specific service or activity, the strength of the link between the fee and the service provided may vary considerably, as may the relation between the amount of the fee and the cost of providing the service. Where the recipient of a service pays a fee clearly related to the cost of providing the service, the levy may be regarded as requited and under the definition of §1 would not be considered as a tax. In the following cases, however, a levy could be considered as 'unrequited':

   a) where the charge greatly exceeds the cost of providing the service;

   b) where the payer of the levy is not the receiver of the benefit (e.g., a fee collected from slaughterhouses to finance a service which is provided to farmers);

   c) where government is not providing a specific service in return for the levy which it receives even though a licence may be issued to the payer (e.g., where the government grants a hunting, fishing or shooting licence which is not accompanied by the right to use a specific area of government land);

d) where benefits are received only by those paying the levy but the benefits received by each individual are not necessarily in proportion to his payments (e.g., a milk marketing levy paid by dairy farmers and used to promote the consumption of milk).

12.   In marginal cases, however, the application of the criteria set out in §1 can be particularly difficult. The solution adopted — given the desirability of international uniformity and the relatively small amounts of revenue usually involved — is to follow the predominant practice among tax administrations rather than to allow each country to adopt its own view as to whether such levies are regarded as taxes or as non-tax revenue.[4]

13.   A list of the main fees and charges in question and their normal[5] treatment in this publication is as follows:

Non-tax revenues:	court fees; driving licence fees; harbour fees; passport fees; radio and television licence fees where public authorities provide the service
Taxes within heading 5200	permission to perform such activities as distributing films; hunting, fishing and shooting; providing entertainment or gambling facilities; selling alcohol or tobacco; permission to own dogs or to use or own motor vehicles or guns; severance taxes

14.   In practice it may not always be possible to isolate tax receipts from non-tax revenue receipts when they are recorded together. If it is estimated that the bulk of the receipts derive from non-tax revenues, the whole amount involved is treated as a non-tax revenue; otherwise, such government receipts are included and classified according to the rules provided in §32 below.

Royalties

15.   The ownership of subsoil assets in the form of deposits of minerals or fossil fuels (coal, oil, or natural gas) depends upon the way in which property rights are defined by law and also on international agreements in the case of deposits below international waters. In some cases, either the ground below which the mineral deposits are located, the deposits themselves or both may belong to a local or central government unit.

16.   In such cases, these general government units may grant leases to other institutional units that permit them to extract these deposits over a specified period of time in return for a payment or series of payments. These payments are often described as 'royalties' but they are essentially rent that accrues to owners of natural resources in return for putting these assets at the disposal of other units for specified periods of time. The rent may take the form of periodic payments of fixed amounts, irrespective of the rate of extraction, or, more commonly, they may be a function of the quantity, volume, or value of the asset extracted. Enterprises engaged in exploration on government land may make payments to general government units in exchange for the right to undertake test drilling or otherwise investigate the existence and location of subsoil assets. Such payments are also recorded as rents even though no extraction may take place. These payments are therefore classified as non-tax revenues.

17.   The same principles apply when other institutional units are granted leases that permit them to fell timber in natural forests on land owned by general government units. These payments are also classified as non-tax revenues.

18.   These rents or royalties paid to general government should not be confused with taxes on income and profits, severance taxes, business licenses, or other taxes. If the payments are levied on the profits from the extraction activity, then they should be classified as taxes on incomes, profits and gains (1000). In addition, any severance payments that are imposed on the extraction of minerals and fossil fuels from reserves owned privately or by another government should be classified as taxes. Payments related to the gross value of production should be classified as other taxes on goods and services (5128). Payments for

a license or permit to conduct extraction operations should be classified as taxes on use of goods and on permission to use goods or perform activities (5213).

Fines and penalties

19.   In principle, fines and penalties charged on overdue taxes or penalties imposed for the attempted evasion of taxes should not be recorded as tax revenues. However it may not be possible to separate payments of fines or other penalties from the revenues from the taxes to which they relate. In this case the fines and penalties relating to a particular tax are recorded together with the revenues from that tax and fines and penalties paid with revenue from unidentifiable taxes are classified as other taxes in Category 6000. Fines not relating to tax offences (e.g., for parking offences), or not identifiable as relating to tax offences, are also not treated as tax revenues.

A.3 Basis of reporting

Accrual reporting

20.   The data reported in this publication for recent years are predominantly recorded on an accrual basis, i.e. recorded at the time that the tax liability was created. Further information is provided in the footnotes to the country table in Chapter 5 of the Report.

21.   However, data for earlier years are still predominantly recorded on a cash basis, i.e. at the time at which the payment was received by government. Thus, for example, taxes withheld by employers in one year but paid to the government in the following year and taxes due in one year but actually paid in the following year are both included in the receipts of the second year. Corrective transactions, such as refunds, repayments and drawbacks, are deducted from gross revenues of the period in which they are made.

22.   Data on tax revenues are recorded without offsets for the administrative expenses connected with tax collection. Similarly, where the proceeds of tax are used to subsidise particular members of the community, the subsidy is not deducted from the yield of the tax, though the tax may be shown net of subsidies in the national records of some countries.

23.   As regards fiscal monopolies (heading 5122), only the amount actually transferred to the government is included in government revenues. However, if any expenditures of fiscal monopolies are considered to be government expenditures (e.g., social expenditures undertaken by fiscal monopolies at the direction of the government) they are added back for the purpose of arriving at tax revenue figures (see §65 below).

The distinction between tax and expenditure provisions[6]

24.   Because this publication is concerned only with the revenue side of government operations, no account being taken of the expenditure side, a distinction has to be made between tax and expenditure provisions. Normally there is no difficulty in making this distinction as expenditures are made outside the tax system and the tax accounts and under legislation separate from the tax legislation. In borderline cases, cash flow is used to distinguish between tax provisions and expenditure provisions. Insofar as a provision affects the flow of tax payments from the taxpayer to the government, it is regarded as a tax provision and is taken into account in the data shown in this publication. A provision which does not affect this flow is seen as an expenditure provision and is disregarded in the data recorded in this publication.

25.   Tax allowances, exemptions and deductions against the tax base clearly affect the amount of tax paid to the government and are therefore considered as tax provisions. At the other extreme, those subsidies which cannot be offset against tax liability and which are clearly not connected with the

assessment process, do not reduce tax revenues as recorded in this publication. Tax credits are amounts deductible from tax payable (as distinct from deductions from the tax base). Two types of tax credits are distinguished, those (referred to here as wastable tax credits) which are limited to the amount of the tax liability and therefore cannot give rise to a payment by the authorities to the taxpayer, and those (referred to as non-wastable tax credits) which are not so limited, so that the excess of the credit over the tax liability can be paid to the taxpayer.[7] A wastable tax credit, like a tax allowance, clearly affects the amount of tax paid to the government, and is therefore considered as a tax provision. The practice followed for non-wastable tax credits[8] is to distinguish between the 'tax expenditure component',[9] which is that portion of the credit that is used to reduce or eliminate a taxpayer's liability, and the 'transfer component', which is the portion that exceeds the taxpayer's liability and is paid to that taxpayer. Reported tax revenues should be reduced by the amount of the tax expenditure component but not by the amount of the transfer component. In addition, the amounts of the tax expenditure and transfer components should be reported as memorandum items in the country tables. Countries that are unable to distinguish between the tax expenditure and transfer components should indicate whether or not the tax revenues have been reduced by the total of these components, and provide any available estimates of the amounts of the two components. Further information is given in Chapter 1 of the Report, which illustrates the effect of alternative treatments of non-wastable tax credits on tax to GDP.

Calendar and fiscal years

26.   National authorities whose fiscal years do not correspond to the calendar year show data, where possible, on a calendar year basis to permit maximum comparability with the data of other countries. There remain a few countries where data refer to fiscal years. For these the GDP data used in the comparative tables also correspond to the fiscal years.

A.4 General classification criteria

The main classification criteria

27.   The classification of receipts among the main headings (1000, 2000, 3000, 4000, 5000 and 6000) is generally governed by the base on which the tax is levied: 1000 income, profits and capital gains; 2000 and 3000 earnings, payroll or number of employees; 4000 property; 5000 goods and services; 6000 multiple bases, other bases or unidentifiable bases. Where a tax is calculated on more than one base, the receipts are, where possible, split among the various headings (see §32 and §81). The headings 4000 and 5000 cover not only taxes where the tax base is the property, goods or services themselves but also certain related taxes. Thus, taxes on the transfer of property are included in 4400[10] and taxes on the use of goods or on permission to perform activities in 5200. In headings 4000 and 5000 a distinction is made in certain sub-headings between recurrent and non-recurrent taxes: recurrent taxes are defined as those levied at regular intervals (usually annually) and non-recurrent taxes are levied once and for all (see also §47 to §50, §53, §54 and §79 for particular applications of this distinction).

28.   Earmarking of a tax for specific purposes does not affect the classification of tax receipts. However, as explained in §39 on the classification of social security contributions, the conferment of an entitlement to social benefits is crucial to the definition of the 2000 main heading.

29.   The way that a tax is levied or collected (e.g., by use of stamps) does not affect classification.

Classification of taxpayers

30.   In certain sub-headings distinctions are made between different categories of taxpayers. These distinctions vary from tax to tax:

a) Between individuals and corporations in relation to income and net wealth taxes

The basic distinction is that corporation income taxes, as distinct from individual income taxes, are levied on the corporation as an entity, not on the individuals who own it, and without regard to the personal circumstances of these individuals. The same distinction applies to net wealth taxes on corporations and those on individuals. Taxes paid on the profits of partnerships and the income of institutions, such as life insurance or pension funds, are classified according to the same rule. They are classified as corporate taxes (1200) if they are charged on the partnership or institution as an entity without regard to the personal circumstances of the owners. Otherwise, they are treated as individual taxes (1100). Usually, there is different legislation for the corporation taxes and for the individual taxes.[11] The distinction made here between individuals and corporations does not follow the sector classification between households, enterprises, and so on of the System of National Accounts for income and outlay accounts. The SNA classification requires certain unincorporated businesses[12] to be excluded from the household sector and included with non-financial enterprises and financial institutions. The tax on the profits of these businesses, however, cannot always be separated from the tax on the other income of their owners, or can be separated only on an arbitrary basis. No attempt at this separation is made here and the whole of the individual income tax is shown together without regard to the nature of the income chargeable.

b) Between households and others in relation to taxes on immovable property

Here the distinction is that adopted by the SNA for the production and consumption expenditure accounts. The distinction is between households as consumers (i.e. excluding non-incorporated business) on the one hand and producers on the other hand. However, taxes on dwellings occupied by households, whether paid by owner-occupiers, tenants or landlords, are classified under households. This follows the common distinction made between taxes on domestic property versus taxes on business property. Some countries are not, however, in a position to make this distinction.

c) Between households and others in relation to motor vehicle licences

Here the distinction is between households as consumers on the one hand and producers on the other, as in the production and consumption expenditure accounts of the SNA.

d) Between business and others in relation to the residual taxes (6000)

The distinction is the same as in c) above between producers on the one hand and households as consumers on the other hand. Taxes which are included under the heading 6000 because they involve more than one tax base or because the tax base does not fall within any of the previous categories but which are identifiable as levyable only on producers and not on households are included under 'business'. The rest of the taxes which are included under the heading 6000 are shown as 'other' or non-identified.

Surcharges

31.   Receipts from surcharges in respect of particular taxes are usually classified with the receipts from the relevant tax whether or not the surcharge is temporary. If, however, the surcharge has a characteristic which would render it classifiable in a different heading of the OECD list, receipts from the surcharge are classified under that heading separately from the relevant tax.

Unidentifiable tax receipts and residual sub-headings

32.   A number of cases arise where taxes cannot be identified as belonging entirely to a heading or sub-heading of the OECD classification and the following practices are applied in such cases:

   a) The heading is known, but it is not known how receipts should be allocated between sub-headings: receipts are classified in the appropriate residual sub-heading (1300, 2400, 4520, 4600, 5130, 5300 or 6200).

b) It is known that the bulk of receipts from a group of taxes (usually local taxes) is derived from taxes within a particular heading or sub-heading, but some of the taxes in the group whose amount cannot be precisely ascertained may be classifiable in other headings or sub-headings: receipts are shown in the heading or sub-heading under which most of the receipts fall.

c) Neither the heading nor sub-heading of a tax (usually local) can be identified: the tax is classified in 6200 unless it is known that it is a tax on business in which case it is classified in 6100.

A.5 Commentaries on items of the list

1000 — Taxes on income, profits and capital gains

33.   This heading covers taxes levied on the net income or profits (i.e. gross income minus allowable tax reliefs) of individuals and enterprises. Also covered are taxes levied on the capital gains of individuals and enterprises, and gains from gambling.

34.   Included in the heading are:

a) taxes levied predominantly on income or profits, though partially on other bases. Taxes on various bases which are not predominantly income or profits are classified according to the principles laid down in §32 and §81;

b) taxes on property, which are levied on a presumed or estimated income as part of an income tax (see also §47(a), (c) and (d));

c) compulsory payments to social security fund contributions that are levied on income but do not confer an entitlement to social benefits. When such contributions do confer an entitlement to social benefits, they are included in heading 2000 (see §39);

d) receipts from integrated scheduler income tax systems are classified as a whole in this heading, even though certain of the scheduler taxes may be based upon gross income and may not take into account the personal circumstances of the taxpayer.

35.   The main subdivision of this heading is between levies on individuals (1100) and those on corporate enterprises (1200). Under each subdivision a distinction is made between taxes on income and profits (1110 and 1210), and taxes on capital gains (1120 and 1220). If certain receipts cannot be identified as appropriate to either 1100 or 1200, or if in practice this distinction cannot be made (e.g., because there are no reliable data on the recipients of payments from which withholding taxes are deducted) they are classified in 1300 as not-allocable.

Treatment of credits under imputation systems

36.   Under imputation systems of corporate income tax, a company's shareholders are wholly or partly relieved of their liability to income tax on dividends paid by the company out of income or profits liable to corporate income tax. In countries with such systems,[13] part of the tax on the company's profits is available to provide relief against the shareholders' own tax liability. The relief to the shareholder takes the form of a tax credit, the amount of which may be less than, equal to, or more than the shareholder's overall tax liability. If the tax credit exceeds this tax liability the excess may be payable to the shareholder. As this type of tax credit is an integral part of the imputation system of corporate income tax, any payment to the shareholders is treated as a repayment of tax and not as expenditure (compare the treatment of other tax credits described in §25).

37.   As the tax credit under imputation systems (even when exceeding tax liability) is to be regarded as a tax provision, the question arises whether it should be deducted from individual income tax receipts (1110) or corporate income tax receipts (1210). In this Report, the full amount of corporate income tax paid is shown under 1210 and no imputed tax is included under 1110. Thus, the full amount of the credit reduces the amount of 1110 whether the credit results in a reduction of personal income tax liability or whether an actual refund is made because the credit exceeds the income tax liability. (Where, however, such tax credits are deducted from corporation tax in respect of dividends paid to corporations the amounts are deducted from the receipts of 1210).

1120 and 1220 — Taxes on capital gains

38.   These sub-headings comprise taxes imposed on capital gains, 1120 covering those levied on the gains of individuals and 1220 those levied on the gains of corporate enterprises, where receipts from such taxes can be separately identified. In many countries this is not the case and the receipts from such taxes are then classified with those from the income tax. Heading 1120 also includes taxes on gains from gambling.

2000 — Social security contributions

39.   Classified here are all compulsory payments that confer an entitlement to receive a (contingent) future social benefit. Such payments are usually earmarked to finance social benefits and are often paid to institutions of general government that provide such benefits. However, such earmarking is not part of the definition of social security contributions and is not required for a tax to be classified here. However, conferment of an entitlement is required for a tax to be classified under this heading. So, levies on income or payroll that are earmarked for social security funds but do not confer an entitlement to benefit are excluded from this heading and shown under personal income taxes (1100) or taxes on payroll and workforce (3000). Taxes on other bases, such as goods and services, which are earmarked for social security benefits are not shown here but are classified according to their respective bases because they generally confer no entitlement to social security benefits.

40.   Contributions for the following types of social security benefits would, *inter alia*, be included: unemployment insurance benefits and supplements, accident, injury and sickness benefits, old-age, disability and survivors' pensions, family allowances, reimbursements for medical and hospital expenses or provision of hospital or medical services. Contributions may be levied on both employees and employers.

41.   Contributions may be based on earnings or payroll ('on a payroll basis') or on net income after deductions and exemptions for personal circumstances ('on an income tax basis'), and the revenues from the two bases should be separately identified if possible. However, where contributions to a general social security scheme are on a payroll basis, but the contributions of particular groups (such as the self-employed) cannot be assessed on this basis and net income is used as a proxy for gross earnings, the receipts may still be classified as being on a payroll basis. In principle, this heading excludes voluntary contributions paid to social security schemes. When separately identifiable these are shown in the memorandum item on the financing of social security benefits. In practice, however, they cannot always be separately identified from compulsory contributions, in which case they are included in this heading.

42.   Contributions to social insurance schemes which are not institutions of general government and to other types of insurance schemes, provident funds, pension funds, friendly societies or other saving schemes are not considered as social security contributions. Provident funds are arrangements under which the contributions of each employee and of the corresponding employer on his/her behalf are kept in a separate account earning interest and withdrawable under specific circumstances. Pension funds are separately organised schemes negotiated between employees and employers and carry provisions for

different contributions and benefits, sometimes more directly tied to salary levels and length of service than under social security schemes. When contributions to these schemes are compulsory or quasi-compulsory (e.g., by virtue of agreement with professional and union organisations) they are shown in the memorandum item (refer to Table 5.37 of the Report).

43.　　Contributions by government employees and by governments in respect of their employees, to social security schemes classified within general government are included in this heading. Contributions to separate schemes for government employees, which can be regarded as replacing general social security schemes, are also regarded as taxes.[14] Where, however, a separate scheme is not seen as replacing a general scheme and has been negotiated between the government, in its role as an employer, and its employees, it is not regarded as social security and contributions to it are not regarded as taxes, even though the scheme may have been established by legislation.

44.　　This heading excludes 'imputed' contributions, which correspond to social benefits paid directly by employers to their employees or former employees or to their representatives (e.g., when employers are legally obliged to pay sickness benefits for a certain period).

45.　　Contributions are divided into those of employees (2100), employers (2200), and self-employed or non-employed (2300), and then further sub-divided according to the basis on which they are levied. Employees are defined for this purpose as all persons engaged in activities of business units, government bodies, private non-profit institutions, or other paid employment, except the proprietors and their unpaid family members in the case of unincorporated businesses. Members of the armed forces are included, irrespective of the duration and type of their service, if they contribute to social security schemes. The contributions of employers are defined as their payments on account of their employees to social security schemes. Where employees or employers are required to continue the payment of social security contributions when the employee becomes unemployed these contributions, data permitting, are shown in 2100 and 2200 respectively. Accordingly, the sub-heading 2300 is confined to contributions paid by the self-employed and by those outside of the labour force (e.g., disabled or retired individuals).

3000 — Taxes on payroll and workforce

46.　　These consist of taxes payable by enterprises assessed either as a proportion of the wages or salaries paid or as a fixed amount per person employed. They do not include compulsory social security contributions paid by employers or any taxes paid by employees themselves out of their wages or salaries

4000 — Taxes on property

47.　　This heading covers recurrent and non-recurrent taxes on the use, ownership or transfer of property. These include taxes on immovable property or net wealth, taxes on the change of ownership of property through inheritance or gift and taxes on financial and capital transactions. The following kinds of tax are excluded from this heading:

a)　taxes on capital gains resulting from the sale of a property (1120 or 1220);

b)　taxes on the use of goods or on permission to use goods or perform activities (5200); see §76;

c)　taxes on immovable property levied on the basis of a presumed net income which take into account the personal circumstances of the taxpayer. They are classified as income taxes along with taxes on income and capital gains derived from property (1100);

d)　taxes on the use of property for residence, where the tax is payable by either proprietor or tenant and the amount payable is a function of the user's personal circumstances (pay, dependants, and so on). They are classified as taxes on income (1100);

e) taxes on building in excess of permitted maximum density, taxes on the enlargement, construction or alteration of certain buildings beyond a permitted value and taxes on building construction. They are classified as taxes on permission to perform activities (5200);

f) taxes on the use of one's own property for special trading purposes like selling alcohol, tobacco, meat or for exploitation of land resources (e.g., United States severance taxes). They are classified as taxes on permission to perform activities (5200).

4100 — Recurrent taxes on immovable property

48.   This sub-heading covers taxes levied regularly in respect of the use or ownership of immovable property.

- these taxes are levied on land and buildings;
- they can be in the form of a percentage of an assessed property value based on a national rental income, sales price, or capitalised yield; or in terms of other characteristics of real property, (for example size or location) from which a presumed rent or capital value can be derived.
- such taxes can be levied on proprietors, tenants, or both. They can also be paid by one level of government to another level of government in respect of property under the jurisdiction of the latter.
- debts are not taken into account in the assessment of these taxes, and they differ from taxes on net wealth in this respect.

49.   Taxes on immovable property are further sub-divided into those paid by households (4110) and those paid by other entities (4120), according to the criteria set out in §30(b) above.

4200 — Recurrent taxes on net wealth

50.   This sub-heading covers taxes levied regularly (in most cases annually) on net wealth, i.e. taxes on a wide range of movable and immovable property, net of debt. It is sub-divided into taxes paid by individuals (4210) and taxes paid by corporate enterprises (4220) according to the criteria set out in §30(a) above. If separate figures exist for receipts paid by institutions, the tax payments involved are added to those paid by corporations.

4300 — Estate, inheritance and gift taxes

51.   This sub-heading is divided into taxes on estates and inheritances (4310) and taxes on gifts (4320).[15] Estate taxes are charged on the amount of the total estate whereas inheritance taxes are charged on the shares of the individual recipients; in addition the latter may take into account the relationship of the individual recipients to the deceased.

4400 — Taxes on financial and capital transactions

52.   This sub-heading comprises, inter alia, taxes on the issue, transfer, purchase and sale of securities, taxes on cheques, and taxes levied on specific legal transactions such as validation of contracts and the sale of immovable property. The heading does not include:

a) taxes on the use of goods or property or permission to perform certain activities (5200);

b) fees paid to cover court charges, charges for birth, marriage or death certificates, which are normally regarded as non-tax revenues (see §11);

c) taxes on capital gains (1000);

d) recurrent taxes on immovable property (4100);

e) recurrent taxes on net wealth (4200);

146

f) once-and-for-all levies on property or wealth (4500).

4500 — Other non-recurrent taxes on property16

53. This sub-heading covers once-and-for-all, as distinct from recurrent, levies on property. It is divided into taxes on net wealth (4510) and other non-recurrent taxes on property (4520). Heading 4510 would include taxes levied to meet emergency expenditures, or for redistribution purposes. Heading 4520 would cover taxes levied to take account of increases in land value due to permission given to develop or provision of additional local facilities by general government, any taxes on the revaluation of capital and once-and-for-all taxes on particular items of property.

4600 — Other recurrent taxes on property

54. These rarely exist in OECD member countries, but the heading would include taxes on goods such as cattle, jewellery, windows, and other external signs of wealth.

5000 — Taxes on goods and services

55. All taxes and duties levied on the production, extraction, sale, transfer, leasing or delivery of goods, and the rendering of services (5100), or in respect of the use of goods or permission to use goods or to perform activities (5200) are included here. The heading thus covers:

   a) multi-stage cumulative taxes;
   b) general sales taxes — whether levied at manufacture/production, wholesale or retail level;
   c) value-added taxes;
   d) excises;
   e) taxes levied on the import and export of goods;
   f) taxes levied in respect of the use of goods and taxes on permission to use goods, or perform certain activities;
   g) taxes on the extraction, processing or production of minerals and other products.

56. Borderline cases between this heading and heading 4000 (taxes on property) and 6100 (other taxes on business) are referred to in §47, §52 and §78. Residual sub-headings (5300) and (5130) cover tax receipts which cannot be allocated between 5100 and 5200 and between 5110 and 5120, respectively; see §32.

5100 — Taxes on the production, sale, transfer, leasing and delivery of goods and rendering of services

57. This sub-heading consists of all taxes, levied on transactions in goods and services on the basis of their intrinsic characteristics (e.g., value, weight of tobacco, strength of alcohol, and so on) as distinct from taxes imposed on the use of goods, or permission to use goods or perform activities, which fall under 5200.

5110 — General taxes on goods and services

58. This sub-heading includes all taxes, other than import and export duties (5123 and 5124), levied on the production, leasing, transfer, delivery or sales of a wide range of goods and/or the rendering of a wide range of services, irrespective of whether they are domestically produced or imported and irrespective of the stage of production or distribution at which they are levied. It thus covers value-added taxes, sales taxes and multi-stage cumulative taxes. Receipts from border adjustments in respect of such taxes when

goods are imported are added to gross receipts for this category, and repayments of such taxes when goods are exported are deducted. These taxes are subdivided into 5111 value-added taxes, 5112 sales taxes, 5113 turnover and other general taxes on goods and services.

59.   Borderline cases arise between this heading and taxes on specific goods (5120) when taxes are levied on a large number of goods, for example, the United Kingdom purchase tax (repealed in 1973) and the Japanese commodity tax (repealed in 1988). In conformity with national views, the former United Kingdom purchase tax is classified as a general tax (5112) and the former Japanese commodity tax as excises (5121).

5111 — Value-added taxes

60.   All general consumption taxes charged on value-added are classified in this sub-heading, irrespective of the method of deduction and the stages at which the taxes are levied. In practice, all OECD countries with value-added taxes normally allow immediate deduction of taxes on purchases by all but the final consumer and impose tax at all stages. In some countries the heading may include certain taxes, such as those on financial and insurance activities, either because receipts from them cannot be identified separately from those from the value-added tax, or because they are regarded as an integral part of the value-added tax, even though similar taxes in other countries might be classified elsewhere (e.g., 5126 as taxes on services or 4400 as taxes on financial and capital transactions).

5112 — Sales taxes

61.   All general taxes levied at one stage only, whether at manufacturing or production, wholesale or retail stage are classified here.

5113 — Turnover and other general taxes on goods and services

62.   These are multi-stage cumulative taxes and taxes where elements of consumption taxes are combined with multistage taxes. These taxes are levied each time a transaction takes place without deduction for taxes paid on inputs. Multi-stage taxes can be combined with elements of value-added or sales taxes.

5120 — Taxes on specific goods and services

63.   Excises, profits generated and transferred from fiscal monopolies, and customs and imports duties as well as taxes on exports, foreign exchange transactions, investment goods and betting stakes and special taxes on services, which do not form part of a general tax of 5110, are included in this category.

5121 — Excises

64.   Excises are taxes levied as a product specific unit tax on a predefined limited range of goods. Excises are usually levied at differentiated rates on nonessential or luxury goods, alcoholic beverages, tobacco, and energy. Excises may be imposed at any stage of production or distribution and are usually assessed as a specific charge per unit based on characteristics by reference to the value, weight, strength, or quantity of the product. Included are special taxes on individual products such as sugar, sugar beets, matches, and chocolates; taxes levied at varying rates on a certain range of goods; and taxes levied on tobacco goods, alcoholic drinks, motor fuels, and hydrocarbon oils. If a tax collected principally on imported goods also applies, or would apply, under the same law to comparable domestically produced goods, then the revenue from this tax is classified as arising from excises rather than from import duties. This principle applies even if there is no comparable domestic production or no possibility of such production. Taxes on the use of utilities such as water, electricity, gas, and energy are regarded as excises rather than taxes on

specific services (5126). Excises exclude those taxes that are levied as general taxes on goods and services (5110); profits of fiscal monopolies (5122); customs and other import duties (5123); or taxes on exports (5124).

5122 — Profits of fiscal monopolies

65.   This sub-heading covers that part of the profits of fiscal monopolies which is transferred to general government or which is used to finance any expenditures considered to be government expenditures (see §23). Amounts are shown when they are transferred to general government or used to make expenditures considered to be government expenditures.

66.   Fiscal monopolies reflect the exercise of the taxing power of government by the use of monopoly powers. Fiscal monopolies are non-financial public enterprises exercising a monopoly in most cases over the production or distribution of tobacco, alcoholic beverages, salt, matches, playing cards and petroleum or agricultural products (i.e. on the kind of products which are likely to be, alternatively or additionally, subject to the excises of 5121), to raise the government revenues which in other countries are gathered through taxes on dealings in such commodities by private business units. The government monopoly may be at the production stage or, as in the case of government-owned and controlled liquor stores, at the distribution stage.

67.   Fiscal monopolies are distinguished from public utilities such as rail transport, electricity, post offices, and other communications, which may enjoy a monopoly or quasi-monopoly position but where the primary purpose is normally to provide basic services rather than to raise revenue for government. Transfers from such other public enterprises to the government are considered as non-tax revenues. The traditional concept of fiscal monopoly is not generally extended to include state lotteries, the profits of which are usually accordingly regarded as non-tax revenues. However, they can be included as tax revenues if the prime reason for their operation is to raise revenues to finance government expenditure. Fiscal monopoly profits are distinguished from export and import monopoly profits (5127) transferred from marketing boards or other enterprises dealing with international trade.

5123 — Customs and other import duties

68.   Taxes, stamp duties and surcharges restricted by law to imported products are included here. Also included are levies on imported agricultural products which are imposed in member countries of the European Union and amounts paid by certain of these countries under the Monetary Compensation Accounts (MCA) system.[16] Starting from 1998, customs duties collected by European Union member states on behalf of the European Union are no longer reported under this heading in the country tables (in Chapter 5 of the Report). Excluded here are taxes collected on imports as part of a general tax on goods and services, or an excise applicable to both imported and domestically produced goods.

5124 — Taxes on exports

69.   In the 1970s, export duties were levied in Australia, Canada and Portugal as a regular measure and they have been used in Finland for counter-cyclical purposes. Some member countries of the European Union pay, as part of the MCA system, a levy on exports (see note 16 to §68). Where these amounts are identifiable, they are shown in this heading. This heading does not include repayments of general consumption taxes or excises or customs duties on exported goods, which should be deducted from the gross receipts under 5110, 5121 or 5123, as appropriate.

5125 — Taxes on investment goods

70. This sub-heading covers taxes on investment goods, such as machinery. These taxes may be imposed for a number of years or temporarily for counter-cyclical purposes. Taxes on industrial inputs which are also levied on consumers [e.g., the Swedish energy tax which is classified under (5121)] are not included here.

5126 — Taxes on specific services

71. All taxes assessed on the payment for specific services, such as taxes on insurance premiums, banking services, gambling and betting stakes (e.g., from horse races, football pools, lottery tickets), transport, entertainment, restaurant and advertising charges, fall into this category. Taxes levied on the gross income of companies providing the service (e.g., gross insurance premiums or gambling stakes received by the company) are also classified under this heading. Tax revenues from bank levies and payments to deposit insurance and financial stability schemes are provisionally included here for the 2012 edition. The detailed classification is set out in §108.

72. Excluded from this sub-heading are:

  a) taxes on services forming part of a general tax on goods and services (5110);

  b) taxes on electricity, gas and energy (5121 as excises);

  c) taxes on individual gains from gambling (1120 as taxes on capital gains of individuals and non-corporate enterprises) and lump-sum taxes on the transfer of private lotteries or on the permission to set up lotteries (5200);[17]

  d) taxes on cheques and on the issue, transfer or redemption of securities (4400 as taxes on financial and capital transactions).

5127 — Other taxes on international trade and transactions

73. This sub-heading covers revenue received by the government from the purchase and sale of foreign exchange at different rates. When the government exercises monopoly powers to extract a margin between the purchase and sales price of foreign exchange, other than to cover administrative costs, the revenue derived constitutes a compulsory levy exacted in indeterminate proportions from both purchaser and seller of foreign exchange. It is the common equivalent of an import duty and export duty levied in a single exchange rate system or of a tax on the sale or purchase of foreign exchange. Like the profits of fiscal monopolies and import or export monopolies transferred to government, it represents the exercise of monopoly powers for tax purposes and is included in tax revenues.

74. The sub-heading covers also the profits of export or import monopolies, which do not however exist in OECD countries, taxes on purchase or sale of foreign exchange, and any other taxes levied specifically on international trade or transactions.

5128 — Other taxes on specific goods and services

75. This item includes taxes on the extraction of minerals, fossil fuels and other exhaustible resources from deposits owned privately or by another government together with any other unidentifiable receipts from taxes on specific goods and services. Taxes on the extraction of exhaustible resources are usually a fixed amount per unit of quality or weight, but can be a percentage of value. The taxes are recorded when the resources are extracted. Payments from the extraction of exhaustible resources from deposits owned by the government unit receiving the payment are classified as rent.

5200 — Taxes on use of goods or on permission to use goods or perform activities

76.   This sub-heading covers taxes which are levied in respect of the use of goods as distinct from taxes on the goods themselves. Unlike the latter taxes – reported under 5100 –, they are not assessed on the value of the goods but usually as fixed amounts. Taxes on permission to use goods or to perform activities are also included here, as are pollution taxes not based upon the value of particular goods. It is sometimes difficult to distinguish between compulsory user charges and licence fees which are regarded as taxes and those which are excluded as non-tax revenues. The criteria which are employed are noted in §11–12.

77.   Although the sub-heading refers to the 'use' of goods, registration of ownership rather than use may be what generates liability to tax, so that the taxes of this heading may apply to the ownership of animals or goods rather than their use (e.g., race horses, dogs and motor vehicles) and may apply even to unusable goods (e.g., unusable motor vehicles or guns).

78.   Borderline cases arise with:

  a) taxes on the permission to perform business activities which are levied on a combined income, payroll or turnover base and, accordingly, are classified following the rules in §81;

  b) taxes on the ownership or use of property of headings 4100, 4200 and 4600. The heading 4100 is confined to taxes on the ownership or tenancy of immovable property and – unlike the taxes of 5200 – they are related to the value of the property. The net wealth taxes and taxes on chattels of 4200 and 4600 respectively are confined to the ownership rather than the use of assets, apply to groups of assets rather than particular goods and again are related to the value of the assets,

5210 — Recurrent taxes on use of goods and on permission to use goods or perform activities

79.   The principal characteristic of taxes classified here is that they are levied at regular intervals and that they are usually fixed amounts. The most important item in terms of revenue receipts is vehicle licence taxes. This sub-heading also covers taxes on permission to hunt, shoot, fish or to sell certain products and taxes on the ownership of dogs and on the performance of certain services, provided that they meet the criteria set out in §11–12. The sub-divisions of 5210 are user taxes on motor vehicles paid by households (5211) and those paid by others (5212). Sub-heading 5213 covers dog licences and user charges for permission to perform activities such as selling meat or liquor when the levies are on a recurring basis. It also covers recurrent general licences for hunting, shooting and fishing where the right to carry out these activities is not granted as part of a normal commercial transaction (e.g., the granting of the licence is not accompanied by the right to use a specific area which is owned by government).

5220 — Non-recurrent taxes on use of goods and on permission to use goods or perform activities

80.   This section covers non-recurrent taxes levied on the use of goods or on permission to use goods or perform activities and taxes levied each time goods are used. It includes taxes levied on the emission or discharge into the environment of noxious gases, liquids or other harmful substances.

  • Payments for tradable emission permits issued by governments under cap and trade schemes should be recorded here at the time the emissions occur. No revenue should be recorded for permits that governments issue free of charge. The accrual basis of recording means that there can be a timing difference between the cash being received by government for the permits and the time the emission occurs. In the national accounts, this timing gives rise to a financial liability for government during the period.

- Payments made for the collection and disposal of waste or noxious substances by public authorities should be excluded as they constitute a sale of services to enterprises.

81.   Other taxes falling under heading 5200 that are not levied recurrently are also included here. Thus, once-and-for-all payments for permission to sell liquor or tobacco or to set up betting shops are included provided they meet the criteria set out in §11–12.

6000 — Other taxes

82.   Taxes levied on a base, or bases, other than those described under headings 1000, 3000, 4000 and 5000, or on bases of which cannot be considered to be related to any one of these headings, are included here. Where taxes are levied on a multiple base and it is possible to estimate the receipts related to each base the separate amounts are included under the appropriate headings. If separate amounts cannot be estimated and it is known that most of the receipts are derived from one base, the whole of the receipts are classified according to that base. Otherwise, they are classified here. Other revenues included here are presumptive taxes not included elsewhere in the classification system, taxes on individuals in the form of a poll tax or capitation tax, stamp taxes not related to financial and capital transactions nor falling exclusively on a single category of transaction, expenditure taxes where personal deductions or exemptions are applied and unidentifiable tax receipts. A subdivision is made between taxes levied wholly or predominantly on business (6100) and those levied on others (6200).

A.6 Conciliation with National Accounts

83.   This section of the tables provides a re-conciliation between the OECD calculation of total tax revenues and the total of all taxes and social contributions paid to general government as recorded in the country's National Accounts. Where the country is a member of the European Union (EU), the comparison is between the OECD calculation of total tax revenues and the sum of tax revenues and social contributions recorded in the combination of the general government and the institutions of the EU sectors of the National Accounts.

A.7 Memorandum item on the financing of social security benefits

84.   In view of the varying relationship between taxation and social security contributions and the cases referred to in §39 to §45, a memorandum item collects together all payments earmarked for social security-type benefits, other than voluntary payments to the private sector. Data are presented as follows (refer Table 5.37 of the Report):

a) Taxes of 2000 series.

b) Taxes earmarked for social security benefits.

c) Voluntary contributions to the government.

d) Compulsory contributions to the private sector.

Guidance on the breakdown of (a) to (d) above is provided in §39 to §45.

A.8 Memorandum item on identifiable taxes paid by government

85.   Identifiable taxes actually paid by government are presented in a memorandum item classified by the main headings of the OECD classification of taxes. In the vast majority of countries, only social security contributions and payroll taxes paid by government can be identified. These are, however, usually the most important taxes paid by governments (refer to Table 5.38 of the Report).

A.9 Relation of OECD classification of taxes to national accounting systems

86.   A system of national accounts (SNA) seeks to provide a coherent framework for recording and presenting the main flows relating respectively to production, consumption, accumulation and external transactions of a given economic area, usually a country or a major region within a country. Government revenues are an important part of the transactions recorded in SNA. The final version of the 2008 SNA was jointly published by five international organisations: the United Nations, the International Monetary Fund, the European Union, the Organisation for Economic Co-operation and Development, and the World Bank in August 2009. The *System* is a comprehensive, consistent and flexible set of macroeconomic accounts. It is designed for use in countries with market economies, whatever their stage of economic development, and also in countries in transition to market economies. The important parts of the SNA's conceptual framework and its definitions of the various sectors of the economy have been reflected in the OECD's classification of taxes.

87.   There are, however, some differences between the OECD classification of taxes and SNA concepts that are listed below. They arise because the aim of the former is to provide the maximum disaggregation of statistical data on what are generally regarded as taxes by tax administrations.

  a) OECD includes compulsory social security contributions paid to general government in total tax revenues. Imputed and voluntary contributions plus those paid to private funds are not treated as taxes (§8 and §10 above);

  b) there are different points of view on whether or not some levies and fees are classified as taxes (§11 and §12 above);

  c) OECD excludes imputed taxes or subsidies resulting from the operation of official multiple exchange rates or from the central bank paying a rate of interest on required reserves that is different from other market rates;

  d) there are differences in the treatment of non-wastable tax credits

88.   As noted in §1 and §2, headings 1000 to 6000 of the OECD list of taxes cover all unrequited payments to general government, other than compulsory loans and fines. Such unrequited payments including fines, but excluding compulsory loans can be obtained from adding together the following figures in the 2008 SNA

- value-added type taxes (D.211);
- taxes and duties on imports, excluding VAT (D.212);
- export taxes (D.213);
- taxes on products, excluding VAT, import and export taxes (D.214);
- other taxes on production (D.29);
- taxes on income (D.51);
- other current taxes (D.59);
- social contributions (D.61), excluding voluntary contributions;
- capital taxes (D.91).

A.10 The OECD classification of taxes and the International Monetary Fund (GFS) system

89.   The coverage and valuation of tax revenues in the GFS system and the 2008 SNA are very similar. Therefore, the differences between the OECD classification and that of the 2008 SNA (see §87 above) also apply to the GFS. In addition the International Monetary Fund subdivides the OECD 5000 heading

into section IV (Domestic Taxes on Goods and Services) and section V (Taxes on International Trade and Transactions). This reflects the fact that while the latter usually yield insignificant amounts of revenue in OECD countries, this is not the case in many non-OECD countries.

A.11 Comparison of the OECD classification of taxes with other international classifications

90.   The table below describes an item by item comparison of the OECD classification of taxes and the classifications used in the following:

a) System of National Accounts (2008 SNA);

b) European System of Accounts (2010 ESA);

c) IMF Government Finance Statistics Manual (GFSM2014).

91.   These comparisons represent those that would be expected to apply in the majority of cases. However in practice some flexibility should be used in their application. This is because in particular cases, countries can adopt varying approaches to the classification of revenues in National Accounts.

	OECD Classification			2008 SNA	2010 ESA	GFSM2014
1000	Taxes on income, profits and capital gains					
	1100	Individuals				
		1110	Income and profits	D51-8.61a	D51A	1111
		1120	Capital gains	D51-8.61c, d	D51C, D	1111
	1200	Corporations				
		1210	Income and profits	D51-8.61b	D51B	1112
		1220	Capital gains	D51-8.61c	D51C	1112
	1300	Unallocable as between 1100 and 1200				1113
2000	Social security contributions					
	2100	Employees		D613-8.85	D613	1211
	2200	Employers		D611-8.83	D611	1212
	2300	Self-employed, non-employed		D613-8.85	D613	1213
	2400	Unallocable as between 2100, 2200 and 2300				1214
3000	Taxes on payroll and workforce			D29-7.97a	D29C	112
4000	Taxes on property					
	4100	Recurrent taxes on immovable property				
		4110	Households	D59-8.63a	D59A	1131
		4120	Other	D29-7.97b	D29A	1131
	4200	Recurrent net wealth taxes				
		4210	Individual	D59-8.63b	D59A	1132
		4220	Corporations	D59-8.63b	D59A	1132
	4300	Estate, inheritance and gift taxes				
		4310	Estate and inheritance taxes	D91-10.207b	D91A	1133
		4320	Gift taxes	D91-10.207b	D91A	1133
	4400	Taxes on financial and capital transactions		D59-7.96d; D29-7.97e	D214B, C	114114; 1161
	4500	Other non-recurrent taxes on property		D91-10.207a	D91B	1135
	4600	Other recurrent taxes on property		D59-8.63c	D59A	1136
5000	Taxes on goods and services					
	5100	Taxes on production, sale and transfer of goods and services				
		5110	General taxes on goods and services			
			5111 Value-added taxes	D211-7.89	D211; D29G	11411
			5112 Sales taxes	D2122-7.94a; D214-7.96a	D21224; D214I	11412

	5113	Other general taxes on goods and services		D214-7.96a	D214I	11413
5120		Taxes on specific goods and services				
	5121	Excises		D2122-7.94b; D214-7.96b	D21223; D214A, B, D	1142
	5122	Profits of fiscal monopolies		D214-7.96e	D214J	1143
	5123	Customs and other import duties		D2121-7.93	D2121; D21221, 2	1151
	5124	On exports		D213-7.95a	D214K	1152-4
	5125	On investment goods				
	5126	On specific services		D2122-7.94c; D214-7.96c	D21225; D214E, F, G, H; D29F	1144; 1156
	5127	Other taxes on international trade and transactions		D2122-7.94d D29-7.95b D29-7.97g D59-8.64d	D21226; D29D; D59E	1153; 1155-6
	5128	Other taxes on specific goods and services				1146
5130		Unallocable between 5110 and 5120				
5200		Taxes on use of goods and on permission to use goods or perform activities				
5210		Recurrent taxes on use of goods and on permission to use goods or perform activities				
	5211	Motor vehicle taxes households		D59-8.64c	D59D	11451
	5212	Motor vehicles taxes others		D29-7.97d	D214D; D29B	11451
	5213	Other recurrent taxes on use of goods and on permission to use goods or perform activities		D29-7.97c, d, f D59-8.64c	D29B, E, F; D59D	11452
5220		Non-recurrent taxes on permission to use goods or perform activities				11452
5300		Unallocable as between 5100 and 5200				
6000	Other taxes					
6100		Payable solely by business				1161
6200		Payable by other than business, or unidentifiable		D59-8.64a, b	D59B, C	1162

A.12 Attribution of tax revenues by sub-sectors of general government

92.   The OECD classification requires a breakdown of tax revenues by sub-sectors of government. The definition of each sub-sector and the criteria to be used to attribute tax revenues between these sub-sectors are set out below. They follow the guidance of the 2008 SNA and GFSM 2014.

Sub-sectors of general government to be identified

a)   *Central government*

93.   The central government sub-sector includes all governmental departments, offices, establishments and other bodies which are agencies or instruments of the central authority whose competence extends over the whole territory, with the exception of the administration of social security funds. Central government therefore has the authority to impose taxes on all resident and non-resident units engaged in economic activities within the country.

b)   *State, provincial or regional government*

94.   This sub-sector consists of intermediate units of government exercising a competence at a level below that of central government. It includes all such units operating independently of central government in a part of a country's territory encompassing a number of smaller localities, with the exception of the administration of social security funds. In unitary countries, regional governments may be considered to

have a separate existence where they have substantial autonomy to raise a significant proportion of their revenues from sources within their control and their officers are independent of external administrative control in the actual operation of the unit's activities.

95.   At present, federal countries comprise the majority of cases where revenues attributed to intermediate units of government are identified separately. Spain is the only unitary country in this position. In the remaining unitary countries, regional revenues are included with those of local governments.

c)   Local government

96.   This sub-sector includes all other units of government exercising an independent competence in part of the territory of a country, with the exception of the administration of social security funds. It encompasses various urban and/or rural jurisdictions (e.g., local authorities, municipalities, cities, boroughs, districts).

d)   Social security funds

97.   Social security funds form a separate sub-sector of general government. The social security sub-sector is defined in the 2008 SNA by the following extracts from paragraphs 4.124 to 4.126 and 4.147:

"Social security schemes are social insurance schemes covering the community as a whole or large section of the community that are imposed and controlled by government units. The schemes cover a wide variety of programmes, providing benefits in cash or in kind for old age, invalidity or death, survivors, sickness and maternity, work injury, unemployment, family allowance, health care, etc. There is not necessarily a direct link between the amount of the contribution paid by an individual and the benefits he or she may receive." (Paragraph 4.124).

"When social security schemes are separately organised from the other activities of government units and hold their assets and liabilities separately from the latter and engage in financial transactions on their own account they qualify as institutional units that are described as social security funds." (Paragraph 4.125).

"The amounts raised, and paid out, in social security contributions and benefits may be deliberately varied in order to achieve objectives of government policy that have no direct connection with the concept of social security as a scheme to provide social benefits to members of the community. They may be raised or lowered in order to influence the level of aggregate demand in the economy, for example. Nevertheless, so long as they remain separately constituted funds, they must be treated as separate institutional units in the SNA. (Paragraph 4.126).

"The social security funds sub-sector (of general government) consists of the social security funds operating at all levels of government. Such funds are social insurance schemes covering the community as a whole or large section of the community that are imposed by government units." (Paragraph 4.147).

98.   This definition of social security funds is followed in the OECD classification with the two following exceptions which are excluded

*   Schemes imposed by government and operated by bodies outside the general government sector, as defined in §3 of this manual; and
*   Schemes to which all contributions are voluntary.

Supra-national Authorities

99.   This sub-sector covers the revenue-raising operations of supra-national authorities within a country. In practice, the only relevant supra-national authority in the OECD area is that of the institutions of the European Union (EU). As from 1998, supra-national authorities are no longer included in the *Revenue Statistics*, to achieve consistency with the SNA definition of general government which excludes

them. For example, income taxes and social security contributions collected by European Institutions and paid by European civil servants who are resident of EU member countries should not be included. However the specific levies paid by the member states of the EU continue to be included in total tax revenues and they are shown under this heading.

Criteria to be used for the attribution of tax revenues

100.   When a government collects taxes and pays them over in whole or in part to other governments, it is necessary to determine whether the revenues should be considered to be those of the collecting government which it distributes to others as grants, or those of the beneficiary governments which the collecting government receives and passes on only as their agent. The criteria to be used in the attribution of revenues are set out in §101 to §104 which replicate paragraphs 3.70 to 3.73 from the 2008 SNA.

101.   In general, a tax is attributed to the government unit that

> *a)* exercises the authority to impose the tax (either as a principal or through the delegated authority of the principal),

> *b)* has final discretion to set and vary the rate of the tax

102.   Where an amount is collected by one government for and on behalf of another government, and the latter government has the authority to impose the tax, and set and vary its rate, then the former is acting as an agent for the latter and the tax is reassigned. Any amount retained by the collecting government as a collection charge should be treated as a payment for a service. Any other amount retained by the collecting government, such as under a tax-sharing arrangement, should be treated as a current grant. If the collecting government was delegated the authority to set and vary the rate, then the amount collected should be treated as tax revenue of this government.

103.   Where different governments jointly and equally set the rate of a tax and jointly and equally decide on the distribution of the proceeds, with no individual government having ultimate overriding authority, then the tax revenues are attributed to each government according to its respective share of the proceeds. If an arrangement allows one government unit to exercise ultimate overriding authority, then all of the tax revenue is attributed to that unit.

104.   There may also be the circumstance where a tax is imposed under the constitutional or other authority of one government, but other governments individually set the tax rate in their jurisdictions. The proceeds of the tax generated in each respective government's jurisdiction are attributed as tax revenues of that government.

Levies paid by member states of the European Union

105.   The levies paid by the member states of the EU take the form specific levies which include

> *a)* custom duties and levies on agricultural goods (5123),

> *b)* gross monetary compensation accounts (5123 if relating to imports and 5124 if relating to exports); and

> *c)* Steel, coal, sugar and milk levies (5128).

106.   The custom duties collected by member states on behalf of the EU are recorded

- on a gross of collection fee basis;
- using figures adjusted so that duties are shown on a 'final destination' as opposed to a 'country of first entry' basis where such adjustments can be made. These adjustments concern in particular

duties collected at important (sea) ports. Although the EU duties are collected by the authorities of the country of first entry, when possible these duties should be excluded from the revenue of the collecting country and be included in the revenue of the country of final destination

107.   This is the specific EU levy that most clearly conforms to the attribution criterion described in §99 above. Consequently as from 1998, these amounts are footnoted as a memorandum item to the EU member state country tables (in Chapter 5) and no longer shown under heading 5123. However the figures are included in the total tax revenue figures on the top line for all the relevant years shown in the tables.

A.13 Provisional classification of revenues from bank levies and payments to deposit insurance and financial stability schemes

108.   The OECD have adopted the following interim approach to reporting revenue from bank levies plus deposit insurance and stability fees for the 2012 and subsequent editions of *OECD Revenue Statistics*. It is recommended that the amounts should be recorded under category 5126.

- Compulsory payments of stability fees, bank levies and deposit insurance should generally be treated as tax revenues where the payments are made to General Government and allocated to the governments' consolidated or general funds so that the Government is free to make immediate use of the money for the purposes that it chooses. This principle would apply regardless of whether the Government is promising to make payments to guarantee the banks' customer deposits in some future contingency.
- If the compulsory payments are made to general government and placed in funds that are earmarked to be entirely channelled back to the sector of the economy that comprises the companies that are subject to the payment, they would still generally be treated as tax revenues on the grounds that the funds would be available for the government and would reduce its budget deficit, the fee is unrequited for an individual entity and the amounts raised could be unrelated to any eventual pay out to depositors or expenditure on wider support for the financial sector.
- Payments to made to the smaller long-standing schemes for insuring 'retail' deposits, where the payment levels are consistent with the costs of insurance should be classified as fee for service.
- Any payments which involve governments realising the assets of a failed institution or receiving a priority claim on its assets in liquidation in order to fund payments of compensation to customers for their lost deposits would be treated as a fee for a service as opposed to tax revenues.
- Compulsory payments that are made to funds operated outside the government sector and non-state institutions backed by the deposit takers and all payments to voluntary schemes should not be treated as tax revenues.

Notes

1. All references to SNA are to the 2008 edition.

2. See section A.12 of this guide for a discussion of the concept of agency capacity.

3. It is usually possible to identify amounts of social security contributions and payroll taxes, but not other taxes paid by government.

4. If, however, a levy which is considered as non-tax revenue by most countries is regarded as a tax — or raises substantial revenue — in one or more countries, the amounts collected are footnoted at the end of the relevant country tables, even though the amounts are not included in total tax revenues.

5. Names, however, can frequently be misleading. For example, though a passport fee would normally be considered a non-tax revenue, if a supplementary levy on passports (as is the case in Portugal) were imposed in order to raise substantial amounts of revenue relative to the cost of providing the passport, the levy would be regarded as a tax under 5200.

6. A more detailed explanation of this distinction can be found in the special feature, 'Current issues in reporting tax revenues', in the 2001 edition of the *Revenue Statistics*.

7. Sometimes the terms 'non-refundable' and 'refundable' are used, but it may be considered illogical to talk of 'refundable' when nothing has been paid.

8. A different treatment, however, is accorded to non-wastable tax credits under imputation systems of corporate income tax (§36–38).

9. This is not strictly a true tax expenditure in the formal sense. Such tax expenditures require identification of a benchmark tax system for each country or, preferably, a common international benchmark. In practice it has not been possible to reach agreement on a common international benchmark.

10. Unless based on the profit made on a sale, in which case they would be classified as capital gains taxes under 1120 or 1220.

11. In some countries the same legislation applies to both individual and corporate enterprises for particular taxes on income. However, the receipts from such taxes are usually allocable between individuals and enterprises and can therefore be shown in the appropriate sub-heading.

12. For example, "…sufficiently self-contained and independent that they behave in the same way as corporations…….(including) keeping a complete set of accounts" (2008 SNA, section 4.44).

13. In Canada — a country also referred to as having an imputation system — the (wastable) tax credit for the shareholder is in respect of domestic corporation tax deemed to have been paid whether or not a corporation tax liability has arisen. As there is no integral connection between the corporation tax liability and the credit given against income tax under such systems, these credits for dividends are treated, along with other tax credits, on the lines described in §25.

14. This may also apply where a scheme for government employees existed prior to the introduction of a general social security scheme.

15. In the 2008 SNA these are regarded as capital transfers and not as taxes (see section A.8).

16. This is the system by which the European Union adjusts for differences between the exchange rates used to determine prices under the Common Market Agricultural Policy and actual exchange rates. Payments under the system may relate to imports or exports and where these amounts are separately

identifiable they are shown under the appropriate heading (5123 or 5124). In this Report, these amounts are shown gross (i.e. without deducting any subsidies paid out under the MCA system).

17. Transfers of profits of State lotteries are regarded as non-tax revenues (see also §67).

Annex B. Interpretative Guide to non-tax revenue in Revenue Statistics in Asian and Pacific Economies

Table of contents

1. Coverage ....

2. Grants ....

3. Property income ....

4. Sales of goods and services..

5. Fines, penalties and forfeits..

6. Other social contributions ....

7. Miscellaneous and unidentified revenue ....

Notes ....

1. Coverage

The definition of non-tax revenues and the main subcategories identified in this publication generally correspond to the concepts laid out in the 2014 IMF Government Finance Statistics Manual (GFSM). Non-tax revenues refer to increases in government net worth resulting from transactions other than tax revenues. They exclude funds arising from the repayment of previous lending by governments or from borrowing, or proceeds derived from sales of fixed capital assets, stocks, land and intangible assets or private gifts.

Non-tax revenues are made up of the following elements.

2. Grants

The GFSM 2014 states "Grants are transfers receivable by government units from non-resident government units or international organisations without the receipt of any goods, services, or assets in return. Grants are normally receivable in cash, but may also take the form of the receipt of goods or services (in kind)". These transfers are un-refundable and unrequited. Grants encompass reparations and gifts given for particular projects or programmes. The term "grants" is not used to refer to transfers to or from non-governmental units and excludes inter-governmental transfers. The remission of funds collected by one government for another in an agency capacity should not be shown as receipt of a grant by the beneficiary government but as its direct receipt of revenue.

3. Property income

This category includes income to government arising from their ownership of property, enterprises, financial assets, or intangible assets when government units place them at the disposal of other units. Sales of non-financial assets such as the sales of lands are not recorded as revenue because disposal of such an asset does not increase the net worth. Similarly, repayments on loans and loan disbursements are not revenue. Property income may take the form of dividends, interest, land rents, royalties, or withdrawals from entrepreneurial income. The main components are:

- Interest and dividends: Interest is the revenue earned by the government unit from a financial asset by putting it at the disposal of another institutional unit. Dividends are the revenue earned by placing equity funds at the disposal of a corporation (resident or non-resident corporation). This category also consists of profits of state-owned enterprises except those classified as fiscal monopolies (see §62-§64 of the OECD Interpretative Guide to tax revenue in Annex A), export and import monopoly profits (see §70-§71 of the same document) or those providing public utilities such as rail transport, electricity, post offices and other communications. In this category are included revenue from public financial institutions such as the central banks' profits, profits transferred or distributed from the operation of monetary authority functions outside the central bank and the profits of state lotteries transferred to the government. Transfers from public utilities enterprises are recorded as non-tax revenue under "sales of goods and services" whereas profits for fiscal, export or import monopolies are classified as tax revenue.

- Rents or royalties: Rent is the revenue generated from natural resources, such as land, mining, or oil resources, when a government unit places these at the disposal of private or foreign entities. The rents received relate to a resource lease-giving agreement for the exploitation and extraction of a natural resource by the lessee in return for a payment. Payments for exploration rights are also treated as rent. Rents should not be confused with other payments a government may receive related to the exploitation of subsoil and similar assets, such as severance taxes, business licenses, or other taxes (e.g. value added taxes, excises, taxes on exports, etc.). They should also not be taken to mean incomes from the rental of buildings and equipment, which are treated as sales of goods and services. Revenues from rents and royalties are in some cases difficult to establish and depend on the agreement between the government unit and the lessee. For example rents, royalties and taxes such as corporate income taxes and VAT are sometimes encompassed in a single payment to the general government. In such cases the revenue should be classified under the category to which the majority of revenue belongs (see §71 of Annex A for further explanation.)

- Other property income: This includes revenue earned by a government unit placing funds at a disposal of quasi-corporations.[1] Conceptually this source of revenue is equivalent to that of dividends from a corporation but by definition, quasi-corporations cannot distribute income in the form of dividends. This category of "other property income" also includes retained or reinvested earnings, i.e. the percentage of distributable revenue not paid out as dividends, but retained by the corporation or quasi-corporation on foreign investment; property income from investment income disbursements and unidentified property income.

4. Sales of goods and services

Revenue under the category "sales of goods and services" is generally reported on a gross basis, without deduction of costs. Since these costs can represent a significant proportion of revenues, they cannot be regarded in total as funds available for governments to finance their general activities. This contrasts with tax revenues, where the collection costs are usually a small proportion of revenue. This difference implies that it may not be meaningful to sum tax and non-tax revenues as part of a calculation of generally available funds.

The proceeds of sales of nonfinancial assets such as the sale of buildings or lands are not classified as revenues since their disposal does not increase the net worth.

Sales of goods and services consist of:

- Sales by market establishments.[2]
- Administrative fees for services (i.e. fees for drivers' licences, passports, visas, court fees, harbour fees, fees for birth, marriage or death certificates, patent registrations, radio and television licenses when public authorities provide general broadcasting services).
- Administrative fees that are sales of services associated with a regulatory function of government (such as fees for the inspection of premises before delivering a business licence) and considered to be proportional to the cost of producing the service are included in this category. If the fee in return for the service provided by the government unit is disproportionate, then the fee will be classified as a tax. Specific examples of fees that are considered taxes include fees for permission to perform activities such as hunting, fishing and shooting; and fees for business registration where this is a legal requirement for the business to operate.
- Sales by nonmarket establishments such as fees at government hospitals, tuition fees at government schools and admission fees to museums and parks.
- Leasing of buildings and equipment.

5. Fines, penalties and forfeits

The GFSM 2014 states "Fines and penalties are compulsory transfers imposed by courts of law or bodies for violations of laws or administrative rules. Out-of-court agreements are also included (...). Forfeits are amounts deposited with a general government unit pending a legal or administrative proceeding, and that will be transferred to the unit upon resolution". For example traffic fines are included here. Fines and penalties charged on overdue taxes or penalties imposed for the evasion of taxes should be recorded in this category and not as taxes. However if it is not possible to separate the amounts paid in taxes and fines, the whole amount should be classified under the tax to which the fine relates (see §14 of Annex A for further explanation).

6. Other social contributions

This category includes the actual and imputed contributions to social insurance schemes operated by governments as employers on behalf of their employees that do not create a future defined liability. This category also includes the sum of the total voluntary contributions.[3] Excluded from this category are any contributions to funds in which the contributions of each participant and of his employer on his behalf are kept in a separate account earning interest and withdrawable under specified circumstances or any contributions to a pension fund autonomous to the general government. This category is not included in this publication.

7. Miscellaneous and unidentified revenue

This category consists of unidentified non-tax revenues or those that do not fit into any of the other categories listed above. It includes revenue such as gifts and transfers from individuals, private non-profit institutions, nongovernmental foundations, corporations, or sources other than governments and international organisations. Major non-recurrent payments receivable in compensation for extensive damages or serious injuries not covered by insurance policies are also included, such as payments of compensation for damages caused by major explosions; oil spillages; or payments receivable for damage to property other than payments from an insurance settlement.

Notes

[1] Quasi-corporations are unincorporated enterprises that exercise some functions of corporations, but have not been granted separate legal personality by statute.

[2] A market establishment is an establishment that charges economically significant prices.

[3] The IMF includes these contributions as part of their total of social security contributions.

Lightning Source UK Ltd.
Milton Keynes UK
UKHW050651310820
369099UK00001B/1